THE NURTURING FATHER

THE
NURTURING
FATHER

Journey
Toward
the
Complete Man

Kyle D. Pruett, M.D.

WARNER BOOKS

A Warner Communications Company

Selections from this book first appeared in *The Psychoanalytic Study of the Child*, Vol. 38 (1983), Vol. 40 (1985), Yale University Press and in *Frontiers of Infant Psychiatry*, Vol. 2 (1984), Basic Books.

Warner Books, Inc., 666 Fifth Avenue, New York, NY 10103

 A Warner Communications Company

Printed in the United States of America

First Printing: January 1987

10 9 8 7 6 5 4 3 2 1

Library of Congress Cataloging-in-Publication Data

Pruett, Kyle D.
    The nurturing father.

    Bibliography: p. 303
    Includes index.
    1. Fathers—United States—Psychology. 2. Father and child—United States. 3. Love, Paternal.
I. Title.
HQ756.P78 1987   306.8'742   85-40917
ISBN 0-446-51269-9

Book design by H. Roberts

For Leslie, Emily, and Lisa

the real authors of this particular nurturing father; who have endured and given so much of late.
This book is yours as much as mine.

And to my parents;

my father for sharing his lifelong love affair with words, ideas, and the human condition; and to my mother for sharing her affection and respect for, and flawless skill with children; hers, mine, and yours.

ACKNOWLEDGMENTS

Book writing is a dicey business. The reader is forever in the front row staring back at the author, wondering how he will handle the passionate disorder of thoughts and ideas that rush to grab center stage. Thank God one is not alone out there. As this book grew, so did my indebtedness to my loving family (my first and best critics), my dear friends, and smart gifted colleagues at Yale and Warner.

My gratitude to Al Solnit for providing a climate and space for academic excellence and social responsibility in clinical research, even after the quest for quick and simple answers made such excellence more expensive. My enduring and warm thanks to my perpetual teacher, Sally Provence, whose creative study of, service to, and loving respect for the complexity of early life experience never ceases to amaze and feed me. My medical students and residents (especially Michael Gilbert) who have helped directly by working beside me, and indirectly by asking all those marvelous questions. To Alan Gurwitt who has been unfailingly supportive of my work and the understanding of fatherhood, even when we read our papers to nearly empty convention rooms in the early days of fatherhood research.

To dear friends and smart colleagues Kirsten Dahl, Liz Loewald, Paul and Nancy Cotton, Julian Ferholt, and Jim Herzog for support, affectionate criticism, wit, humor, and good food.

To my brother Gordon; running, singing, fathering, muffin-eating, traveling companion who set a wondrous pace, and for reading the manuscript and saying the right things. To my brother Bryce, who has anchored my perception of a strong nurturing father in his own rich soil, and for keeping the faith. To Susan Bingham, for reading the manuscript in her sickbed, and offering such harmonically correct and creative advice. Steven Fleck, for his devotion to detailed reading of the manuscript, and his world class understanding of people who belong to families.

At Warner, Fredda Isaacson, for her persistent and deft devotion to my ideas and the correctness of their form. To Larry Kirshbaum, Nansey Neiman, and Bernie Shir-Cliff for their infectious enthusiasm and respect for my words.

Finally, this book has several sponsors. First are the families themselves who permitted me the remarkable privilege of watching them live their lives during a difficult and intimate period of life that no one does perfectly. Their openness, energy, patience, and generosity affected me deeply. This book is as much their progeny as mine. Second, has been the sponsorship of Freya Manston whose steadfast, affectionate nudging gently pushed this book out of my head and onto paper. I cannot thank her enough.

To all the children who helped me write this book.

CONTENTS

THE NURTURING FATHER

INTRODUCTION

The Youngs occupied the top floor of a two-family house on the quiet main street in one of New England's old, semirural, dormant mill towns. A weathered "Room for Rent" sign with a faded telephone number stuck out of the tall grass of the front yard. Like the house, the covered steps leading up the back were in moderate repair. A note in good calligraphy was taped to the Youngs' door, informing visitors that "The Youngs may be found in the garage if there is no answer."

I went back down the stairs and through the even taller grass of the backyard to the garage. Rock and roll at a reasonable volume was making its way outside through the partially opened door. Mr. Young yelled from somewhere inside, "I saw you comin', Doc. Come on in and meet my girl. We're busy back here." As he finished his greeting, a tall, bearded young man wearing a blue denim bib apron appeared from the side room and extended both his hands for a handshake.

This wiry, intense man, so warmly welcoming, was nineteen-year-old Allen Young. He was the youngest father in my study of families in which the father was home raising the children. He explained, "We're back here developing prints. This is my darkroom. Sometimes it's even a studio when all this photographic junk isn't in here."

Pushing herself up and down in a Jolly-Jump-Up seat suspended between two tripods was "his favorite subject," a nine-month-old charmer named Nancy. Nancy had been staring at me without blinking since I'd come through the door. I was feeling thoroughly "checked out" as I bent down to say "hello" at her father's invitation. Nancy began to bounce up and down, squealing vigorously, as she contentedly gummed an unemployed lens cap. Allen said, "You guys get acquainted. I've got to take a second and finish up back here."

The room we were in seemed to be half of an old garage, partitioned off and flooded with light fixtures. On the walls were three very large photographic prints of highly abstract black and white emulsions, looking like partially blurred time-lapse exposures of the night sky. Mr. Young came back to find me staring at these pieces and asked, "Do you recognize her? That's Nancy, four months— seven months—and this one's eight months. You know, those sound pictures they take with sonar before the baby's born? These are Polaroid two by four footers my uncle did for me from the ones the technician gave us. Great, huh?"*

Yes, these were pictures worth a thousand words, each about who this father was and what he felt about his "favorite subject."

Mr. Young suggested that we move to the house because he had to get lunch ready for Nancy. As he leaned over to extract Nancy from her seat, she held up her arms in anticipation of being picked up, all the while keeping her eyes fixed on me. She was displaying classic stranger awareness, a hallmark of the seven- to nine-month-old's response to "outsiders"—very interested, but very cautious. As her father gathered her up in his arms, I became aware of the strong physical likeness between father and daughter. She too was wiry and intense, but also warmly interactive. There was a sense of a good "fit" here, both in physiology and temperament.

---

*Sonograms or "echoes" are now in common use to follow the growth of the fetus through all three trimesters, especially if the obstetrician feels that the pregnancy bears close watching. Ultrasound waves are capable of great accuracy. One of Nancy's "portraits" in fact caught her sucking her thumb in utero during the seventh month.

Once in the kitchen, Mr. Young turned on the same radio station that had been playing in the garage. "She likes this song"—and indeed she appeared to be making the most of its strident rhythms.

Seated in the kitchen, Allen Young and I at the kitchen table and Nancy in her four-wheeled walker, Mr. Young spontaneously began this first interview by describing how it happened that he was home with Nancy while Barbara, his twenty-year-old wife, was out "keeping us afloat." When they'd married seventeen months before, Allen was working at his family's auto salvage business, and Barbara was a waitress in a busy, well-known local restaurant, both of them "pulling down pretty good money for people our age." They had been planning "to do it the regular way" all along. Allen's family would help out with a little extra cash if and when Barbara decided to stop working to "start a family." Everything "looked okay."

In the seventh month of the pregnancy, however, Allen's family business got into trouble for some alleged EPA violations at the junk yard, and they had to cease operation temporarily. Allen suddenly no longer had a job. Shortly thereafter, Barbara started to have trouble with her pregnancy; mild toxemia and a urinary tract infection were but a few of her difficulties. Nancy herself came three weeks early, and Barbara had planned to ask her mother to come to help out. But, three days after Nancy's early birth, Barbara's mother underwent an "urgent mastectomy" for breast cancer.

Allen described the situation: "So there I was, the only one with nothing to do. So I started helping out. I felt so clumsy at first even holding her. The birth was one thing. That was great. But the lookin' after was somethin' else."

He had attended the birth only because Barbara's insistence had compelled him to be there. When it was clear that she was going into early labor, "She made me promise to go in with her. She was real scared. I wasn't as frightened as she was. I was more afraid of feeling turned off, grossed out, or even getting sick. Newborn babies are *sooo* ugly, and I knew Barbara would be really hurting. But the delivery went okay. We'd done some Lamaze stuff, and it went pretty smooth. Barbara had wanted a girl for a first child. She was an only child and thought she'd know more about girls.

"The nurse handed the baby to me and I was afraid to take her. She was so little—so little—I'd never held anything that was alive and so little. She was screeching bloody murder when they sponged her off! Then they wrapped her up and gave her to me, to *me* to show Barbara—*me*—the klutz! Later the doctor told me that Barbara had arranged all that!

"Nancy was a dynamite little number. She had my nose, but thank God she had her mother's face—so perfect—God, I was high for two weeks!" (He still looked intoxicated to me as he related this story months later.) "She opened those big baby blues and looked right at me. Her smile still is like that—look, she knows we're talking about her! She's so damn smart."

That summer, now five years ago, I began, with the help of some fathers and daughters like the Youngs, a study of families in which the father served as the primary caregiver to his children, "the main man," as one wife referred to her husband. The study of men and babies had intrigued me even before I had become a father. As a medical student in Boston, I'd encountered some pretty sick babies at Boston City Hospital. I can clearly recall the seemingly magical ability of one barrelchested, unemployed Black father to stop his tiny preemie's crying. He would hum in a deep beautiful voice as he touched his son with rough hands, somehow getting close to that fragile little body in spite of the maze of tubes, glass, and beeping monitors that separated them. It worked every time. Something special was happening here. What could it be?

Years later, as I taught a course on Personality Development in Young Children to Yale medical students, questions about *paternal* nurturing capacities began to occur more and more frequently. A question asked by one of my students stands out in my memory: "Dr. Pruett, what if the mother is too sick, or just isn't there for some reason, and the father takes the place of the mother? What will happen to the baby?"

As a teacher born to a family of teachers and married to a teacher, I had learned early of that special mixture of anxious embarrassment (quickly concealed) and an itchy tingle that comes with those marvelously creative, usually naive, probing questions to which one has no answer. This question certainly qualified as one of those.

I had not the vaguest notion of how to respond.

I polled my friends and scholarly colleagues about any data or studies that they'd encountered which addressed this question of the primary nurturing father. Nothing.

I went to the Gothic caverns of the Yale Library and ordered up a computer search of all published literature on the development of infants and young children raised by their fathers. I scoured those fields of study I thought the most likely sources of relevant material: child development, psychology, psychiatry, pediatrics, developmental psychology, and sociology. The reference librarian cocked his head to the side and said soberly, "That should be interesting, but I wouldn't hold my breath on that one if I were you."

The computer printed out one entry. Only one. And

that turned out to be a product of computer error. Initially, I had been intrigued. That feeling was rapidly turning into burning interest in finding the answer to the question.

It has proven to be a most timely subject. This circumstance of the primary nurturing father is sometimes called the role-reversed family. (I personally loathe that term because it seems such quick and dirty shorthand for what turns out to be an extremely complex collage of issues of identity, creativity, and parental satisfaction for both men and women.) All of us in the myriad disciplines that comprise the field of child development have noticed that fathers and their babies are finding themselves in increasing physical and emotional contact with one another, though for many different reasons. We have begun to notice powerful, ofttimes good, though complicated, happenings and attitudes as a result of this new proximity, especially when viewed in the context of the nurturing domain of the whole family. This particular familial arrangement of the child-rearing father, a kind of "natural experiment," as one study father described it, seemed the best place to start filling this curious hole in our knowledge of families, fathers, and their babies.

Ultimately, this book is about the universal manifestations of paternal identity—a paternal identity which unfolds in the lives of certain men and families who have found themselves wrestling with a particularly compelling version of fatherhood. These men have discovered themselves to be "unbelievably important" to their children. In their stories, we will see the impact and power of that experience on their lives, their mates, and their children. Their stories depict fathering by men who earn hourly wages, work in Fortune 500 companies such as United Technologies, are unemployed, or wear hard hats. A few had never held a child in their arms before the birth of their own. But like Mr. Young, they show us over and over again their joy in their children. We see the growth of intimacy in their daily child care and the response of the child to the father. We also see the gradual erosion of the father's awkward "klutzy" feeling at his baby's birth, and its replacement with a profound, informed commitment to the well-being of his child.

It has always been my belief that the best investigations of the human experience begin with the simplest questions. What *does* happen to these babies, to these men, and to these women? Because the tide of family life and adult male and female development is turning in the direction of bringing fathers and babies together, should we not find out whether this is good for these babies and/or their families? If the babies are fine, we need to know. If they are not, we certainly need to know. What are the effects of primary father care on the baby's development, not to mention the developing fathers and mothers themselves?

It is the custom in my field of study to present the early findings and ideas stimulated by such research to a forum of one's colleagues for advice and (one hopes) helpful criticism. At my first opportunity to present some of my early results, I was gratified by an unusually enthusiastic response. Dr. Stanley Greenspan, Chairman of the Research Committee of the American Psychoanalytic Association, a highly distinguished group of clinicians and scholars, called the work "pioneering and vitally significant to our understanding of the complex phenomenon of fathers and their children."

It is certainly a complex phenomenon. But it is also a phenomenon of extraordinary richness, powerful emotional forces, immense potential, and unbounded creativity. Excavating and exploring the vast riches of the territory called paternal nurturing are long overdue.

The number of men involved as primary caretakers

of their children is small, though rapidly expanding. But their very existence bears witness to a change of enormous proportion in the way that men see their lives and nurturing capacities. A most interesting speaking invitation I recently received was to address my twentieth Yale college reunion class on the subject of men and their familial relationships. The invitation came not from the humanities committee or the Alumni Office, but from a reunion committee of my classmates, comprised of investment bankers from Morgan Stanley and Manufacturers Hanover, corporate attorneys from Citicorp, and highly successful businessmen. They felt that the one thing we all had in common was what had happened to us as men over the past twenty years—not as businessmen, or academic men, or Yalies, or soldiers, or salesmen—but as men.

Surprised as I was by the invitation, I was wholly unprepared for the response to my brief speech about men, familial relationships, and male nurturing capacities. The forum ran over its allotted time by an hour, and its reverberations were felt throughout the remainder of the reunion.

Some two hundred of these men, many of whom said they would neither have "bothered" nor "dared" to attend such a public discussion two decades before, were now embroiled in sharing stories of their own relationships with their children and their own fathers, with an intensity that amazed me. During the discussion, raised hands crowded the air as these men excitedly interrupted and amplified upon one another's stories about the effect of these relationships on their lives, both personal and business. I could not believe my eyes or ears. Was this happening in 1985?

The discussion was finally brought to a close because we had to vacate the lecture hall. The last man to speak introduced himself as a nonfather, whom I knew to be a highly successful merger broker. "I've been sitting here feeling that I'm beginning to understand a change lots of us have seen in the business world over the past five years. It's an increasing move away from the hierarchical, dictatorial management of leadership style—some of us call it the 'old boy patriarchy.' It's being gradually replaced with a more caring, respectful style in dealing with one's employees. It's clear to me that this awakening of nurturing feelings we're talking about here doesn't exist just in fathering. It really seems to be affecting relationships known to all of us."

It *is* affecting all of us, and that's the reason for this book. To understand how and why this extraordinary thing has happened, we turn to the study of the babies of primary nurturing fathers, the fathers themselves, and their spouses, with special emphasis on the singular impact of the baby/father connection. Their stories woven together are the fabric of this book. As the only continuing study of its kind, its revelations are remarkable and profound.

1

The
Father
Problem

"It just felt so silly going back to work after she was born." The 26-year-old, first-time father and salesman chatted casually after we had admired photographs of each other's children while we waited at the airport. "Of course, I knew I had to—it was the thing I *should* do as a father. But I felt that once I left, I might not ever get back into that place with her—you know—when I held her in the delivery room while they cleaned up my wife? That look—God, it melted my soul. I wondered if she felt it?" (Long pause.) "No, that's crazy... my wife is great with her, just great. Besides, what would I *do* with her, anyway?" His "backing off" was palpable.

The problem has been with us probably always. It sits there across time and history, leaving most cultures to struggle with it in their own fashion. What *is* a man to do with a baby, his baby, of his flesh, yet not really from his body? It so often seems exclusively "hers" from even before the beginning of its life. Is he to know this infant only by profile, from casual touch? Must he seek permission from her, the "gatekeeper," to enter this "kindergarten," this child's place? Even after he somehow gains entrance to the kindergarten, what is he to do?—hold, feed, protect, be tender, talk, teach, tease, play, listen, work, hang out? Moreover, what is he to feel?—pride, shame, embarrassment, ignorance, helplessness? Such quandaries from the personal, inner life of the father form one-half of the father problem.

The other half of the father problem lies out there, beyond and outside the kindergarten. It is composed of all the familial and social reverberations of the father/baby

---

connection. As a man attaches himself to his baby, what happens to his real, "traditional" fathering role? Who will guard and protect, watch over the hearth fire, hunt and gather, punch the clock, acquire, or climb the corporate ladder while he idles with his child?

Woven together, these two halves constitute the father problem. I believe it plagues, saddens, and confuses many among us, men and women. The old identities for father-nurturer (the distant, remotely involved patriarch, perpetually absent from the nursery) are creaking and groaning under the strain of a profound historical shift that is putting fathers and children in ever-increasing contact with one another. As a result, the father problem is not likely to go away.

This historical shift is formidable in its own right, fueled by at least a half dozen powerful events and currents in the late twentieth century that continue to ebb and flow, perpetually reshaping the familial landscape. First is the advent of extensive use of birth control in the present century. This has had the effect of allowing the choice to become a parent to be consciously controlled by both mother and father. Unprepared, "surprised," or "tricked" fathers can make resentful, unhappy parents to often un-wanted and bewildered babies. The choice to be parents, and the timing of parenthood, can now be a more rational-ly shared decision, giving more equal footing to the father. He, in turn, is more likely to be ready, involved, and invested in a planned baby right from the start.

Second is the phenomenal movement into the work force enjoyed by, if not forced upon, women over the last two decades, especially women of childbearing years. Day care, extended family care, babysitting (purchased and shared), have all begun to fill the gap. But more fathers are becom-ing involved in filling this gap themselves, though no one knows how prevalent or even welcome such filling-in may be.

Third is the ongoing turmoil within the nuclear family, manifest in the soaring divorce rate of the late 1970s. The questioning of familial values and sexual stereotypes continues unabated. Together, such currents have further swept along the evolution of father care whether as custodial, shared custodial, or single parent. Certainly, a man's fathering is powerfully influenced by his continuing relationship with the divorced spouse. Such arrangements have often decisively changed the father's nurturing role, sometimes for better, sometimes for worse, as we shall see in greater detail in Chapter 14.

Fourth, the slow but persistent softening of sexual stereotyping continues apace, allowing men to be more open in revealing their internal, more nurturing, emotional, less aggressive, and less competitive selves. This permits some relaxation of the grip of rigid "masculinity." Campbell's Soup advertisements, which feature men making menu choices for their children, and the phenomenal popularity of movies such as *Tootsie, Kramer vs. Kramer,* and *Mr. Mom,* all serve as witness that something profound is happening here.

I was stunned at a recent rock concert I attended with my daughters to hear the lead singer introduce two of the group's instrumentalists as "brand-new fathers," setting off more than even the usual screaming and jumping about, both on and off the stage. This softening, largely sponsored, even canonized, by the women's movement of the last twenty years, has permitted more men and women to take seriously the father's often powerful though frequently unfamiliar, if not hidden, wish to be a central figure in the life of his child.

Finally, the work-at-home phenomenon that characterized family life before the Industrial Revolution appears to be returning with some popularity. Computer terminals at home, home businesses, cottage industries, and so on are permitting work to be done by men and women in a setting which permits contact with children in a daily, integrated rhythm. Such decentralization of the workplace certainly holds far-reaching implications for the family as a whole.

The impact of all this change and movement is neither simple nor deniable. It has made many men aware, as they labor in the old traditional ways of the father's place, of a yawning paternal emptiness which leaves them feeling uncertain, confused, and often unfinished as men.

Certainly some aspects of the father's role have changed, especially at the very beginning of his child's life. As many as 62 percent of all births, in some studies, are now being attended by fathers.[1] This surely is some progress from the time when humorist Russell Baker was confined to the "Father Room" at the hospital, for his "third attempt to win an Academy Award for playing fifth wheel at a parturition." Having been sent home by the obstetrician, he missed the delivery. Upon returning to the hospital early the next morning, he asked to see his new son. "The nurse's eyes accused me [of going home] and, having convicted me, she refused to let me hold my son until the afternoon."[2]

Despite the current, more hopeful beginnings, fathers often find themselves soon after the delivery withdrawing awkwardly or being asked to withdraw by the wardens of infancy—mothers, grandmothers, pediatricians, Russell Baker's nurse, even Gerbers, Johnson & Johnson, etc. Few men have explored the territory of child care. They have had neither the socialization nor the practice—much less the role models—to aid them through such moments of rebuff or uncertainty. As a result, most back away silently and compliantly, though often longingly, seeking comfort and praise instead for doing what they are *supposed* to do: working, making money, providing, protecting, being responsible, toughening up, and, in general, adhering to the established canons of masculinity. With such a decision the father often seals his fate in "the male predicament," described by theologian James Dittes as the "stultifying effect of living life according to culturally defined ideas of manliness...the father renounces his innate tenderness, vulnerability, and wish for intimacy, 'acting' instead, as though he is in charge—the boss—the manipulator."[3]

In spite of all we feel we've accomplished as a society in encouraging men and women to evolve to their fullest humanity, the evolution continues at a glacial pace. Sacred stabilities still shape our views, social policies, habits, and expectations. They are unmistakably present in frequent, recognizable justifications like, "While it is fine, even wonderful, for women to work, their only *real* job is to be a mother" or "While it is fine, yes wonderful, for a man actively to father and raise his children, his only *real* job is to make money and support his family."

The time to change this message has arrived.

The "me generation" of the late 1970s is now suffering from growing self-doubt. The benefits of "acquisitive Yuppyism" (you *can* have it all) are leaving many men wondering, "Is that all there is?"

A 22-year-old, already affluent computer-wizard first-time father, who was at the hospital after his six-month-old son had recovered from a life-threatening respiratory illness, told me, "Things will never be the same again for me. I used to think 'With my brains and money nothing could touch me'—and I thought it was *supposed* to be like that. I don't even think I could cry. Now I am worried that I feel *too* much—you know—can't get it back together? But I will, I always do. I hope I don't forget, though. I feel like I know my son so well now. I took every breath with him for four days and nights."

Though this father is less likely, as a result of his painful experience, to suffer that feeling of an empty paternity, the sense of himself as a purposeful, present, loving father does not spring full-blown from the birth of his child.

It begins from within and frequently needs help from without. It is often tough going from the outset. One of the most tenacious obstacles to a man's discovery and sponsorship of his own nurturing capacities is the early and often reinforced lesson that the economic security of his family is his most sacred, possibly only, legitimate domain. Men learn early that the "correct" way to father is *indirectly*: loving by fostering, securing, protecting, guiding, sponsoring—not necessarily by touching or holding. The economic fabric of society seems to depend on this view. Society fosters the impression of a direct correlation between economic security and the distance a man keeps from his children and, by implication, his nurturing self.

The long-term results of adopting this view were evident in a poignant conversation I had with an old high school classmate on returning from New England to Indianapolis for my twentieth Shortridge High School reunion. He had been rather dissolute in his youth, but through personal connections and uncanny business acumen had amassed several successful businesses and was planning to retire shortly. But he saddened perceptibly as I asked if he felt he had enough now to make him happy: "Happy? What's that? My community thinks I've succeeded, but I've blown it with my kids—clear out of the water. They have almost nothing to do with me. I mostly sign checks for them now. I missed the important things in their lives, like the times when they needed real stuff from me, not just money, but time and ears and someone to help with the feelings they poured out. I thought I was doing it right—like my dad did with me. But it's a real heartache for me now."

His story was echoed in further conversations with other old friends at this gathering. Though financial and social success were more rule than exception, a certain emptiness was all too evident as many of them talked about being fathers to their children. In contrast, many of the women had often been through much more personal struggle and growth than the men, especially in their families and careers, and seemed more vital, more interesting, somehow more "complete" as people.

As I thought about the encounters on the way back home, I was struck by the curious "push me, pull you" rhythm of these last two decades in all of our lives. We all *had* been through a lot. A flood of women of all ages had returned to work or had just begun to work outside their homes. Men had had to grapple with the impact of that phenomenon on their personal lives, their families, their jobs, and their image of themselves as "masculine." Wifehood and especially motherhood had been in such flux that a complementary turbulence in fatherhood had received little attention until fairly recently.

As more men become involved with their children, women now must contend with this development and its effect on their lives, personally and professionally. As men have had to deal with the complex and powerful changes in women's roles as they spend more time on their careers and less time in mothering, so too must women begin to deal with men's struggles to secure identity as nurturers despite the inadequate, restrictive old conceptions of the man's and father's work. To put it simply: Women had to deal with the men's response when the women wanted more time "out" of the home; men now must deal with the women's response as men want more time "in."

As I listen to the men of my own generation, I hear the father problem in many variations. Steve, the 35-year-old father of three, the last a four-month-old boy: "While I'm carrying my son around with me on errands, someone may pause to admire, asking if I'm babysitting today. That automatically triggers a kind of slow, smoldering sizzle in my gut. Usually, I just let it pass. But I don't forget it. It makes me just boil. I'm *not* a babysitter. I'm a father!"

The intensity of pain experienced as a result of this "empty paternity" view of father as babysitter varies widely. At the extreme end of the spectrum is the lacerated, divorced father who has lost his children. His kind are the walking wounded of the father-problem wars. Near this same location on the spectrum are the welfare fathers whose families are financially rewarded or reimbursed for their absence and nonfathering. At the other end where the pain is less severe but still present are the men who, like my high school classmate, slowly neutralize the nurturing essence of their fathering.

All these men are suffering from the long-standing reverberations and neglect of the father problem. It is to the lives and stories of the primary nurturing fathers that we turn to seek understanding of how the problem can be solved.

Primary nurturing fathering is not necessarily wholly new nor avant-garde. As we recall the frighteningly high incidence of maternal death in childbirth prior to the twentieth century, it is obvious that there must not always have been enough women, even in extended-family situations, to carry on child care, and fathers were probably much more often involved than we can document from this historical distance.

Although this book may focus on men who are functioning in a nontraditional role as primary nurturing parents, the truths and questions generated by their experiences have far-reaching implications. Their stories give us a wider view of the whole terrain of paternal identity and a clearer vision of male identity itself.

Such a discussion of paternal identity in these changing times is not only long overdue, it is fundamental to understanding the integrity of the contemporary family as a nurturing unit. In the portraits offered in this book of real, identifiable, not particularly unusual families, you will see all our society's assumptions about fatherhood, paternal identity, and paternal nurturing put to the test. You will discover that there are measurable, positive effects upon children when fathers are actively involved in their care and nurture. You will see how important factors such as self-esteem, sexual identity, cognitive growth, curiosity, and social relatedness are all affected, and how the life of the father too is changed, often profoundly. As the study of these families reveals, there are fundamental changes afoot in the recognition of the father problem and in the ways it can be resolved. There will be no going back from such awakenings.

2

The Underground Father

Surprising as it may seem, we already know much about men as parents that is striking in its power, clarity, and consistency. Yet, though this information is often found in the literature of behavioral or social science, it is rarely brought to public attention. Bits and pieces appear in newspapers and magazines around Father's Day, popping up as spring peepers do on early April days—and having about as much impact. It is as though we either do not believe what we know or prefer to ignore it, consigning the facts to a kind of underground circulation.

In a number of other cultures, fathers are not relegated to babysitter status, nor is their ability to be primary nurturers so readily dismissed. In fact, in some societies men are so involved with fathering that their bodies and their psychologies may undergo dramatic changes before the birth of their children. We have evidence that in our own society men can rear and nurture their children competently and that men's methods, although different from those of women, are imaginative and constructive. We have learned that a man can make a significant, often profound difference in the whole life of his child *directly*, and not just through "loving his child's mother."

We have harvested these facts from researchers and families because it "seems to matter" inherently, but we can't seem to get them out of the warehouse into the marketplace. Yet that is precisely where they are most needed—to influence social policy, to inform families about their choices about children and child-rearing, and to aid the pursuit of happiness for both adults and children. So let's inventory the warehouse.

The transition from adult male to father is a much more complex task than just hanging on like an appendage to a mate who carries a pregnancy and delivers a fetus. Fathers are often profoundly involved with pregnancy and childbirth and seem to have been so for a long time and across many cultures. The most primitive and obvious reactions to pregnancy are physiological (bodily) experiences: They are many and varied. Toothaches and transient migrating gum pain, with no apparent explanation, for example, are so common that experienced and understanding dentists may ask the symptomatic patient about his wife's "condition."[1] During his wife's pregnancy, a man may also develop unusual food cravings. Once we got smart enough to start asking at our prenatal clinics about weight gain in fathers, remarkably common especially among first-time fathers, we discovered they were indulging in an amazing variety of consumables. Large quantities of milk, eggs, pickles (yes, dill), and ice cream were suddenly desirable, along with even more exotic foods such as pomegranates and cactus pears. In the Yucatan, a woman's pregnancy is considered confirmed when her spouse begins to have food cravings.[2]

Vague, nonspecific gastrointestinal disorders in men with pregnant spouses are reported as commonplace by many physicians, midwives, and clinics. One-fourth of all expectant fathers in a large study of normal pregnancies in Rochester showed up in the doctor's office during their mates' pregnancies with gastrointestinal symptoms they did not have before or after the pregnancy. No one even knows how many of the other fathers suffered from but did not seek help for such symptoms. Their nausea, cramps, diarrhea, even vomiting, had no explainable source other than the mate's pregnancy. Such symptoms parallel those experienced by women in the first trimester. Typically, it might not even have occurred to the suffering, expectant father that his symptoms could have some relationship to his wife's pregnancy.[3]

None of these involvements can compare in drama to that of *Couvade*, a ritualized custom observed in some primitive South Pacific cultures in which the expectant father undergoes a simulated pregnancy and delivery. He enters the men's hut late in his mate's pregnancy, takes to bed when she begins prelabor, and stays there throughout her labor and delivery. With intense, hysterical writhing and moaning, twisting and turning, he simulates female labor in graphic detail. The belief abroad in the men's hut at such rituals is that the man is easing his spouse's pain, not vicariously but actually, and that by so doing he is protecting his wife and his offspring from harm.[4]

A man's emotional responses to his wife's pregnancy may be less dramatic than the physical ones, but they are nonetheless remarkably prevalent and powerful. Depression and worry, especially about one's adequacy as a provider and protector, is almost universal (in mild form) in some studies of expectant fatherhood. I recall most clearly a medical school friend who became preoccupied with home security measures in his apartment in Boston's South End the week after his wife's pregnancy was confirmed. It busied and entertained him throughout the entire gestation. He remained impervious to suggestions from his friends that spending most weekend hours and fair sums of money visiting burglar alarm and security business establishments was being a bit overzealous.

We have gradually come to understand that mood changes in the pregnant father are to be expected, not feared. The rhythm of sexual activity also changes, though probably for many complex reasons. Some men experience a dip in libido, or sexual drive, especially during the second half of the pregnancy, beginning often at the time of four to five months, precisely when women may experience an increase in theirs. The men who can talk about such private matters tell different stories about this change. Some feel less erotically attracted to their spouse's body now that intercourse could somehow be dangerous to their mate or to the growing fetus.

Dreams, with troublesome themes, may also disturb men during their mates' gestation. Little wonder that unconscious work is required to deal with this profound body and mind response. Dreams about a spouse or child being in danger were quite common in the men I studied, a finding corroborated by several other investigators.[5]

In this sampling of the rapidly expanding body of new information about paternal expectancy, we come back repeatedly to the same bottom line; namely that even before the birth of his child, the father's life, his body, and his mind are quite busy making ready in ways of which he may have only a passing awareness. My security-obsessed colleague was both amazed and amused when he brought his healthy wife and son home from the hospital to his four-room fortification, aware for the first time that he may have overdone his mission as "protector."

But what about the "real" thing—the birth of his child?

We now are certain beyond doubt that the relationship between father and child begins very early indeed, certainly at birth, but as we have already seen, usually in some fashion even before. Fathers who are present at the birthing are more verbal about their babies, more accurate in describing them, and more intimately attached to them. They are also more engrossed in their babies and competent in the handling of them, or as one mother put it, "more deeply in love" with their babies from the first days than are men who have not attended the birth. Martin

Greenberg, a San Francisco psychiatrist, reported a decade ago that the *traditional* new fathers he observed were so "engrossed" with their babies that they described their infants as "beautiful and perfect" and wanted to spend hours gazing at or touching them.[6]

A particularly talkative and jovial maintenance worker of Greek ancestry at the Child Study Center, where my office is, knew of my interest in fathers and babies and came to my office door one morning the week after his second child had been born to say that he had some "evidence" for me. His first child, a son, had been "sickly and fragile" from early in his life and "my wife and the doc never let me near him." (He indeed had been "thrown out" of the delivery room when his wife began to hemorrhage briefly because of a minor placental laceration.) "I probably could have stayed. But this time, doc, Zeus was not going to drag me out of there—God, she was fabulous—fabulous! Her head came out and she opened her eyes and looked at me—*right at me*—I swear to God! Her shoulder popped out and then the rest of her just slid right out. Perfect. Just perfect! The doc cut the cord and put her on my wife's belly, and I touched her. I was sort of afraid because she was so small and soft. Perfect and small. My hands looked so big and rough. But she opened her eyes again when I touched her—like she liked it! A shiver went up my back."

I thought as I listened, what a lucky little girl and mother. There appears to be no turning back from such experiences. This father seems hooked for good.

This is certainly not to say that all is forever blessed. These early months are very complex. For the first-time parent especially, things will never be the same again. The couple is now an asymmetrical triangle. There are now at least three sides to every question. The old rhythms of the couple's life are now distorted beyond recognition, as is intimacy. The "paternity blues" may put in a brief appearance in the first three months.[7] This period is also known as the "fourth trimester," because fathers are so often separated or excluded from direct dealings with the newborn that it might as well still be in utero.

In a study of a middle-class population of families, Martha Zaslow, a clinical psychologist from the National Institute of Child Health and Human Development, found that two-thirds of first-time fathers described some feelings of "the blues" in the first four months.[8] Explanations ranged from feeling inadequate in helping their spouses with their problems in "new mothering" to feeling a frustrating loss of control over their own lives. Interestingly, the less direct contact he had with his baby, the more "blue" the father, and consequently the more contact the mother had with the baby.

Which comes first?

We don't know, but it does appear that the more vigilant and rigid the mother is as a "gatekeeper" to restrict the father's access to his baby, the less her husband and baby interact, and the more exclusively she and her baby interact. Is this freeze-out or freeze-in?

Once he becomes a father, how does a man actually deal with his infant? We know for certain (and again our knowledge is kept underground) that men can be competent, capable, creative caretakers of newborns. This is all the more remarkable given that most men are typically raised with an understanding that they are destined through some natural law to be ineffective nurturers, at least directly. The research on the subject, some of it now decades old, says this assumption is *just not so.* And it says it over and over again, in data from many different disciplines.

Developmental psychologists, pediatricians, child psychiatrists, and psychoanalysts have all been scrutinizing the young father of late, and there is a surprising unanimity in what they see and describe. Men nurture, interact with, and rear competently but differently from women: not worse, not better...differently.[9] A most unhelpful adage has helped keep many fathers at arms' length from their children. "Father knows best" (a frequently empty maxim) should be changed to "Father knows different."

Beginning with a parent's first and most critical job, infant feeding, we can sample some of the best of this research about how (differently) a man cares for his baby. Two developmental psychologists, Ross Parke and Doug Sawin, carefully observed and videotaped fathers and mothers while they bottle-fed their newborns. Feeding one's baby may or may not be an easy job, depending upon the temperament of the baby and the capacity of the feeder to adapt to the baby's attentiveness to and pace of consumption. Sensitivity and reciprocity are essential, as well as the ability to decide when to burp or continue feeding, when enough is enough, when to arouse the sleepy baby who has not fed adequately, and when to soothe and settle the overstimulated infant. Parke and Sawin found that fathers fed their babies as effectively and efficiently as did their spouses.[10] They solved the feeding problems, burped and stroked, awakened and soothed appropriately and, most important, got as much milk into their babies in the allotted time as did their spouses. This rather surprising finding held true whether or not the fathers had extensive experience with babies before their own were born.

Needless to say, men typically have very little infant care experience, much less babysitting or childhood play to prepare them for parenting. Yet they seem to know more than we, or even they, expect. To illustrate, I have often noticed that men in newborn nurseries and delivery rooms speak to their infants using a vocal pitch higher than their normal conversational voice. It is well known by neonatalogists (pediatric specialists in the care of newborn babies) that newborn infants respond better to higher than lower pitched verbal stimuli. Yet most men are not even aware they are altering their pitch, and certainly few have been told to do so. How do they know?

Anthropologists and ethologists such as Konrad Lorenz have suggested that the very nature and appearance of the human infant elicits powerful nurturing responses in both men and women. Erik Erikson has credited the profound helplessness of the human infant as the force evoking nurturing responses from both men and women.[11] Lorenz suggested that the baby's wobbly limbs, the high forehead, short face, and chubby cheeks elicit inborn instinctual, not learned, attachments.[12] These same researchers have also concluded that there are innate biological mechanisms over and above breast-feeding that produce the female's superior attunement to her baby, ultimately determining her greater involvement with the child.

But this is hardly borne out by the newly discovered facts. In 1978, Michael Lamb, a developmental psychologist and consistent researcher into the role of the father in the development of the child, decided to study this supposed "biological superiority" of women.[13] Men and women volunteers were shown a videotape of a crying, obviously distressed infant, followed by another tape of a comfortable, cooing baby. The response of the male's nervous and circulatory systems to the tape of the upset infant—i.e., quickened pulse rate, increased rate of respiration, overall alertness of the senses—and the subsequent relaxation response to the comforted infant was indistinguishable from that of the female. Researchers concluded that social determinations outweighed biological influences (which are undoubtedly present) in shaping the sensitivity of mothers and fathers to their babies' needs.

If we can believe, as the research suggests we should, that men are not bad for or dangerous around babies (as was the prevailing wisdom twenty years ago) how then do they behave with babies? Here again the research speaks loud and clear. In a 1975 study, Parke and Sawin studied first-time parents and found intriguing, important differences in the way fathers and mothers handle their children.[14] Mothers picked up their babies and held them intimately close to neck and breasts, handling and often talking in a gentle, soft, low-keyed manner. Fathers seemed to want always to *do* something with their babies when they picked them up. They were playful and provocative, tickling, nudging and roughhousing, somewhat more with their sons than their daughters, though not in every case. These findings were later expanded to include the observation that fathers used more play and games in general than did mothers.

Henry Biller, another developmental psychologist, began a series of studies in 1974 to examine a growing hunch that mothers and fathers interacted quite differently when their babies tried to explore the environment.[15] He observed men encouraging their babies' curiosity and urging them to attempt to solve intellectual and physical challenges, persistently fostering their child's sense of mastery over the outside world, functioning as a kind of "socializer/coach."

I recently found myself across the aisle from a young working couple in their early twenties and their thirteen-month-old adopted daughter on an economy, red-eye flight back to Hartford from Washington, D.C. The father had carried his daughter on board in the so-called "football position" with her back cradled in the curve of his left arm, sitting upright on his left hand, tucked in tight and safe against her father's left side. She met the eyes of the passengers, viewing the world en face with her father. After they were settled, she indicated her interest in the fresh-air ports overhead by pointing excitedly and gesturing. Her father held her up to touch and explore. The mother giggled anxiously when her daughter began to squeal loudly with delight over the discovery of the feeling of the air rushing over her fingers (making perhaps too much noise). The child then tried to roll over, precariously balanced on her father's hands. From her perch, over the heads of most of the passengers, she began to play peek-a-boo with anyone whose gaze she could capture. The mother terminated the game, playfully calling her a "flirt."

This fathering style of initiating more physical, rough and tumble, unusual, and exciting forms of play differs from a mother's style. Mothers in Biller's study tended to engage in more conventional toy-mediated acts of play, picking up their children to engage in caretaking and nurturing activities.

Do the babies respond to their fathers' novel, complex, interactive style? You bet they do. There have been several studies of fathers and their infants which focus on the effect the baby and father have upon each other. A group of Harvard pediatricians, led by T. Berry Brazelton and Michael Yogman, have noticed that by the time babies are eight weeks old, they are already responding quite differently to fathers and mothers.[16] At only six weeks of age, babies will hunch their shoulders and lift their eyebrows, as though in anticipation that "playtime has arrived" when their fathers appear. When the same six-week-olds see or hear mothers, they seem to expect more routine, serious, or functional business, such as feeding or diapering.

Fathers often notice such anticipations (or even invitations) in their babies, and they have a profound effect on them. These face-to-face differences in play, modulation, and verbal and physical contact are mutually appreciated by child, mother, and father, thereby justifying the father's feeling that there is something special afoot here. The infant's skill in evoking and shaping parenting may be more enduringly powerful than either inborn or biological parental predispositions.

The bottom line here seems to be that the father's involvement, undoubtedly promoted by such responses from his baby, has measurable positive effects in its own right on the development of the child. Intellectual competence is one observable effect. Frank Pedersen, psychologist at the National Institute of Child Health and Human Development, has found that the more actively involved a six-month-old baby has been with his or her father, the higher that baby's scores on certain tests of mental and motor development.[17] Similarly, Ross Parke, examining children over the first eight weeks of life, has found that the more fathers were involved in the everyday repetitive (even boring) aspects of care, such as bathing, feeding, dressing, and diapering, the more socially responsive the babies were.[18] In addition, Parke also found such babies were able to withstand stressful situations better.

In the traditional family, father has always been acknowledged to play two vital roles in the lives of his children. First, he helps his offspring develop a sense of their own competence and independence outside the powerful intimacy of the mother/child couple. Second, he contributes powerfully to the sexual identity formation of his children.[19] These concepts are so important that they merit closer scrutiny, beginning with the idea of father as promoter of independence.

Right from the beginning, the father is experienced by the infant as a person who is different from the mother—in style, smell, appearance, size, sound, texture, and in overall presence. Usually, he simply is not around as much. When he is there, he seems to matter, but in ways different from the mother. He is usually the most "significant other" in his baby's life and, as such, helps the baby learn about comings and goings, transitions, separations, and nonmother nurturing. The infant learns, through the father's in-and-out schedule, how to develop a mental image of something longed for and trusted, though not always actually present.

Because the child is accustomed to separations from the father, the child often turns more decisively to him for help in differentiating itself from its mother. When the "terrible twos" (which usually are not so terrible) arrive, the father is actively pursued by the child as the parent who is already seen as separate, novel, interesting, and a source of adventure.

How does the father gain this importance?

First, he earns it through his presence and attention. Second, he must to some extent be permitted it by the child's mother. Third, the baby accepts him and is usually ready at the slightest hint to take him up on this togetherness. This readiness seems to be promoted by the interesting unpredictable rhythms of the father's appearance and disappearance, and his novel, unique handling style, so different from mom's.

The earliest research into the father's impact on the development of his child centered on his other vital roles, such as his contribution, through father/child interactions, to his child's sexual identity formation. This early interest centered on the way a father differentiates, or shapes, his child's sexual identity to conform with the norms of gender/role expectations. Sociologist Eleanor Maccoby has pointed to the father's role in rendering his sons "masculine" and his daughters "feminine."[20] In studies of infant interaction, men roughhouse more with their sons than daughters but read more to their daughters. They use different language in describing their female and male children, and the list goes on and on (as we shall see in Chapter 3). Many such studies may be of limited value, however, because of the failure to examine carefully the stereotypic male/female interactions between the *parents* first, before reaching valid conclusions about sexual stereotyping among their children.

As we shall see later, primary nurturing fathers do not tend to treat their sons much differently from their daughters. In fact, these particular fathers resemble traditional mothers, in that they seem less occupied with shaping gender-appropriate behavior and beliefs in their children than are traditional fathers.

The hospital labor action crisis in England in 1973, when so many doctors were on strike, offered an unusual opportunity to see how father presence during home delivery affected birthing experiences and safety.[21] The doctors were not delivering in hospitals, but would assist at home. In this unusual (at least for late twentieth-century Western culture) situation, many mothers and fathers, not ideologically or even physically prepared for home birth, were stuck with no alternative to it. When all the factors that might have complicated the births, such as mothers over thirty, first births, and Rh-negative mothers, were analyzed, the most significant and relevant factor that militated *against* birth complications and further illness in the child and mother was the father's presence and aid at the birth. It is unfortunate that the researchers failed even to interview the fathers for their own responses to the events. Only half of the fathers present had expressed a wish to be present when they had thought the birth would be in-hospital, so the men in this group could not be considered counterculture, nontraditional fathers.

Interestingly, fathers attending births is a reversion to an old pattern that predates the assertions of medical, especially hospital, control over the customs of birth. In preindustrial America, fathers routinely assisted in births. A typical nineteenth-century birthing scene would have the laboring mother sitting on her husband's lap, bracing her back against his chest and her hands pushing against his upper thighs or knees, while he massaged her abdomen, assisting with each contraction. This position was sometimes called the "father chair."

Today's fathers are known to have beneficial effects on the birthing process, now that they have breached the delivery room doors again. Another British study, this one by the National Childbirth Trust, concludes that father presence "reduces the terror, loneliness, sensory deprivation and confusion of labor, especially protracted labor, resulting in decreased birth complications."[22]

Finally, one of the most dramatic findings in the research into father infant care is its relationship to subsequent sexual abuse of children. Whether the child is the father's or someone else's, if a man is involved in the physical care of his child before the age of three, there is a dramatic reduction in the probability that that man will be involved later in life in sexual abuse of children in general as well as his own.[23,24] The humanization of both father and child inherent in such activity erects a strong barrier against later exploitation of that intimacy.

The growing body of data verifying the relevance of fathers in the lives of their children, some of it now decades old, makes me wonder why it is not put to work.

An attorney in his early thirties, a father of three daughters, had asked to review some of my research and inquired about father/infant research in general. He sat on a state commission, impaneled to draft some "sane legislation" to help judges deal with child custody disputes. So often these disputes hinge, rightly or wrongly, upon the "fitness of parenting" issue. When he called from New Hampshire after reviewing the material I sent summarizing my findings to date, he said, "You know it is really very amazing, this stuff. There is a kind of strong commonsense logic and clarity about most of it. It is so interesting. As a father, I feel I know a lot of it to be true. I asked my wife to read it, to compare her response to see if it differed from mine, but it didn't, not in any important ways. Thanks. It's going to make my job easier. It should help the judges."

Yes, it will help the judges. More important, it will help us all. Yet, why is it so hard for our society to acknowledge fathering as a truly vital issue? Why do many of the men we will meet in this book feel so lonely, isolated, even excluded and ridiculed by friends and occasionally family for giving their parental role such seminal importance in their lives? Why is it so hard to take such men and their children seriously? Are we truly that much more comfortable as a society with the image of the "Life with Father" despot, who reigns benevolently over his family but in truth has little if any nurturing power or authority beyond administration? We accept images of skillful executives and bureaucrats, providers, entertainers, protectors, yes—but not of down-to-earth, flesh-and-blood nurturers.

My research leads me in two different directions to determine why the nurturing father still remains an almost underground phenomenon. First, I see all the societal controls and demands for men to keep their distance. Their job is to stabilize, stimulate, and protect the economic life of the family, if not society as a whole, and to make certain that the home fires don't go out.

My second belief is that men have not done themselves any favors here. Men's resistance to acknowledging their nurturing selves has, with the aid of the "experts," helped them avoid what they fear to be the innate vulnerability of the nurturing role. To discover how men have done themselves in, we turn to articles and books such as Mark Gerzon's *A Choice of Heroes*[25] or Arthur and Libby Colman's *Earth Father: Sky Father*,[26] which reexamine the male role in American society. To quote Jim Dittes, again from his book *The Male Predicament*, as he examines stereotyped ideas about what it means to be manly: "Acting supremely in control, in charge of his life, and many others, culturally programmed and automated to be strong and un-needy, he yells in his own ears 'be a man.' The narrow rigidity of this role as boss-manipulator, renounces, if not precludes many satisfactions of human relationships."[27] Dittes suggests this predicament is more manmade than womanmade. (More on this later in Chapter 12.)

Finally, it seems that the underground father is struggling his way out of the catacombs and into the daylight, elbowing and bellycrawling under and around the barbed wire of the old masculine stereotypes. He knows it may yet be possible to be emotional and vulnerable enough to nurture without feeling or looking like a victim. An interesting indicator of this change in attitude is the fact that the 1985 Yale graduating class asked Senator Paul Tsongas of Massachusetts to address it on its Class Day. He is a hero who is not a minion of Wall Street, the playing fields, the theater of war, Madison Avenue, the Oval Office, Hollywood, or Broadway—he is a father facing a fatal illness who decided to go home to his family.

3

Teaching the Boys Not to Cry

Four healthy, active five- and six-year-olds were happily "playing house" in the doll corner of Mrs. Kits' kindergarten. As a consultant, I was a frequent visitor here, usually with a few medical students in tow. Together, we saw the following drama unfold.

Three boys and one girl were intimately engaged in solving the daily problems of life through acting out the everchanging drama of domestic existence. After several comfortable moments, the trouble began. Sarah, who was directing this "play" about mommies and their babies, ordered Adam (whom she had designated to portray "the bad baby brother") to "go sit in the corner for being naughty." Adam responded by robustly feigning tears and pleading loudly, "Mommy, don't make me go, I'll be good—I'll be good," all the while sobbing convincingly.

Sarah, apparently undone by Adam's vigorous response, suddenly put down the purse and cooking utensils she'd been carrying about as symbols of her mother power, and in a state of agitation, left the doll corner to go get Mrs. Kits. In an anxious, pressured voice, she urged Mrs. Kits to discipline Adam. Sarah: "Come on, Mrs. Kits, Adam is crying and he's not supposed to. You're supposed to teach Adam not to cry. Girls can cry okay, and so can mommies. But boys can't do that, it's not fair. Even in pretend babies. You teach Adam not to cry."

I wondered what else Sarah might have wanted Mrs. Kits to "teach" Adam about the proper boundaries of male emotionality. Has five-year-old Sarah already learned that the rules of our society are different for boys and girls when it comes to the expression of feelings?

What might Sarah have meant in her earnest plea to Mrs. Kits?

She seemed to be saying, "Keep the boys off my property." Tears, feelings, maybe even babies, are "mine." It's true that Sarah's position is developmentally an important and healthy one for her to take at this age. After all, she has only recently mastered some of the fundamental differences between maleness and femaleness.

Yet, she articulates clearly one of the twentieth century's major confusions when dealing with people of differing sex as human beings. She is confusing Adam's boy*ness* with what she feels are appropriate boy*ish* doings. She is certain that Adam is a boy, a child whose sex, or gender, is male. But Sarah is irritated with this male, because his behavior is *not* in keeping with her ideas of the rules or roles for male children. What she's doing, innocently enough, is confusing Adam's gender *identity* with Adam's emerging gender *role*.

Adults do this, however, and they do it with destructive frequency. When they do this, it is much less innocent and imposes a much more critical limitation on both man and womankind. (In Chapter 11 we shall turn to examining the confusion of gender identity with gender role and its place in interfering with a completed sense of self for women and men.)

In this chapter, however, we began with the story of the development or suppression of a crucial element in the nurturing skill of our male children—the capacity for emotionality, tenderness, and empathy. How does such capacity develop, and what do we as a society do to foster or discourage the survival of this quality from its universal presence in childhood into adulthood?

Nurturing requires the abiding capacity for caring physically and emotionally for dependent beings. It is achieved best in the context of uniquely human feelings such as empathy, love, compassion, self-sacrifice, and the wish to protect the nurtured object from harm. How has it happened that so many men have come to their adulthood so removed and uncertain as nurturers? Is such a capacity by definition an exclusively feminine province? Not so, as we shall see.

Emotionality, the innate capacity to feel and respond to feeling, appears to be inborn, or "prewired" in all human infants. Adult interaction is the essential irreplaceable element that stimulates, indeed permits, its *ongoing* development and expression. Consequently, what the nurturing adults expect from a child in the way of emotional interaction plays a large role in helping a particular child bring its emotional capacities to fruition. Such expectations appear to vary considerably for male and female babies.

Widely respected research has shown that adults, both men and women, will talk to, feed, handle, and play with a baby differently if that baby is wearing boy's clothing than they will if the same baby is reintroduced later dressed as a girl.[1,2] The "boy" (dressed in blue, of course) is played with and jostled about more, talked to less, and more often held away from the adult's body. Words such as "strong...big...independent" are used more often to describe the "boy" babies. The "girl" (dressed in pink) is talked to more often, played with less, read to and cuddled more. Words such as "soft" and "little" are used more often. The *same* baby is responded to differently because of apparent sex difference.

Despite cultural and societal notions, I would guess that had this experiment been done in Ming China, Medici Florence, or Czarist Russia, it still would have yielded marked differences in the adult treatment of the child, depending on the culture's accepted behavior toward each sex.

Much of the early fatherhood research in the 1960s and 1970s focused on this sexual difference question, especially as it related to the ways mothers and fathers dealt with their female and male offspring. The research produced a list of *interactional* behaviors based on sex difference and is worth recounting here.[3,4,5]

Mothers talk more and are more involved with their daughters, and fathers with their sons. Fathers are more rough and tumble and unpredictable in their play, somewhat more so with sons, though not in every case. Children at three and a half years of age are treated by their fathers with more regard for their sex role differences than by their mothers.

Parental expectations regarding sex role differences in their children are also worthy of review. Middle-class schoolchildren, according to a study by University of California behavioral psychologists Jean and Jack Block,[6] are expected by both mother and father to be different in these ways: Boys are to be more independent, responsible, assertive, ambitious, and strong-willed, and to *control* their feelings. Girls are to be more obedient, dependent, thoughtful, well mannered, attractive, trustworthy, and capable of intimacy. A boy's world is more external, less sheltered or supervised, and he is expected to "learn from experience." A girl's world is more circumscribed and insulated, and she is more protected from experience and the unexpected.

This familiar old list of parental expectations, if present before birth, obviously leads to profoundly different ways and philosophies of handling and raising one's children. The list itself is linked to gender/role expectations as established within cultures and individuals; and as we have seen, for better or for worse, often has remarkably little to do with one's potential as a human being.

Such parental expectations are powerfully conveyed to children from very early in life and have a lot to do with whether a child feels acceptable. The adult world says a great deal to children like Mrs. Kits' kindergartners through such stereotypes. The "list makers" would certainly side with Sarah rather than Adam on the issue of "appropriate behavior." Sarah's behavior is seen according to the lists (none of which, by the way, leaves much room for the survival of open emotionality in boys) as gender-appropriate.

But what of Adam? Should we worry about him? What if the roles were reversed, and a purse-toting, dress-wearing Adam complained to Mrs. Kits about *Sarah's* tears? Would anyone notice?

As a society, ours tends to be more tolerant of cross-gender behavior in girls than in boys. What's more, recent evidence suggests that girls may cross gender boundaries more often than boys. In general, we set narrower limits of tolerance of cross-gender behavior in boys and are more upset by deviations outside those limits. It has long been noted in child guidance clinics that "effeminate" boys are referred for psychological help much more frequently than are "tomboyish" girls. In an important prospective longitudinal study of sexual identity development in children, psychologist Katherine Williams and psychiatrist Richard Green of the State University of New York at Stony Brook found that society offered far greater latitude to tomboyish girls than to effeminate boys:

> Tomboyish behavior does not usually elicit negative reactions and is more commonly viewed as positive or as a developmental stage not worthy of much alarm. Thus, girls may dress extensively in culturally masculine style or boys clothes, play sports with boys, take a male role when playing house and play with stereotypically masculine toys and not receive deviant labels and sanctions from parents, peers or professionals in the same way that boys who engage in stereotypical feminine behaviors do. (page 721)[7]

Should we worry more about Adam than Sarah? Probably not. He's working, too, hoping to be reassured by Mrs. Kits about the "rules" of expected gender/role behavior. Meanwhile, what is to happen to that wonderfully vital "feminine" part of Adam to which Sarah objects, the part that would have had him tending the babies in the kitchen when he was a year younger *before* the normal gender stereotyping reached the kindergarten? What will happen to the freewheeling, swashbuckling, independent side of Sarah that brought her such pleasure in her prekindergarten days?

Teacher and school-administration attitudes are very important in softening or hardening the normal kindergarten gender/role rigidity. It is very hard not to get drawn in. But if the adults remain aware that flexibility can be most helpful here, teacher support for less restrictive role expression can help boys and girls feel free to explore their whole minds and selves to include and tolerate the full range of "male" and "female" qualities of the self in the classroom. An example of such an excursion of awareness for one teacher is provided in one of my favorite monographs. "Boys and Girls: Superheroes in the Doll Corner" is written by an obviously gifted teacher, Vivian Paley, who teaches at the University of Chicago Laboratory Schools.[8] She tells simply how hard, but rewarding, it was for her personally to examine her own unwitting contribution to the sexual stereotyping of her young charges (male and female) during a carefully documented school year in kindergarten: "If I have not yet learned to love Darth Vader, I have at least made some useful discoveries while watching him at play. As I interrupt less, it becomes clear that boys' play is serious drama, not morbid mischief." (p. xii)

Dramatic in their awesome influence on sex typing

are the media. Children spend ten times as many hours with television males and television fathers than they do with their own real ones. What do they learn of male emotionality here? The television male is typically two-dimensional, usually ridiculously stereotyped, symbolic, seductive, violent, and romantically adventuresome. Cartoon males of course are the most absurd of all.

A small group of contemporary TV males who *are* fathers stands out as evidence of some improvement of late in the portrayal of nurturing capacities in men: Bill Cosby in his show, or "Punky Brewster's" adoptive father, or father Steven Keaton in *Family Ties*. All of these characters are variously drawn and acted so as to give more permission for men to appear affectionate, nurturing, wrong, emotional, even dependent, and more remarkably, in each case without massive defection by advertisers. There is even an occasional commercial for Campbell's Soup or McDonald's that shows fathers interacting in competent and real ways with their children, not just as bumbling fools who "barely survive until Mom comes home." A recent "Team Xerox" ad features the expectant face of a six- or seven-year-old daughter pressed against the windowpane with the caption "The real reason for getting my office running smooth is waiting for me at home." That's a beginning, but a greater victory would be if it were the face of an Adam instead of a Sarah.

Despite some small gains in the thawing of sexual stereotypes on the tube and the box, the media must be subject to our constant vigilance. Unlike school, where children's and adults' gender/role expectations interact with one another in an ongoing organic way over the school year and therefore *can* sometimes be eased, television and radio are seen by an audience that is absolutely passive. As such, these media can be considered even more omnipotent by our children, especially the young ones. That's why adults must be tuned in also, to be ready to subject that omnipotence to the reality test by constantly reminding their youngsters that "*General Hospital* sells laundry detergent, food, shampoo, and fantasies, not depictions of real adults who know how to solve life's real problems."

There is of course another institution that oftimes works against a flexible view of gender roles—the "advice of experts." "Experts" as such are a historically root-bound lot. What is "expert" in one age may seem absurd in another.

Phillipe Ariès, the great historical chronicler of *Centuries of Childhood,* noted that it was acceptable during the Middle Ages for adults to play with children's genitals (1965).[9] Other "experts" did not outlaw infanticide until A.D. 374, and then only because of the emergence of a new concept called "maternal nurturance."[10] Puritan fathers were specifically forbidden by the experts to touch, hold, or play with their children before "breeching" (age six) because of the threat to paternal authority. Nineteenth-century pediatricians discouraged men from ever playing with their children, lest they interfere with the maternal/ infant bond.

Although not strictly limited to the field of "expert" advice, a classic example of the destructive and constructive power of adult gender/role expectations occurs during the adolescent years in the way that adults educate boys about the role of emotionality and commitment in the sexual arena. Most sex education programs for males somehow manage to ignore the fact that there is more than a casual relationship between sex and fathering. Males are taught about contraception, sexually transmitted disease, unwanted pregnancy, and reproduction but almost never about intercourse as an ongoing, active, decision-making process in procreation, pregnancy, birth, and even child-rearing. To compound such "oversight," there is almost always a much greater emphasis on the involvement of the female. This is certainly a very effective way to keep men away from "their" children, both physically and emotionally.

This separation of contraception from family planning for males perpetuates the father's distancing of the act of sex from procreation and limits his possible participation in conscious parenting. Young men are then forced to stick to archaic positions regarding sexuality that hide their uncertainty and anxiety. This may result in increasingly defensive sexual postures (boasting, promoting the idea of "sexual performance on demand") and becomes even more devaluing when coupled with the peer pressure against being sexually inexperienced. One young National Honor Society member recently told me, "You only think about the father end of sex when you get caught. Otherwise it's irrelevant."

Tragically, by adulthood, most male gender/role typing is so rigid that many men won't even ask whether or not they are on the right subway, much less seek out information about family planning or sexuality. They are supposed to be independent, to be decisive, and never to need instruction. The mark of clear gender separation and differentiation toward which Adam and Sarah set out at five is now so far overshot that forthright, independent, competent women are considered unfeminine, and empathic, emotionally forthcoming, competently nurturing men are regarded as unmanly. By young adulthood, it is not at all unusual for men who are close to or interested in children (other than their own siblings) to be questioned regarding their gender orientation, whether they are day-care workers, residents in psychiatry, or training candidates in child analysis.*

Once we have carefully examined this universal business of observed sexual difference in children, it is very important to remember that the person doing the observing, whether in research or real life, is an adult—behaving, thinking, and seeing according to his or her *own* views of sexual difference. Consequently, the only truly valid notion of sexual difference is the one that embraces the interaction *between* a particular child's and a particular adult's *concepts* of sexual difference. In close contact, it is not possible to hide the sex of a child from its parent nor the sex of the parent from its child. Whether the interaction is same sex or cross sex powerfully affects and shapes the adult's and the child's behavior. The failure to appreciate the interactional nature of expressed sexual difference is a fatal flaw in much of the otherwise interesting research cited above. This oversight is all the more serious when we consider how adults' expectations, wishes, dreams, and fears for their children so powerfully affect the way they raise, handle, and interact with their own or other offspring.

An example of children's expectations that are most probably rooted in some adult opinion somewhere recently found its way to our home. Periodically I am honored by a request from one of our daughters to come to talk to her class about some aspects of my research. Emily's eleven-year-old fellow fifth graders had just finished watching some of my videotapes of fathers and young children together. A bright male classmate sitting next to Emily

---

*At the recent 1985 Fall Meetings of the American Psychoanalytic Association in New York City, Dr. Theodore Shapiro, Professor of Psychiatry and Pediatrics and Director of Child and Adolescent Psychiatry at Cornell University Medical College, when discussing some of my work, recalled being "held in suspicion" for his interest in children and infants when he began his training in child psychiatry.

leaned over to her to whisper a question: "Does your Dad *have* to work with those kids? What a weird job for a Dad." I've heard countless similar sentiments from adults.

Were Adam to continue on his prescribed journey toward the limitation and constriction of his emotionality, he'd probably think it was a "weird job for a Dad," too. The discouragement of innate emotionality in males like Adam strikes me as an absurd squandering of an essential human quality in half of the species! Active male nurturance promotes the healthy growth and development of our young. When it is present, fulfillments abound that were previously unimagined. The cost is simply too great in incomplete lives, marriages, and families for us to carry on teaching the boys not to cry.

As we turn now to meet the families of the nurturing fathers, discover their histories, and learn of their kin, we shall see for ourselves what happens when men, with the help of their children, cease to fear their capacity for intimacy or emotionality.

4

The Nurturing Fathers and Their Kin

I was fairly certain there were not legions of families out there in which mothers did the breadwinning and fathers the child-rearing, but I estimated that I would need at least a dozen to conduct "hypothesis-generating research." This is a kind of observational study that is conducted on questions so new that researchers are not yet certain what to examine or which questions are the most relevant to ask. Such investigations, whether about people or photons, are called "pilot" studies, in the sense that "to pilot" means to "lead through unfamiliar waters." A dozen seemed an arbitrary but still scientifically valid, symmetrical number of families, and the time I planned to allot to the project, between teaching time and patient care for the next two years, seemed sufficient to the task.

My plan was to recruit six families the first summer and six the second, when my academic schedule eased enough for me to conduct research. I would study the babies and their parents, distill the important questions, and then embark more efficiently at some later date on the study of many more families over a longer time.

I began my search for these families by spreading the word among colleagues and friends that I intended to do a study of the primary nurturing father and his child in families, especially those with children under two years of age. It seemed important to focus the study of such parenting when it has the greatest impact, those first two years of life when attachments are first formed and the rate of human growth and development is so rapid.

I also drew up a list of fifty pediatricians whom I

knew in the surrounding cities and towns. I included the local primary care centers and clinics, too, because I was interested in the whole socioeconomic range of family life, not just the upwardly mobile middle class. As a teacher in child psychiatry, child development, and pediatrics in a large medical center, I spend a good deal of time collaborating and agonizing with pediatricians over the families in their practices. As I knew many of them personally, it seemed a natural place to begin. I sent out a letter from which this excerpt is taken:

With your help I hope to assemble a small cohort of families which contain fathers who have primary caretaking responsibilities for their infants or toddlers (from newborn up through 24 months of age). Even though the parenting may be shared with the mother, I am primarily interested in fathers who bear the major responsibility for care giving (e.g., working mother, student father at home, dual career family, etc.). This arrangement need not be considered long-term, but one which in your judgment, allows for the formation of a primary affectional tie between the father and infant.

In-depth interviews, an hour-and-a-half to two-and-a-half hours in total, will be conducted with the father. An extended home visit will be conducted as well, in order to meet and interview other significant family members, most importantly the mother. This will also permit the observation of the family unit as a whole. The infant will have a comprehensive developmental evaluation, using the Yale Developmental Schedules.

The information from the developmental assessment will be available to the pediatrician if desired. The same information will also be shared in a supportive manner with the family in order to enhance the understanding of these infants, but also to support the fathers and mothers in what some may consider a rather vulnerable parenting effort....

If my colleagues remembered getting the letter, a typical response was "I don't have any of those in my practice...never seen one...rare as hens' teeth...good luck!" Soon I learned to ask more detailed questions, such as, "Do you have any families in your practice where the father usually brings the child in for illnesses or for well-baby check-ups?" It had occurred to me that this question might be necessary because some of the families I sought might not even think of themselves in the way *I* was describing them, and so their physicians might not see them that way either. Meanwhile, I also learned to ask the pediatricians to check with their head nurse or receptionist. In some practices, these staff members turned out to be a more reliable source of family data, as the doctor was often so focused on the health and welfare of the baby that he tended to treat father-presence as a kind of ongoing exception.

As the efficiency of my inquiry increased, so did the yield. One pediatrician called back to say, "Come to think, I *do* have this guy who brings his daughter in all the time. My receptionist called and he's interested in being in the study." One of the senior pediatricians in the community called to tell me that "*two* of my families were interested, not none as I said the first time. I'd seen both mothers only in the hospital after the birth. I just thought the father was doing the 'well-baby visit' as an interested escort. I could have even more! I'll keep my eyes open."

To my astonishment, I was soon faced with a wholly unforeseen problem. I suddenly had nine families that met the criteria, not the six for whom I had budgeted research time. (The same dilemma was to present itself the following summer.) Even more amazing, I was only at the tenth name in the alphabetical list! Was it possible that there were *hundreds* of such families out there, not just dozens as I had guessed? That in itself was the first intriguing question. How many *are* there out there? There were simply no reliable data anywhere, including the United States Census Bureau, about what the prevalence of such families might be in our general population.

I decided to recruit some help. I invited some interested medical students to join me as summer research assistants so that I could include the extra families in the study. My medical school sponsors summer fellowships for a few medical students who wish to pursue research questions that intrigue them and may help them develop their skills in research. Several gifted students joined the study each summer from then on as note takers, recorders, and literature searchers.

My recruitment effort, however, soon hit yet another snag. Even more families cropped up in these same ten practices. (I had long since abandoned my alphabetical list.) The word was spreading quickly. I began to notice that families were interested in being in the study not only to tell their stories or learn more about their babies but because they were often quite lonely. "We would love to be in your study... are there any more of us out there... are we going to meet any of the other families in the study?" My original study plan, or protocol, did not call for contact between the families. I wanted to study each one separately and not have the results affected by the families' sharing and conveying one another's stories or experiences. Besides, the study was not designed in any way to modify these families' lives. Nevertheless, the parents sounded quite isolated and uncertain. Why? Would they in fact resemble one another? How real would this "aloneness" I heard in their voices turn out to be?

The study focused separately but equally on information from various places in the family's life. Some of the data would come from direct observation, what the researchers behold with their eyes, often referred to as "hard data." An example here is the direct examination of the baby or infant's developmental abilities. I would use standardized assessment schedules to test the baby myself and would not rely solely on what the pediatrician or parents could tell me about what the child could or could not do. This was of primary importance. *How* the babies of such families are doing has a kind of "proof of the pudding" validity to it. If the babies are doing okay, common sense tells us these children are not at risk developmentally. If they are not doing well, we need to start worrying about why.

Other directly observable "hard data" on the baby *within* the family would be collected in a series of home visits and interviews with the couple, again giving the researcher a chance to witness these parents conducting the business of everyday life with their children.

Equally intriguing and important is the information drawn from the parents' reports. These are sometimes called indirect, or "soft," data because they are not events observed by the researcher but instead are the results of parents' historical perceptions and memories. Though viewed as somewhat less reliable factually, such data are of a different but equal vitality because they comprise the family's story of itself. The story embraces the family's view of its own inception, major landmarks, social and economic context, secrets, strengths and weaknesses, and continuity through history and tradition—its legacies, dreams, and wishes for its future. My research design required and encouraged both kinds of data, because I believed that one is useless without the other, a left hand which knows not of the right.

Equally useless was just one look. In the case of child and family development, two looks separated by time are exponentially more valuable than a doubly careful look once. So the families were told we would need to meet with them again after one year to "catch up" with them and their babies.

This was the plan. We would all start together and go on to chart routes through unfamiliar waters. To review: We planned a small clinical investigation of intact families in which the father serves as primary caretaker of the family's children. The study would address four different areas: (1) the development of infants from 2 to 22 months (these were the ages of the children who were found for study), (2) the psychological characteristics of the fathers and the mothers, (3) the fathers' nurturing patterns, and (4) the marital relationships.

And so we began.

Seventeen families were finally recruited from in and around the large New England industrial and academic community where I lived and worked.

The families ranged across the socioeconomic spectrum from those on welfare to blue-collar and white-collar workers and professionals. A few fathers were unemployed, but the rest were graduate students, blue-collar workers, sales representatives, artists, computer programmers, real estate brokers, lawyers, writers, or small businessmen. If employed, they had incomes ranging from $7,000 to $125,000 a year. The mothers were nurses, teachers, secretaries, lawyers, sales representatives, real estate brokers, blue-collar workers, or welfare recipients. If employed, they had incomes ranging from $8,000 to $75,000 per year.

Of the seventeen children, eight were male and nine were female infants. The parents ranged in age from 19 to 36 with a mean age of 24 for fathers and 25 for mothers. Surprisingly, all the children except one were first-born, though this was not part of the research design.

The average age at marriage for these couples had

been 23 for men and 24 for women. Of the 34 adults, three had been married previously; one man and two women. The man, 26, was married three years before his wife died in an auto accident. One 30-year-old woman had been married for three years when her first husband died. The other was 22; her marriage had lasted less than a year and had ended in an uncontested, mutually agreed upon divorce.

The fathers were first interviewed in their own domain—at home while caring for their children. Detailed histories were taken not only about the choice to stay home with the baby but also about their own lives and families of origin, their parents, their growing up, their previous experience with children. During this extended first visit, usually 90 minutes in length, observations were recorded of the father/infant interaction in a natural setting during the process of typical child care or "male care" as one father called his "job." But the main focus was on the stories the men told of their own lives and experiences. Would we discover some recurring factor that would predict such unique parental behavior?

Here is their group portrait.

All seventeen fathers reported themselves as having been traditionally reared, their fathers breadwinners, their mothers raising the children and caring for the home. Thirteen of the group came from intact families. The other four had lived predominantly with their mothers before beginning their own families (one had lived with his father from the age of 12, after a bitter divorce). They had on the average two siblings with a range from none to seven.

Six of the men had attended private school for all or part of their secondary education. Fifteen of the seventeen men had spent most of their post–high school years living away from home, while the other two remained with their families. Of these, one worked and the other commuted to college.

All seventeen fathers reported that as teenagers,

they seemed headed toward the expected role of breadwinner, protector, or provider. Few even considered fathering
as a role. *None* would have predicted as teens that they
would be rearing their own children.

As would be expected of adolescent males, few recalled
giving any thought as teenagers to what might be gained or
lost by actively nurturing a child. The immediacy of controlling their own instinctual needs during this notoriously
agitated era seemed to eclipse interest or reflection about
the needs of *any* children in their lives, present or future.
Often when these men did think about fathering as teenagers, it was in terms of pride in siring an offspring as an
exhibition of fertility or potency and not of fulfilling a
dream to nurture competently or of "being immortal."
Only four of the seventeen men reported active memories
of anything more than casual involvement with young
children or infants as teenagers. Three of these were involved with infants born into their immediate families.
One father lived transiently during his adolescence with a
family friend who sheltered at-risk foster children.

To put it simply, the bulk of these men regarded
themselves as having developed normally (based on their
own stories) and in step with their traditional social and
familial values.

Taken as a whole, this was an unremarkable group
with little to distinguish it from any other predominantly
middle-class collection of young men who would self-
select for such a study. However, some subtle subgrouping
proved interesting with regard to *when* during the conception and pregnancy process the families decided that the
fathers would "mother." Early during my contact, I asked
when the families had decided on this arrangement of
child care, and they all shared only one decision characteristic. *None* of the families considered this a permanent
situation at its inception.

At the outset, the families' "decision phase" could be grouped roughly into thirds: the first third (six families) decided that the father would be primary caregiver prior to the pregnancy, the second third (another six families) made that decision during the pregnancy, and the final third (five families) made it during the neonatal period, around the time of the baby's birth.

The early-deciding group of men tended to be professionals, graduate students, upper socioeconomic people. A typical example was the father who decided to "take some time off from his career" (education) while the wife pursued hers (retail sales) and would care for the baby because it seemed either "fair or interesting or both to do for a while." The attempt to time conception carefully was a hallmark of this group.

The middle third was often similar in reasoning but was typically influenced by some change in the mother's feeling about staying home with a baby after she'd begun carrying it around inside her. Or, it had become increasingly clear that the mother's job or career would be jeopardized by maternity leave but that the father's economic status was changing anyway or that his established career could better withstand a leave of absence.

The late-deciding third was in some ways the most interesting one to me. These families often had the decision "forced" upon them at the last moment, usually for economic reasons; for example, when the father lost his job while mother retained hers. Not surprisingly, this group contained the highest number of initially reluctant, uncertain fathers.*

Having described the overall groupings, it is interesting to examine especially the one subgroup of men that

---

*In the end, it also contained fathers who were to stay the longest in the role of primary caregivers and be among its most vocal, committed practitioners.

distinguished itself most clearly from the other fathers. This was the group of "early deciders." Five of the six men who had chosen *earliest* (prior to conception) to serve as the primary nurturing parent tended to describe *their* fathers as "uninvolved" in their lives during their growing up, often most particularly during adolescence. Only here, at the earliest timing in paternal nurturing choice, was there any clustering of common experience.

These five men frequently portrayed their own fathers as "absent...gone a lot...distant." Their nurturant role identifications seemed more strongly associated with their mothers than with their more remote fathers. They also seemed to pair in marriage primarily with women of more independent strivings who did not seek their sole primary fulfillment in life through mothering or nurturing.

As for the middle and late choosers, eight of those eleven men spoke of their fathers in predominant positive terms, irrespective of how physically available they were. This larger group contained no preponderance of either paternal presence or absence.

In searching for any unique aspects of development that might set these seventeen primary nurturing fathers apart from the traditional father, I looked at certain classic constructs of male development which might highlight these men's developmental experience. I chose to examine their masculine identification, feelings of alienation, social adjustment, paternal and maternal identification, and experience with infants and children as revealed in their histories, especially during adolescence.

Masculine Identifications. Physical strength as teenagers was important to these men in compensating for the usual age-appropriate awkwardness. Tenderness and intimacy were typically reported as unwelcome feelings or demands. Sixteen of seventeen had held jobs during high school, typically to make money or "be on my own."

Though often chafing against and longing for an adult male's authority (usually their father's), admiration by girlfriends and others seemed a greater prize.

Alienation. Almost all the study fathers described themselves as having many friends before marriage and belonging to social, athletic, and religious organizations. There was little delinquency or involvement with authoritative correctional agencies. "Belonging" was seen by most of the men as very important. Only one of the seventeen had embraced alienation as a personality style during adolescence; he had been a "self-conscious hippie," a fact he reported as an amusing memory.

Social Adjustment (Behavior and Class). Fourteen of the seventeen fathers said they had begun dating by the last year in high school (the expected contemporary percentage). Typically, most of the men did not regard their first dating experiences as either *friendships* or as especially important relationships. Affirmation of their own sexual identities seemed more important. Intimacy was certainly not a characteristic of such early experiences regardless of social class.*

Father Identification. Signs of rivalrous or competitive relationships with fathers during adolescence were quite obvious during descriptions of these men's teenage years. Yet, in these traditionally raised men who were now being so *untraditional* in their own fathering would we find unique forms of identification with the father?

---

*Psychiatrist George Vaillant in his classic thirty-year study of male psychological health reported that "Social class variables played no role in distinguishing poor fathers from good fathers....Subjects who had grown up in upper-class families, buffered from their parents by many servants, did not make worse fathers than those who had grown up in more closely knit middle-class homes; the latter did not make better fathers than the upwardly mobile socially disadvantaged men who had more of an economic struggle in the early years after college. Many upwardly mobile men are bad fathers, but so are many downwardly mobile men." (page 318)[1]

What I found was that fourteen of the seventeen in the study could be grouped at the polar extremes of paternal closeness; the majority of fathers were either quite close *or* quite distant from their fathers during adolescence. Those men who were close to their fathers while growing up seemed to be reveling in a strong identification with a nurturing, protecting, feeling father. Those men who were distant (the early deciders) may well have been trying to master conflicts felt in relation to their unavailable fathers by nurturing their own babies. Interestingly, few of the men in the study could be called neutral on the subject of father-closeness.

It can be said, therefore, that pleasant memories of being fathered *or* lingering dissatisfaction with the way one was fathered in the past may compel a man once he becomes a father either to repeat or remake his past.

Mother Identification. As all of these men were traditionally raised, their primary nurturing relationships had been with their mothers. Curiously, although mothers were often described as "important...the boss...wearing the pants," there was not a "domineering" or hostile mother described in the group.*

How have these men managed to find themselves so thoroughly nurturing? As Mr. Mellow, a study father whom we shall encounter in greater detail later, concluded thoughtfully toward the end of our first interview: "Talking about this makes me think how odd it is that I have become both the mother *and* a father. I really love it...wouldn't have it any other way."

Like all men who struggle with the meaning of their

---

*Vaillant reports as one of his most impressive findings from the thirty-year study mentioned previously that "the image of the dominating mother seemed more a reflection of a young man's immaturity or of his mother's poor mental health than a reflection of actual strength or dominance in the mother....dominating mothers were rarely strong women and in fact were often emotionally ill. Their power to dominate came more from their, or their son's, view of reality than from their own too loving or powerful nature." (page 298)[2]

role as nurturer, conflicts exist for these fathers between the desire for intimacy with the child and the wish to be a productive, working, creative man of the world. The men in this study have found particularly fulfilling, though far from simple, resolutions which have allowed them to both "father and mother" in ways that have been quite rewarding for them and often for their wives. The success of such resolutions is also evident in the relative, though far from complete, absence of rivalry and competition between the mother and father, especially in the younger couples where it might be more expected.

Experience with Infants and Children. It was a great surprise to find that the study fathers had so little previous experience with young children. The five men who had decided early to nurture their infants tended to have had more experience with children than the rest of the group. Possibly the more interesting segment of the population are the twelve who did *not* have extensive prefathering experiences with children, who seemed to lack the "parent gene." They too were able to form intensely mutual, need-satisfying reciprocity with their infants. That seemed a genuine surprise—one which the families will later explain.

Having looked hard for consistent factors but finding few, we could not draw a clear portrait of *the* classic "father/mother." The diversity of fathering seen in these families equals the diversity of most families' mothering. It was clear that there was no *generic* primary nurturing father discernible or describable here. Nevertheless there is a pervasive, involving, committed fatherliness about these men.

But would such "fatherliness" have been evident in all the men who selected themselves for this study, had we been privileged to meet them earlier in their lives?* I somehow doubt it. While the *capacity* to father is certainly more broadly rooted in biology, it may have less to do with fatherliness per se than does the *expression* of fathering. Although it's not the subject of our discourse here, it is essential to remember the infant's enormous contribution to the development of fatherliness through eliciting, evoking, provoking, promoting, and nudging fathering from men. It does take two to tango.

In sum, these men were not an unusually homogeneous lot with strongly delineated idiosyncrasies that predicted and determined their parenting choices and behavior. Instead we found a predominantly healthy, heterogeneous group of men, with some subtle predispositions, who were deeply committed to raising their children in ways that were of paramount importance to them and to their spouses.

And what of the mothers? Who were these women who were making a choice and living a life as unique as their husbands'? Here is their group portrait.

The women of the study ranged in age from 21 to 36, the mean age being 25. They came from families every bit as diverse culturally and socioeconomically as their husbands. Three of the men had been only children, whereas two of the women were without siblings. The number of siblings was slightly higher for the men than it was for the women, the average size of the father's family being 5.2 and the mother's averaging 4.3 members.

Six of the seventeen mothers were first born, compared to four of the men. One man and one woman were adopted; these two were not married to each other. One couple I have included as married because they had lived

*I agree wholeheartedly with psychoanalyst Theresa Benedek's definition of fatherliness as "an instinctually rooted character trait which enables the father to act toward the child or all children with immediate empathetic responsiveness."[3]

together for five years before becoming parents. They had not married officially because the father's eccentric uncle would have disinherited him if he married before the age of 30. One husband and one wife (from different marriages) had been married previously, the first marriage ending in the wife's death after three years, the second ending in divorce.

Fifteen of the seventeen women still had living mothers. Of these, all but two of those grandmothers disapproved initially of their daughters' and sons-in-laws' child-care arrangements. Thirteen of the original seventeen mothers had had mothers who worked outside the home either full or part time at some point during their childhoods.

The women's educations ranged from eighth grade to graduate degrees in medicine, law, and business. This was exactly the same spread for the husbands, though an extra Ph.D. degree or two was held in the father group. Again, the timing of the choice to have the care of the baby rest primarily with the father presented some interesting correlations.

Those women who chose earliest tended to have higher incomes and more education. Several of these women were at "critical" phases of their careers or educations and had had their babies sooner than they would have preferred. The middle group, who made the fathering decision during the pregnancy, tended to talk about their child care plans as temporary measures. For example, Mrs. James had asked her husband "to take over for a few months while I made my new promotion secure (in a real estate office). Then I'll be able to help out."

The late-deciding group had the lowest income and least education. There were two disadvantaged families in this group whose mothers were earning income "illegally" because of limitations placed on allowable income by state welfare regulations. This was a kind of double jeopardy for these women because they could not be proud of their work since it was always so uncertain. Another one of the late-deciding couples had exchanged nonunion construction jobs because the father had injured himself. Although he was not able to bend over to lift bricks, he could manage a baby. The foreman accepted this man's sturdily built wife as a replacement at the job site! Five years later, *she* is the foreman.

As a group, the women were no more or less homogeneous than the men were. Yet one life choice did separate out one subgroup from the rest, i.e., those who chose to leave or suspend work and stay home full time to care for the children after the birth of a second child. These women had mothers who were somewhat similar. When I looked back at the early histories they gave me at the time of the first interview, I discovered that as a group they tended to describe their own mothers as being "unhappy ...cold...unavailable." One of the group said the only time she ever heard her mother laugh was when she watched the "Honeymooners" on TV. This group of women seemed to feel more strongly identified with their fathers, whom they generally regarded as more nurturing and supportive and more available to them emotionally than their mothers. Such women also reported feeling less competitive with their spouses, and they tended to identify positively with their husband's nurturing of the first baby.

Having met the mothers and fathers, it seems time to meet the babies. Although we had gathered valuable, clear first impressions of the children during the first visit at home with their fathers, the first formal assessment that focused primarily on the children was made at the more laboratorylike setting of the Child Development Unit of the Yale Child Study Center. The children were accompanied by the father and mother if she could make it (and she usually did) to the interview where the standardized assessment instrument I'd chosen to evaluate each child's development, the Yale Developmental Schedule, was used.

The Yale Developmental Schedule is a comprehensive tool originally created at the Yale Child Study Center by Dr. Sally Provence some 25 years ago.[4] It is a composite protocol used widely for research and clinical purposes, consisting of carefully chosen items from several standardized scales (e.g., Gesell, Stanford-Binet, and Merrill Palmer). It provides a reliable matrix for assessing, recording, and following over a time a young child's performance in motor function, problem solving, language, and personal-social skills. It allows the clinician or researcher to compare an individual child's developmental performance with the expected range of competence for children of the same age. The development of the infant or very young child is so complex and so rapid in the early years that one has to evaluate skills and competence carefully in many areas in order to have a valid picture of *how* any child is maturing at a given moment in time.

The Yale schedules have one feature, unique among standardized instruments, which made them quite useful for this study. They can be used to follow a child from birth to its sixth birthday without changing assessment tools. So, if I chose to stretch the study out over time, it would still retain its validity.

The developmental examiner (frequently my role) provides a supportive interaction so that the child can become comfortable enough to do his or her best at some familiar and some novel tasks. Developmental competence is assessed in several areas simultaneously; for example, the child's large and small muscle skills are carefully scored as it solves certain puzzles or block design problems posed during the testing. To illustrate: for the 6-month-old baby to get several small red cubes into a cup or for the 24-month-old to build a tower of 10 cubes is no simple matter. Dexterity, persistence, and comprehension of the task are all required to solve the problem. The *age* of the baby is less reliable as an indicator of its capacities, however, than a careful evaluation of *where* this child is on the well-mapped road of developmental progress. Personal-social functions are then evaluated similarly. Here we look at how involved the child is emotionally with the important people in its life and how competent the child is in eliciting the social interactions so critical to its survival with and without the use of language. Frequently, two sessions were required to get this all done.

Some of the children warmed quickly to the procedure, as though the evaluation itself were an enjoyable game, while others waited and watched carefully, seeming to seek assurance that the examiner or their performance was okay. Eventually, the profiles began to take shape. The developmental competencies of these babies were compared to the age-expected competence of the more typically raised babies represented on the standardized schedules. While there was little cohesive continuity to the group socially, economically, or culturally, as a whole, some intriguing trends emerged.

First, these children raised primarily by men were active, vigorous, robust, and thriving infants. They were also competent. The majority of study infants functioned above the expected norms on several of the standardized tests of development. The youngest group of infants (two to twelve months) performed certain problem-solving tasks on the same level as babies who were often two to six months their senior; personal and social skills were also ahead of schedule. The older babies in the group (12 to 22 months) performed as well.

Secondly, apart from the quantitative scored aspects of these babies' performance, curious qualitative or stylistic characteristics emerged quite frequently; for example, these infants seemed to be especially comfortable with and attracted to stimulation from the external environment.

A third finding, although hard to quantify, looked something like this: Many of the babies seemed to expect that their curiosity, stick-to-itive-ness, or challenging behavior would be tolerated, even appreciated by the adults in their environment, whether they were parents, examiners, or observers. The expectation that play would be rich, exciting, and reciprocated or that block designs or puzzles would eventually succumb to sheer determination was widespread in this group of babies. One of the older children, 22-month-old Amy, knocked over her tower of ten small, red cubes (which she had so carefully and proudly constructed a moment before) with a broad sweep of her closed fist. She sat forward quickly on the edge of her baby chair, and with a broad open-mouthed smile fixed her eyes with excited anticipation on the face of the examiner, as if to say "Okay, guy, let's have some *real* fun!"

As these findings emerged, I realized that I was surprised. Had I expected less? Apparently. As the father of two daughters, I had privately hoped that the babies were doing all right. But *better* than all right would take some explaining. Some of the explaining necessitated a second look at the fathers.

I had expected at the very least that the fathers' uncertainty and lack of preparation for their job as primary nurturing parent would be somehow observable in their babies' developmental profiles. As a psychiatrist, I had been taught to believe that the earlier and better prepared a mind is to meet an obstacle, the more gracefully the obstacle is surmounted. The reverse is also a maxim—the less preparation, the more difficult the obstacle. Another surprise. After the data were analyzed, the *timing* of the decision of the father to be the primary caretaker could not be correlated with how well the child did on developmental examination. The babies of the last-deciding families could not be distinguished from those of the first-deciding families on the basis of developmental testing.

So, the babies were doing well. How about the fathers? Did they demonstrate the capacity to nurture another person adequately, to ensure its survival, and to assure its development as a human being? Could they "read" and understand their babies well enough to feed, change, nap, and comfort on time? Would their responses reasonably conform to the baby's needs?

In a word, yes.

Though as a group they achieved the relationship at different rates, all the fathers had formed the deep reciprocal nurturing attachment so critical to the early development of the thriving human baby. The depth and rapidity of the attachment amazed even them. *How* it happened varies, of course, from man to man and baby to baby. Representative stories will be told in the following chapter.

The fathers as a group reported a similar progression of feelings as they gradually took charge of their babies' lives. Most of the families had an initial three- to eight-week period in which the mother was the primary, or at least coequal, caretaker of the infant. Afterward the mother returned to work, career, or school. This was a critical transition for both parents and babies. But a curiously consistent sequence of realizations was reported by the men.

At first, when the everyday troubles began with the crying or inconsolable infant, the father would think to himself, "What would my wife do?" No surprises here.

The surprises came in the next stage. Anywhere from ten days to a few months later, these men had completely abandoned their mental portrait of themselves as being a "stand-in for mom." Unique caregiving styles flowed forth as the men gradually began to think of themselves as parents in their own right and not just substitutes standing "in loco matris" (in the mother's place). Most of the men kept this feeling to themselves as though they could not quite believe it, or trust it, or maybe shouldn't even have it.

The interactional impact of babies on fathers has, of course, intrigued other researchers. Some tried to find an expression that would adequately describe the father's fascination with his baby. "Engrossment," the word introduced in the early 1970s by psychiatrist Martin Greenberg to encompass the sense of "absorption, preoccupation and interest by the father in the new infant," seems a whispered understatement compared to these fathers' own descriptions of their experiences. These fathers had actively incorporated their infants into their whole lives. They were enraptured *and* enthralled with their babies. There appeared to have been a very literal "taking in" of these babies by their fathers as a profound emotional event.

The fathers also had difficulty believing that they had become so immensely significant to their own infants. A four-month-old girl in the first group stopped eating for two days and developed a week-long sleep disturbance after her father shaved off his beard. She became irritable and inconsolable and avoided her father's gaze when he attempted to comfort her. She would accept her mother's presence and comforting, but only briefly. Only after a neighbor failed to recognize him in the parking lot did it occur to the father that his daughter might be having the same problem.

How can we explain the intensity of such attachment so early in life? How can we understand how rapidly it develops? I think we have to bring the babies in to help find an answer.

The six- or eight-week-old infant of whom the father takes charge is a very different baby from the newborn and enormously more complex. The power of such an infant to evoke in its father a profound commitment to its well-being, through the daily, even tedious, tasks of caregiving, seems to me to dwarf the issues of parental role, gender, or even a specific antecedent experience for the job.*

To show how these remarkable relationships develop I have chosen three families to tell their own stories in detail. These spokesfamilies were selected not necessarily for their eloquence but for the clarity with which they spoke of their lives together. They also reveal certain common threads that wove through the tapestry of the whole group's experience. We first meet the Mellow family. Middle class and of average age, they chose late to parent in this fashion. The father, one of six who had not attended the birth of their babies, is typical of many men who did not begin as fathering enthusiasts. Helen, their daughter, is remarkably clear in telling her own story of this unique parenthood variation.

Next we encounter the Blues and their son Henry. Mr. Blue was a "fathering enthusiast" and, like most of the men in the study, had attended his son's birth. The Blues were typical of the families who chose fairly early (though

---

*A quote from Eric Erikson's *Insight and Responsibility* to clarify the point: "A seeming paradox in life is man's collective power to create his own environment...each individual is born with a naked vulnerability, extending into prolonged infantile dependence. The weakness of the newborn, however, is truly relative. While far removed from any measure of mastery over the physical world, newborn man is endowed with an appearance and response which appeal to those needs; which arouse concern in those who are concerned with his well-being; and which in making adults care, stimulate their active care taking." (page 113)[5]

not actually prior to conception) to parent this way. They also represent the families wherein the father maintains a long-term primary parental role, despite the emergence of severe marital turmoil (an atypical event in the study). Henry, thriving and competent, also speaks loud and clear for the male children in the study.

Finally the Youngs, who represent the younger families in the study, had chosen the latest of all parents to have Allen serve as primary caretaker. Working class (but moving up), the Allens also typify those families who, after the birth of a second child, reverted to a more traditional division of family roles. Nevertheless, their daughter Nancy vividly demonstrates how life in the children's external world is affected by "having a dad for a mom" even for part of the critical early years.

Mrs. Mellow, Mrs. Blue, and Mrs. Young clearly address, according to their separate experiences, the representative joys and dilemmas, blessings and curses, of mothers who yield preeminence in the nurturing domain to their mates. Middle class to working class, late and early deciders, single child and second child, daughters of traditional or working mothers, these three women articulate the various viewpoints on rearing competent children and sustaining successful marriages through some tough times and uncharted waters.

But the main subject in all three family self-portraits is the growth of a life between father and child. What seems to matter greatly to these men and to their families, and a topic to which they return over and over again, is this: the child's ability and power to affect its father's life, and the father's power and ability to allow his life to be affected by his child. This power to influence each other's lives is the news this book has to tell.

5

Helen, Mr. Mellow, and the Briefcase

Helen was ten months old when I first met her family. Her father, Ben Mellow, greeted me at the front door of their modest home when I arrived to conduct the first home visit of the study. He was a short man of robust, stocky build and fair complexion who could have passed for a well-scrubbed longshoreman. At 24, with sandy hair receding noticeably from a widow's peak, he had the look of an older, more experienced man. His wife, Anne, 23, came quickly to the door once I was inside and shook hands firmly. She was intense, precise, and warm in her manner. My first impression that she was of Irish descent was later confirmed. She looked enough like her husband to have been his sister. Their comfortable, two-story house was warmed by a wood-burning stove in the living room. The floor was littered with carefully chosen, durable, attractive toys in moderately good repair. The strains of "Romper Room" music could be heard coming from somewhere in the back of the house.

Helen rounded the corner from the kitchen and teetered into the living room with unsteady gait, apparently having only recently mastered upright locomotion. Her enthusiasm and curiosity drew her toward the stranger standing flanked by her parents in her living room. Her balance, however, was outstripped by her curiosity, and she fell forward onto all fours without missing a stride. Continuing her babble, she came to rest next to an easy chair, against which was propped a briefcase. As the adults took their places about the living room to chat, Helen sat up next to her mother's briefcase and pulled it down across her legs to investigate. Though it was hinge-springing full,

Helen was more interested in the scratches on the surface than the contents of the well-traveled case. Intrigued by the textures, she passed the fingertips of her small hands slowly over the surface, pausing to explore each scuff mark while listening attentively to the adult chatter. I thought as I looked about that this would be a most comfortable and interesting environment, especially at Helen's level two to three feet above the floor.

That first evening, we spent most of two hours talking together about the study, the Mellows' interest in it, and how they had come to decide to care for Helen in this particular way. There was a fresh, inviting, almost crisp atmosphere of anticipation, curiosity, and closeness evident in the Mellow family that never faded.

Ben and Anne Mellow had been married for a year and a half when they decided that it was time to begin a family. They enjoyed each other's company and companionship but did not feel that they wanted to spend their adult lives alone. They were also under some pressure from both sets of parents to "get started making a family." They both giggled comfortably as Ben confided that neither one of them was "too big on sex, so it was good we did not have to work too hard at it to make Helen."

Helen had been delivered by cesarean section, as planned, because of her mother's small pelvic proportions. The pregnancy had been healthy although not particularly happy. The father reported that "the pregnancy wasn't a terrific time for me. I had these dreams of being afraid of my wife, that she was somehow going to hurt me. That bothered me a lot."*

Mr. Mellow had felt a strong desire to become

---

*Several of the fathers in the study reported troubling and disquieting dreams about being in various forms of physical danger from their wives during the final stages of the pregnancy.

involved with the pregnancy because he had a "scientific curiosity about it." Nevertheless, he found it difficult to "find a handle on it." He had attempted to fashion one such handle by keeping a chart and tape measure affixed to the back of the bedroom door to measure his wife's increasing abdominal girth at weekly intervals. He charted the gradual increase with pride and what his wife called "exhibitionism." Such games often ended with his measuring his *own* girth (which was also increasing). During the third trimester, he had begun to exercise more, especially weight-lifting and body-building, favorite forms of tension discharge and physical mastery that he had pursued since his adolescent years.

Mr. Mellow had not attended Helen's birth. He had not planned to even had it not been a cesarean section. (This was a decision he later regretted deeply.) He felt that he "would be in the way. I didn't feel too welcomed by the obstetrician anyway. Anne liked him a lot better than I did."

Though excited and proud after Helen and Anne came home, Ben nevertheless felt intruded upon by his daughter. Consequently, he preferred not to help his wife with child care for the first few weeks. Instead, Ben's mother had come to help because Anne, after her cesarean section, was a "bit less mobile." Anne's mother could not come "because of business." Anne had arranged to take a two-month, half-pay maternity leave from her accounting firm. The couple was considering various forms of infant day care for Helen after Anne was to return to work.

When Anne said soon after the delivery that she was beginning to wonder whether she really wanted to leave her career to stay home and raise Helen, Ben was surprised to find himself rather casually offering to "look after the baby for a while." He reasoned that he could do his marketing data analysis for the utility company that employed him from his home. "I was sick of being on the road and was not really all that happy with my job anyway. I figured that I could use a telephone, a computer terminal, a secretary, and an occasional visit to the office, and we'd see how it worked out. I talked to my boss and the company gave me a kind of half-time paternity leave at one-third pay. My boss called it 'inactive duty.'"

After six weeks at home, Anne was ready to return to work. Unlike the majority of the mothers in the study, she had chosen not to breast-feed, so she felt a bit more mobile. She had been in touch with her office daily for several weeks and "wanted to get back before they really screwed things up around there." She spent two weeks half-time and almost changed her mind about returning to work, because she felt so "torn in two" about leaving Helen. But she stuck with her original plan, because by the third week, she was sure "Ben would do great."

In describing these early days with Helen after Anne returned to work, Ben said, "Suddenly, I began to figure her out. My wife, though she really loved our little girl, never seemed quite able to understand her, maybe because they're so much alike. I don't know. I was reluctant to admit that *I* had figured her out at first. I kept it to myself. But Helen became crystal clear to me. You know, like whether she was either tired, or wanted to eat, or play—that stuff. She responded instantly when I guessed right. That made me feel confident about what I was doing. Really, it was kind of like all of a sudden the feelings of being an outsider left, and I began to feel overwhelmed with the wish to raise her, to develop her the way *I* wanted her developed. It may sound crazy, but I started to almost look forward to her waking up at night just to be with her."

During the first week after his wife had returned to work, he was often anxious: "What was going to happen to *me,* though? I didn't want to watch the soaps and go 'stupid,' so I comforted myself in the afternoon by turning off the TV, and going out to buy a copy of the *Wall Street Journal.* I didn't have the chance to read much of it, but, amazingly, it helped just having it."

Since the beginning, Mr. Mellow had continued to "read" his daughter well. He said, "I eventually developed my own style." He fed her in a fashion different from that of his wife; for example, he allowed Helen more finger play with her food than Anne did.

I had initially speculated that when these new fathers got into everyday difficulties, they would call up images of what their wives would do, but within weeks if not days after the mothers were gone, most of the fathers, like Mr. Mellow, were using their own intuitions about what was useful in particular situations for their babies. They were, with the help of their babies, raising the children in their own unique styles.

Ben initially experienced some guilt about his successful parenting of his daughter and would often attempt to "back off" when his wife returned from work in the evening. Helen, however, usually reacted instantaneously to such withdrawals and would fret or whine plaintively while he was trying to prepare dinner.

This father took much pride in the fact that Helen and he were "very much alike." He reported that his sister-in-law described them as being "almost like twins, both crazy," referring to the mildly hypomanic personality style that led both of them to prefer intense levels of social interaction.

When Anne returned to work somewhat before the end of her allotted eight-week maternity leave, she worried only about her husband "being a softie. In fact, he still is." As evidence, she reported that *she* had been the one to help her daughter end a sleep disturbance at nine months by insisting that Helen "cry it out in bed. I had to make him leave her alone. He was always going in to comfort *her*, he said, but I think they were just playing around."

My next meeting with the Mellows, arranged for a few weeks hence, was scheduled so that I could speak with Ben and Anne alone to get a sense of what their lives were like. During that next home visit, Ben asked that I follow him about on his evening chores, as he needed to get some things done before his wife's return from work. We had set aside this time to do some talking about his growing up and his family of origin. As we gathered in the kitchen to begin our conversation and his preparations for the evening meal, he told me, "I do the work; she provides the music," referring to Helen's animated babbling as she followed him about.

Mr. Mellow started easily, talking about his own family. He was from a middle-class suburban family, the oldest of five children, with two sisters and two younger brothers, led by a father who had been an employee of the Foreign Service. Though he described his family as "very together," Ben, as had all the men in the study to varying degrees, found himself in "hot water" with his family when he originally announced his plans to change his work so that he could raise his daughter.

Ben and Anne had met when they were summer employees of a utility company before graduating from college. He had gone to work for the same company after graduation but had become unhappy with the way his company passed over him for job training and promotions. Meanwhile, Anne had enjoyed a series of promotions and salary increases.

Just prior to the conception of Helen, Anne had gone to work for a subsidiary firm as an accountant. Ben was contemplating a job change amid rumors that his office was soon to be "absorbed," and in the interim, to his wife's surprise and delight, had made his decision to raise Helen.

Mr. Mellow suddenly interrupted this line of thought to say that after our last conversation, he'd remembered that the ten-pound weight gain he experienced during the pregnancy was primarily the result of consuming "large quantities of milk and crackers" during the last trimester.

One of the things that most bothered him in his role as "housefather" was his being the only father he knew who was raising an infant. Early in his days as the "main man," he was invited by several women in the neighborhood to join them on their morning "baby stroll" around their pleasant suburban neighborhood. He resisted initially, reporting a vivid memory of the times his sisters had tried to urge him in taunting, belittling fashion to "play dolls" and push their "babies" around in carriages with them.

"I hated this 'mothers' brigade' at first. But then I noticed it provided relief from the loneliness and tedium of the soap operas, diapers, and laundry. I began to feel some admiration from them for what I was doing, or trying to do, and eventually even of the job I *was* doing raising our daughter. Now we're all fast friends, of course with my wife's permission [chuckle]."

Mr. Mellow described his own childhood as quite comfortable, full of friendships, and enough dating as a teenager and experience with girls "to keep me from feeling freaked out." He had, like most of his peers, done some mild drug experimentation, and as an adolescent enjoyed an increasingly close relationship with his mother. He felt important to her in helping her manage the large family and described her as "the boss, but she stopped short of domineering."

Mr. Mellow's father was away for extended periods on diplomatic business. Between absences, he was home for long uninterrupted stretches of time and was very involved as a father.

But, during Mr. Mellow's adolescent years, his father was gone six or seven months out of the year. "This was probably not such a bad plan, even though I'm sure he didn't work it out that way on purpose. It was when I was beginning to think he was really kind of a turkey that he left. I often managed to feel a little bit better about him while he was gone."

Ben described his mother as "my model. I helped her out a lot, and she taught me how to become a good cook. And I keep a pretty good house. Her mood was always light and stable. We certainly had our bad times, but usually not for long."

He fell silent for a moment to listen for Helen who had cruised out of sight in search of "God-knows-what." He continued, satisfied by some intuition that she was okay.

"You might think that this is surprising, but it was really my wife who wanted kids first, not me. I wanted to get my job rolling. She'd been married for a very short time before we met and had had to have an abortion. She was from an Irish Catholic background, and having the abortion just about tore her apart. I really felt we needed a little more time and I wanted to get my career established, which I guess I did. When we began to think about kids and how to divide up the child care, I decided it really was okay to take a kind of pause in my career and raise our daughter. Anne was much happier in her job than I was in mine."

While we had been talking, Helen had returned to the kitchen and crawled up into Ben's lap and buried her head in his chest. He paused and looked lovingly into the eyes of his daughter, who was just beginning to stir in his arms and said, "But I'm not sure she's ever going to get rid of me."

This theme of resisting separations from the important objects in his life had already affected his feelings about Helen. In order to keep his "finger in the job pie" he had had to leave for ten days on what he called a "job safari" the month before, which had marked the first prolonged separation between him, his wife, and their daughter. He was stunned to find out from his wife during his absence that Helen's appetite had decreased, her mood and temperament had disintegrated, she'd become clingy and was almost perpetually tearful. He reported that he had felt so awful upon hearing this that he had lost *his* appetite. "I'm sure I blew an interview, maybe even on purpose. I took the red-eye flight to get home early."

Ben said that his father had been much more supportive of his parenting choice than his mother, although "she's coming around, mostly thanks to this dynamite little number," he said as he tousled his daughter's curls. He reported occasional pangs of envy as he watched his father play with his daughter, longing for active memories of his father having been so involved with him, but none came. "My father had really been a pal when he *was* there, but for the most part, what I remember most is his being gone." This second visit came to a close just as Anne arrived home, an event celebrated by Helen with much giggling and squealing. We next arranged for Helen to come to "my place."

A vitally important part of the study was the careful examination of the children's development, the so-called "proof of the pudding." Helen was the first child to be evaluated according to the design described in the previous chapter, using first the Yale Developmental Schedules and then a diagnostic play interview. The developmental testing was constructed to examine carefully the overall developmental competence of the children intellectually, physically, emotionally, and socially.

When her father brought her to the child study center, Helen, now eleven months, was a vigorous, bright-eyed, smiling, well-scrubbed little girl who leaned forward immediately from her father's arms to examine my mustache, which bore some likeness to her father's. She looked back and forth between the two faces for a moment, looked at the door of the examining room, and peremptorily ordered, "Go!"

She came into the testing room with no hesitation, clearly expecting and trusting to be dealt with in an amiable, appreciative fashion. She squirmed out of her father's arms onto the floor as soon as she got next to the examining table and its high chair. She held her arms up in the air and ordered "up-up." Once seated on the table, she looked at me wide-eyed, smiled as though to say, "Well, what have you got for me?" She got down to work immediately on the various testing items, most of which were novel experiences for her.

Although 44 weeks at the time of the testing, she exhibited a 52- to 56-week profile in her personal, social, and language function. The quality of her performance was also interesting. Helen would clap her hands in an excited fashion, breaking into a broad smile whenever she successfully assembled a particular puzzle or achieved the desired block design sequence.

Helen's problem-solving skills were equally advanced. But it was her play that was most precocious. She exhibited a broad range of skills with the unfamiliar toys presented to her in the testing situation, often organizing surprisingly complex play involving both her father and me. I felt as though I were in the presence of a budding stage director!

As the obvious competence of his daughter emerged, I invited Helen's father to tell me some of his experience with children prior to his becoming a father to one. His response was typical of much of the fathering population in the study. I was continually surprised to find so little experience with young children in the study fathers. Twelve of the seventeen fathers had few, if any, extensive prefathering experiences with children.

At our next interview, I turned my focus to Anne in order to complete the family portrait. She, too, spoke easily of her family and childhood memories. She was the oldest of four daughters, all born a year apart, beginning when her mother was 21. Her father was a stevedore and her mother had run a yarn and knitting business "out of the sunroom of our house for as long as I can remember."

As I asked her about her growing up, she began thoughtfully. "Money had always been a problem, but there was plenty of everything else," explaining that she had felt comfortable and secure in the family's working-class neighborhood. "The place was always a sea of kids, all ages, plenty to go around. My mother had us early and quick to get us 'out of the way' so she could make a life for herself that would last 'longer than babies do.'" She described her mother's business as "amazingly successful," providing money for travel, college, fun, etc.

Though she still feels close to her mother, her most vivid memories were of her father's support and help at times of the greatest personal need during her growing up. "My mother thinks of children the way a lot of people think of cats. As kittens they're irresistible, but as cats they're something else."

Anne had "always planned to have children" and had fully intended to raise them. She was at a vulnerable stage in her career, having just been promoted when she got pregnant with Helen. "There were three of us competing for one job, these two guys and myself. I knew that this particular job was perfect for me. But I wanted this baby so badly because of losing my first one in a rotten, blessedly short marriage. I was so torn up about it, I just couldn't think about what to do. Ben's decision to stay home with her was just the perfect thing...just perfect, though he and I were the only ones who thought so at the time! My parents did a 'slow roll.' They couldn't begin to understand it. They're coming around, now, but I've really missed their support—especially my father's. It's funny because he's the one who has supported my career so much all along. Though my mother loves me a lot, her business success, which I really admire, I think has sometimes meant more to her than her kids—you know—'the cats,'" and she laughed. At the close of this first evaluation, the Mellows asked that "we stay in touch." In fact, I heard from their pediatrician later that they'd enjoyed being in the study. "Another child is coming and they want this one in the study, too."

Two and a half years after this initial contact with Helen's family, a younger brother, Bruce, was born. I'd heard from the father by phone in the interim that when Helen was about eighteen months old, the Mellows had arranged for some "in-home" babysitting, twelve hours a week. Meanwhile, Ben had returned to 20 hours of office work per week. Six months prior to the birth of his son, he had, with assistance of his company, installed a computer terminal at home (which gave him access to the company's mainframe), allowing him to return as the "house parent." It also allowed the Mellows to plan for some continuity of care after the birth of the second child. Ben had planned to renew his "half-time paternity leave" from his firm and to stay in touch with his business through his computer terminal, but his request was denied. His boss informed him that his company only allowed "one paternity leave per family." As a result, when I interviewed the family at the time that Bruce was four months old, Anne was now the stay-at-home parent, having recently acquired an extended leave of absence (without pay) from her own firm. Helen, now three and one-half, was at nursery school four mornings a week. She had been attending day care three afternoons a week until her brother was born. Now she attended nursery school only.

Ben was not doing so well. Anne had been the first to notice that he'd become less involved at the end of her pregnancy, almost immediately after being informed that he would have to return to his job actively or lose it altogether. Unlike the first pregnancy, he could remember no dreams, and he experienced a weight *loss* instead of gain. At the time of the delivery, and this one he did attend, he had felt elated as he had on first becoming a father but found himself repeatedly handing his son back to his wife after picking him up.

Once Bruce was home from the hospital, Ben did not hear his son's cries at night (again unlike Helen), and his wife had to awaken him to "take his turn" at the night-time feedings. Helen had begun to complain that "Daddy wasn't funny anymore." He reported he was "driving home after work at 50 miles an hour, instead of 60 like before."

Mr. Mellow spontaneously reported during the interview that he was very troubled by the distance he felt between himself and his son. "I don't think it's just the boy-girl stuff. I just don't feel as important in his life. I miss that a lot—*more* than a lot!" Ben's brother, who now worked at the same company, asked him if he were depressed. At first he said no, but he came home to discuss it with his wife and began to wonder if maybe he was.

Anne meanwhile reported feeling "more involved and happy as a mother than I would have ever expected." She was breast-feeding Bruce and finding it "meaningful, though inconvenient." She felt a "little guilty" for not having nursed Helen. As to her husband's role, "Even though he's at work, I *feel* him around the house. I sometimes call him at the office for advice. We're really doing this together, especially on the weekends, my favorite times."

During the period after Bruce's birth, Helen's nursery school teacher reported that she looked listless and somber much of the time. She spoke animatedly and with pride, even exhibitionistically, about her brother but had also regressed to protesting her father's departures in the morning when he dropped her off at nursery school on his way to work. It was hard to tell whether this was due to Helen's feeling displaced by her brother's arrival or that she might have been following her father into some depression.

At the biannual home visit, Helen was found to be a skilled manipulator of all the adult attention available to her. She asked repeatedly what the medical student research assistant observer was doing, and *why* he was writing things down; "Those are secrets and that's *rude!*" Though she did not work at or strive for her father's attention, she stayed in physical, verbal, or eye contact with him throughout the visit while her mother fed and bathed Bruce. Once, when Bruce became briefly inconsolable, Helen looked at her mother and then said with authority and some irritation, "He wants *Daddy*." This comment was followed by her mother's somewhat anxious laugh.

Helen was still the most advanced in her developmental skills of all the children in the study. At 22 months, she had had especially well-developed speech and problem-solving skills. Now at three years eight months, her language continued to be her strongest suit, with vocabulary and work skills occasionally ranging as high as five and one-half to six years. Her problem-solving abilities continued to be equally impressive, and her social competence was more like that of a five-year-old.

Though Helen continued to thrive, this family was involved in a difficult transition, not wholly of its own choosing. Though the mother was doing well, the father had regressed, referring to himself several times as "the odd man out." The denial of the opportunity to father the second child in the manner he wished depressed him significantly, and Helen seemed to be partially following suit. By the time of the reevaluation's completion, however, Mr. Mellow was feeling somewhat healed after he had decided, with his father's advice, to seek legal counsel to challenge his company's paternity leave policies.

His decision, though an intensely personal and risky one for him, serves as witness to what may be required to solve the father problem and free men to develop fully their nurturing capacities.

Mr. Mellow at Twenty-eight, Helen at Six: Life Grows On

Only when I became a father did I begin to notice my own father's tender and intimate nurturing capacities. His lingering glances, his abiding soft strength, his wish to feed which stopped short only at suckling, his endless jokes about my mother's belly, his unfailing memory about my infancy. For the first time in my life, I understood the meaning of the word "generation." A lost secret of our language is that it is really a verb, masquerading as a noun.

——*Attributed to Dostoevsky*

More than two years had passed since we had last seen Helen and the Mellows. She was now six and had been for some time in a developmental phase that I especially looked forward to studying in these families. This is the era when a true sense of self and a mature awareness of physical and sexual role differences begin to develop. If there were to be significant troubles or differences in the way these children thought of themselves as a result of their father's care, it would begin to appear in some detail now.

As the children in the study were now older, more verbal, and more complex emotionally, it would be easier to assess the more subtle aspects of their development and growth and their perceptions of the world about them. By this age, it would be possible to determine more accurately the unique effects, if any, on personality development, when the child has been raised by a father during the crucial early years. This determination is best done by careful evaluation of developmental competence, combined with assessment of the child's inner life, especially as revealed in play.

As I mentioned before in Chapter 4, play is the thing in this era of life. Through play, the child can explore and experiment with his or her perception of and experience with the world. Feelings about the important relationships in life, hopes, and wishes are all part of a rich, ever-changing repertoire. The child solves problems and masters the unhappiness and confusions of everyday life. Play tells us much about the most significant relationships in the child's life. To help us understand what we are to see in evaluating the children who have grown into such complexity, let us first review what should be happening in a six-year-old's inner life.

Aided by the growth of intelligence and perception, children in this phase have ceased to live exclusively within the intimate emotional partnership with the primary nurturing figure, traditionally the mother, but in these families, the father. They have now become fully contributing, even controlling members of the larger family group of siblings, and most especially the secondary nurturing parent. Beginning, rudimentary forms of empathy as well as envy and jealousy of parental intimacies are all in evidence during this transition (sometimes called the oedipal phase).* The relationship of the father in the traditional family becomes increasingly complex the closer the child gets to the fourth year of life. To children of

---

*I mention this developmental phase, an important tenet of psychoanalytic theory, now to lay the groundwork to aid our understanding of the emotional growth of children raised primarily by men. Much of this phase is largely unconscious and lies beyond memory in most children. Anna Freud, Sigmund Freud's daughter and a pioneer in the field of child psychoanalysis, explains the oedipal phase this way: "The child's love for the parent of the opposite sex *creates*, or in the case of the boy, *intensifies*, the already existing rivalry with the parent of the same sex. The boy thus loves the mother, attaches his instinctive desires to her and wishes for [the elimination of] the father who stands in the way; the girls love the father and in the service of the wish to have first place with him, fantasize doing away with the mother. It is this family constellation of the young child for which in [reference to] the Greek myth, the term *oedipus complex* has been introduced." (page 468)[1]

that age, traditional fathers typically seem to possess unlimited quantities of power, strength, and mystery. Although they are clearly loved and admired, they may also be feared.

This dislike and distrust the traditionally reared child feels for the father in his role as a rival for the mother's love is a dilemma for the child, whether male or female. Though such ambivalence has appeared before and is almost never remembered in our adulthood, now it is in full bloom. Only at the beginning of this (oedipal) phase of development do male and female children begin to proceed along fundamentally different paths.

The female child, according to developmental theory, has grown out of her exclusive *attachment to* her mother, beginning instead to copy and *imitate* her mother. In the traditional family, she turns her affection more in the direction of her father, as part of the imitation of her mother as father's companion and mate, seeking his appreciation and approval, often at the expense of her relationship with her mother.

Ultimately, through the unremitting clarity and persistence of the reality that the father does *not* intend to abandon his wife for his daughter, the child recognizes the futility of this wish to have exclusive ownership and control of the parent of the opposite sex. The resulting discouragement and sadness are often almost palpable, but they are essential to the normal developmental process.

Powerful and preoccupying as this scenario may be, it is certainly not the only emotional transaction occurring during the fourth and fifth years of life. Intellectual, physical, and moral growth are surging forward. Yet sexual curiosity certainly does occupy the child's mind during much waking and sleeping time. Investigation into the act of procreation as a normal intellectual extension of the discovery of sexual difference is a favorite, almost universal pastime.

In studying this widespread interest in procreation, psychologists and Freud have postulated both male and female elements in yearning for a baby. Many of the psychoanalytic observers of the 1940s and 1950s suggested that older boys often regress normally to a more "feminine" phase. But, in fear of ridicule and emasculation, they "hide their desire for woman's maternal resources, womb and breasts, behind the facade of male chauvinism and misogyny."[2]

Edith Jacobson, another prominent psychoanalyst in the 1950s, frequently discussed what she believed were the frustrated strivings of the male to assume complete "generative and generational baby-having authority."[3] As we saw in Chapter 3, three- to three-and-a-half-year-old boys frequently express the strong wish to give birth to a baby. At the very least, the three-year-old boy usually is interested in "raising" or "nursing" babies. Similarly, most of his peers are actively exploring the mysteries of childbirth and "where babies come from," or "how they get out."

Now that many of the children of our father-raised population sample were old enough to show us in their play their own attempts to achieve some resolution of these complex questions about sexual and gender identity, would their attempts be unique or different, and if so, would the differences matter? As we shall see, most children at this age are accomplished players and weavers of tales. What were these children's primary identifications going to be by this point in their lives, and what of their primary conflicts?

Enter Helen, bearing her own answers to such questions.

We shall focus heavily on Helen's richly revealing play because in it we find more "proof of the pudding" than if we were to rely solely on discussions with Ben or Anne.

Helen, just six, greeted me with a somewhat over-familiar "Hi" in the waiting room as her father shook my hand to renew our biannual acquaintance of now four years' duration. Helen looked momentarily shy but beamed warmly as we walked silently to the play room. It is customary to conduct such play interviews alone with the child, as children of this age are less distressed by separation from the parent than when they were younger. Furthermore, they often feel less conflicted about revealing charged emotional material in their play when they don't have to worry about parental response.

Helen came with me easily and quickly without a backward glance at her father. She was perky, strongly built, and well coordinated, and she walked in a confident, almost cocky manner into the play room. Helen was dressed in a pink sweatsuit that was a bit short at the midriff, and a pair of work boots. She walked up to the large two-way mirror and preened and groomed momentarily. There was a slightly infantile, lispy quality to her speech that gradually diminished as the session progressed. She seemed almost too comfortable.

After a few moments of somehow feigning both coyness *and* familiarity, she began to set the play table with toy dishes and pots and pans, announcing that "we should have something to eat." She chatted comfortably about her present life situation, describing how her father had been away from home in a nearby town on weekdays for almost three months. (He was apparently returning home on weekends, as his employer required that he do some consultation out of town.) Helen's mother had returned to work full time, and Bruce had just begun to attend Helen's old nursery school and day-care center. Though her father was working twenty in-office hours "downtown," his computer terminal was still at home and he was still, as Helen called him, her "main man."

Helen's chitchat revealed, as we were both eating our "chicken soup," that she liked to eat fast and to "be sloppy," inviting me to appreciate her silliness. "Being sloppy" at the formal dinner table often led to her mother's putting her in her room when she was home in the evening. She reported that her mother needed to discipline her while she was still in her business "good clothes," a fact that seemed to amuse her considerably. Helen seemed to enjoy the contrast between her own sloppiness and well-dressed, strict "business-woman mommies."

Bringing our pretend lunch to an abrupt close, Helen turned toward a collection of toy animals which had caught her eye at the beginning of the session. As though she couldn't hold herself back any longer, she gathered the animals up in her arms and announced that she wanted to "make a farm," converting the playhouse into a barn.

Having now taken charge of the play session in a manner appropriate for her age, she became increasingly relaxed and was clearly enjoying herself. She organized the space competently with the use of blocks as fences, separating the "good animals" from the "sloppy" animals. She became momentarily fascinated with the bodies of the family life dolls (small flexible human figures). Especially interesting to her was the "four-year-old boy" who "seemed to have something loose inside him." She shook the doll vigorously to try to discover the exact nature of the boy's "insides things." During this investigation, she was absentmindedly rubbing her hand tenderly across her tummy, her sweatshirt having worked its way up over her navel.

Next, Helen organized a "sneak attack" on this pleasant little farm scene by the lion and bear puppets, who crept up behind the barn in a competently deceptive way. They were suddenly chased away by the "police guard," the father and mother dolls.

She next assembled a revenge party led by the bull, who sneaked in an equally competent fashion around the rear of the lion's lair. When I complimented her on what a "super sneaker" she was, she reported that she enjoyed getting up in the middle of the night, sneaking into the kitchen, and getting a slice of cake without anybody in her family knowing, "and making a mess." She smiled with a pleasurable complicity in sharing this secret.

Yet another sequence of the doll family's being in danger was introduced by Helen's telling me "this is going to be exciting," as though she needed to rivet my already rapt attention on the next sequence. First she isolated the mother doll in one corner of the barn, then gathered the father, the "two-year-old, the four-year-old, and the seven-year-old" into the other corner of the barn. (All the age designations were decided early in her play and remained consistent.) The following dialogue ensued:

(**H** = Helen, **KP** = Author)
H: The whole family is inside...the little baby has to be near the father...the little baby likes to be near the father.
KP: What makes the little baby want to be near the father?
H: Because the father has to take care and make sure he doesn't wander off and get in trouble with the *big* guys.
KP: Mommies don't do that?

H: The big fathers do that...because they know how to do it good.

KP: How about big mothers?

H: Only the really big, big, *big* mothers can do it. (It appears that mothers must be larger than life to perform this function.)

Helen then orchestrated several other major offensives led by the bull, who "cut and stabbed" the lion with his mighty horns, all with much excited, animated giggling and laughing. The grateful little pig thanked the bull for protecting him.

KP (animating the little pig): Thank you, bull, for protecting us from the lion and bear. You are so powerful!

H: I'm going out there to get that lion and bear and bring them back for dinner...I'm going to bring them back here and we can cook and eat them for dinner.

KP: How is the bear meat?

H: It's really good if you cook it good.

KP: Who cooks dinner?

H (designating the father doll): Him, of course, what did you think? (The designation "dummy" in response to KP's question is strongly implied but courteously deleted.)

When this play sequence was brought to a perfunctory close, and the baby calf was brought in and placed next to its mother, Helen announced, "That's the end of the story, and they lived happily ever after."

KP: Is there a lesson to that story?

H (after a long pause): Yes, the little baby pig should never, never go out because it's too dangerous out there!

Having satisfied her own moral standards of good

nurturing practices, Helen turned her attention to an exploration of the doctor's kit. She conducted a very competent examination of her own chest and abdomen, with the stethoscope giving humorously accurate representations of heart and bowel sounds, all the while coyly exposing her own belly.

She then proceeded to examine her "baby dolls." She announced that the first one was suffering from "an affection of the neck and the bottom" and proceeded to inject medicine into both places with a needleless syringe. She abruptly assigned me the role of the doctor, and assumed for herself the role of the mother, caring for one of the sick babies.

H: My baby is sick and she is crying all the time! She has a problem with her heart beating very slow.

KP: Oh my, that is a serious problem! I think we'd better see if we can help her.

H: She has a very funny feeling in her head, and she's been dreaming about something funny.

KP: My, you certainly do know a lot about your baby.

H: I am a good mommy. I am a *real* good mommy!

KP: I have a special tool that lets us see baby dreams. Shall we use it to see what dreams are bothering your baby? (I appropriated a small plastic microscope for this purpose.)

H: Yes, let's look right now...(she looks excitedly). I see a *hundred* animals...(long pause) fighting!

KP: What are they fighting about?

H: There isn't enough food! There isn't enough to eat!

KP: And that's what bothers your baby?

H: Yes, that's it, yes—that's right! All we need is more food, more food, then she won't cry.

At this point she introduced the father doll into the

story of the office visit for the first time. The father doll held the baby, and a brief dialogue with the doctor ensued in which the father was informed of the diagnosis of the baby's problem. The baby miraculously was cured of his hunger, and the family celebrated by going to a wedding.

Helen was remarkably detailed in her representation of the wedding, including a respectable rendering of a few bars from *Lohengrin*. The baby was part of the wedding ceremony and became extremely excited whenever it came near the father, repeatedly saying "dadoo, dadoo, dadoo."

After being informed that our play session was about out of time, Helen took her final tour of the play room and discovered a pair of guns that she had not yet used. She handed the smaller gun to me, kept the larger one for herself, and announced that she would be the "sheriff," and I was to be a "cowboy, a bad cowboy, who comes to take all the money." She was quite competent in managing the guns and their mechanics.

Abruptly, she became quite silent and somewhat distant, sat down in a chair, and looked off into space, holding the gun tightly in her hands. I commented that she seemed to be thinking about something. She said, "Yes, my daddy doesn't like his yucky job." She just as abruptly recovered and introduced a classic western confrontation between the cowboy and sheriff.

Springing instantly back to life, she action-played a swaggering sheriff who challenged the cowboy to a shoot-out. The shootout, however, was postponed "for tomorrow" when the cowboy, to Helen's surprise, enthusiastically accepted the challenge.

The shootout occurred as planned "the next day," over a bag of gold. The sheriff surprisingly suggested that the combatants lay down their arms and "put up their fists." Helen then proceeded to shadowbox with me with great pleasure and vigor, being careful not to make physical contact with my hands or body. She ended the story with an unexpected turn. She announced that she was going to give the money to the robber, who had now sworn to be good for the rest of his days, "or else..."

This rich play sequence reveals many levels of thinking and feeling, all of which are quite sophisticated, given Helen's age. She demonstrated a broad, healthy range of thought, feeling, humor, moralizing, and relatedness.

Although the themes in her play are age appropriate and are logically connected from the beginning to the end, some of the subtle movements in and around typically male and female representations are quite interesting. Though her repertoire of coping strategies is appropriate, extensive, and in keeping with the expectations for female development, there is a kind of unconflicted "little boy" tinge to it, in her inclusion of gunslingers and attacking bulls. Yet it is woven together with what is considered female interest in body contents and preoccupations with inner spaces. Themes of aggression are combined with reproductive curiosity. Feeding and nurturing play is intermingled with explorations of conscience and right versus wrong, especially in the play involving the mother.

We can also see some acute effects of the father's recent absences, as her pleasure in the gunplay momentarily dissipated when thoughts of her father's decreased presence in her life intruded. Though the mother seems somewhat absent in the play, Helen's own sense of self as revealed in the play is a rich, healthy mosaic of both masculine and feminine interests, pleasures, and identifications.

Just as intriguing as the exploration of gender identity revealed in her play are some broader questions of personal style. Fathers handle their babies differently from mothers in subtle but measurable ways; we have already discussed excavating the underground father. They have the expectation that time together will be fun, spontaneous, and unpredictable. Helen was playing in a way that was remarkably similar to the way that fathers play with their children. This finding was to be repeated again and again throughout the study population. Not only was it evident in Helen's personality, but it seemed to serve as a central organizing feature of the emotional expression of her inner life as well.

But this portrait of Helen, intriguing though it may be, does not fill the canvas. Mr. and Mrs. Mellow have been growing apace, too. Mr. Mellow, after the play interview with Helen, began to "bring me up to date on himself" by showing me a recently compiled photograph album, "with the usual *too many pictures* of the first-born, and too few of the second-born." Ben, who had assigned the job of compilation of the family photograph archive to himself, had discovered something that interested him: "Look at these shots of Bruce, Doc. I'm not in a *single* one—and it's not just because I was taking the pictures. It's because I wasn't there. My father was around that kid more than I was. I was too busy—off feeling sorry for myself because I didn't feel as important in his life as I did in Helen's. Not because I hadn't tried. I was there for the delivery this time. It was powerful and fantastic. I remember holding him when the doc handed him to me—he was so perfect. I just talked to him—talked, talked, talked. I told him about his sister, and his mom and dad, and how handsome he was. He opened and closed his eyes like he was actually listening and interested. Can you believe that? I remember hearing the nurse chuckling at me in the background. I believe that the delivery room stuff is important, but it's not magic. It has already faded a lot in my own memory.

"The stuff that really matters is what happens later on—at home. That was what I missed, and that was something that my company seemed to be denying me. Later I stopped feeling so jealous of my wife and sorry for myself and got to work. My mother didn't help after Bruce's birth, and so I got to know him pretty well. Still, I had the conviction that Bruce was Anne's and that Helen was mine.

"Anne certainly didn't exclude me. In fact, she sought my advice all the time, and that made me feel more involved than I could be time-wise. I also loved the idea that she breast-fed him, even though it sure bothered Helen. When Anne had to return to work, and we arranged for some family day care at a neighbor's home, I got worried that Bruce would become one of those day-care kids—unruly, aggressive, angry about being away from home—you know the kind—they're all over.

"But it was my father who kept on challenging my worries about Bruce. Now that he had done his twenty years and wasn't traveling much, he was around more and had grown real close to Helen. Bruce, too, always turned on like a light bulb whenever he was around.

"When we were walking in the woods last Thanksgiving with the kids, I said to my father that it made me happy to see him loving my kids so much. He said that he guessed he was a better grandfather than father. Then, he launched into one of those 'if I had to do it all over again' lectures."

In this spontaneous outpouring, Mr. Mellow described how he'd recovered from the depression he had been in two years previously. He had had the help of his wife, his father, and Bruce, and he had also done a lot of thinking.

His younger brother, five years his junior, the one who worked at the same utility company, had yelled at him one day not long after Bruce's first birthday to "stop bitching" about how the company had treated him. That set him to thinking about what was important to him after all. He'd stopped wrestling with his company after he had won some of the skirmishes over paternity leave. (His company was offering half-pay paternity leave for eight weeks and subsequent no-pay paternity leave for the same length of time at intervals no shorter than 36 months. Ben called this "a start.") The company *had* responded and was, as both his father and brother pointed out to him, offering more than most corporations.

Ben meanwhile had also come to some beginning terms with his own ambitions. "Career" was a word that did not mean the same to him as it did to his father. A "job" was a means to an end for Ben—the end being freedom to choose and maintain a quality of life that allowed him some success, as well as the opportunity to complete himself as a man, father and husband, and "provider."

Mr. Mellow reported that, while this wasn't a wholly radical view of life among his friends, he had noticed that "my friends seem more comfortable with me when I'm back in the saddle, working. They'd invite me to go bowling, or seek my advice more often when I was on the job than when I was a 'mother.'"

When I asked Ben how raising a child had changed his world view he said, after a long pause, "Hugely...I never used to be a very big ERA person. No one in my family was. My father was very conservative, having been hired during a Republican administration, and my mother was firmly conventional. 'Women love children' by the book. Somehow she managed to separate out her children's families from her politics. But now I'm a *big* ERA person. I watch certain choices being made for Helen and even Bruce at school or day care that remind me of what happened with my company three years ago. You gotta be able to choose for yourself. I think that's what ERA is about, and so we pay our dues, go to the rallies, and take the kids with us!"

Anne, who had listened actively to her husband's soliloquy, then said, "I think he's left the last word for me." She was now 27 and was working full time out of her home and was no longer breast-feeding, she and Bruce having decided "mutually" at seven months to wean. She did feel closer to Bruce than Helen but was not worried about the discrepancy, because "my pediatrician told me that was natural for mothers and sons at this stage."

She went on to expand on her husband's recently described feelings about Bruce. "He's really wrong—he's been very involved—but mostly through me.... I still think it's easier to work full time than it is to stay home and raise a baby, at least for me. It just does not come that naturally, and I really wonder how many other mothers out there are really like me. It's hard to feel so short on intuition, but I think that's what the problem was. My husband actually taught me how to tell when Bruce was hungry as opposed to tired. He could show me the differences between a tired cry and a hungry cry. I felt guilty asking—you know, mothers are *supposed* to know.

"Ben helped later, too, when Bruce was getting a little older. I just could not think of enough diversions when he was upset or hungry and it was too soon to eat. So Ben made out a list of diversion ideas that worked and stuck it on the refrigerator door. I memorized it and it worked— calmed me right down. I thought once of asking my mother about some of these things, but I realized that Ben was better at helping me without making me feel so bad for not knowing.

"It's not that I was short on love or affection, but the

mechanics were sometimes a problem. My milk came in, but my mother's intuition didn't! It had caught me by surprise. I wanted these babies very much. I was so happy pregnant. But looking back, I realized that I did have a lot of mixed feelings about becoming a mother. Who doesn't? The abortion was so important to undo, although I don't think you can ever undo one of those. But it was so important to try that *having* babies meant more to me at first than raising babies.

"My mother was quite proud of my working and my career, but she was pretty hard on me for going back and forth between work and home. She kept on telling me, 'Make up your mind, you are going to really confuse those children.' My father went on worrying quietly about what was 'wrong' with Ben that he wanted to be a mother! I heard this from my next older sister, who I think also worried about the same thing. They tried to support me, but it was real hard for them to believe this was okay. They had consulted their priest, who made matters worse. He told them the proper job for a young mother was to follow in the image of the Virgin Mary, and stay home, and raise babies to the glory of God."

Mrs. Mellow ended our last interview with an affectionate reflection about her parents and in-laws. "They are not moving along as fast as we might like them to in accepting this pattern of family life for their grandchildren, but they keep at it. When you think where they've come from, it's easier to be patient. We just all keep chewing away on this thing together."

They had come far enough for Ben's father to go testify for him at the grievance hearing regarding his company's denial of his second paternity leave. They won, but the grandfather still teased his son, "So you still need your old man to bail you out?"

With the perspective of time, Ben had looked back

over that legal skirmish and was struck by the fact that *all* the people involved were men—lawyers, administrators, managers, antagonist/protagonist—all men! It would seem that the solution to the father problem lies easily as much on the male side of the net as on the female side.

Now let's meet Henry, from the male side.

7

Henry, His Elephant, and the Kangaroo

Mr. Blue answered my knock on the door of their second-floor walk-up apartment in what he was to later describe as his "semiharried style." The door was pulled open rather too fast and revealed a clean-shaven, athletically built young man in his early twenties, wearing a warm smile and well-used painter's coveralls and cradling a giggling baby in his left hand (in the so-called "football" position). With his free hand, he shook my hand firmly and invited me "into this comfortable mess. Park it anywhere. I need to get rid of someone on the phone."

The large upper story of the inner-city old Victorian home was indeed comfortable, randomly scattered with toys, overstuffed chairs, stacks of posterboard, walkers, a crib, a cradle, and lush, thriving plants. It seemed hard to believe there was only one child responsible for all this interesting clutter, but as I was to later corroborate, Henry "seemed plenty" for this family. This first impression of a father and son enjoying each other thoroughly enough to "fill a house" endured throughout my contact with the family.

After the phone call ended, Mr. Blue called me into the kitchen and asked if we could talk there as it was time for Henry's bottle, and "our favorite rocker" was in there. "Besides, it's the warmest room in the house."

He'd made a pot of tea while on the phone and invited me to pour myself a cup and "grab a seat." He took a prewarmed bottle of milk out of a pan on the stove, and Henry squealed with delight. He smiled broadly as his father sat down in the chair he called the "favorite rocker." He explained, "This is breast milk. My wife has to express it every day. Henry is still not weaned, although Susan is thinking some about it." As the young father looked back at his son, Henry reached up to grab the bottle and place the nipple in his own mouth.

While Mr. Blue talked, Henry played with his father's lips and nose, sucking contentedly away. He gradually pulled his hand down to play with the buttons on the coverall breast pocket, pulling repeatedly at it with his right hand. His father looked down, smiled at him and said, "You're sure there's a nipple in there somewhere, aren't you, little guy?"

When I began with my standard questions about ages, dates of marriage, and so on, Mr. Blue said, "Doc, if it won't mess up your interview too much, I want to start with some things I've been thinking about ever since you called and said you were interested in us. You'll get all your information, but I'd like to just tell you some things first, okay? Okay.

"I love looking after my son. But I would never have guessed it. In fact, if my old high school jock buddies ever knew I was doing it, they'd fall over dead from laughing. It wasn't easy at first, but it sure seems natural now. That bothers my wife a little...that it feels natural. She gets a little jealous sometimes. Do other couples like us have that problem?" He did not really wait for an answer and continued, "Anyway, let me tell you the story of this great little guy and where he came from." He started the story of Henry, not with his birth or conception, but with when he had met his wife.

Peter and Susan had gone to the same high school and had not initially cared much for each other. "He was too macho," Susan was to say later, and "She was too straight," said Peter. Things changed later when they worked at the same place at summer jobs. They married after she finished state college and he finished a two-year commercial art program. She worked as a court recorder, and he described himself as a "yet-to-be-discovered commercial artist. Actually that means I am a sign painter." He also worked part time on the weekends as a salesman for a small line of marine hardware. Early in their marriage, Susan had worked part time as a legal secretary.

They had been married two years before Henry was born and had felt "pretty happy to be making it on our own." Mr. Blue had been "particularly keen" on having children. He had always managed to have a discussion with any girlfriend that he got "reasonably serious with" about her feelings and plans about having children.

One year prior to Henry's birth, Susan had a miscarriage which upset her, she said, "more than anything in my whole life," even though the pregnancy had been "a bit of a surprise," hoping as they had to wait another year before starting children. Susan decided to take a full-time job as a court recorder shortly after the loss of the baby to "take care of my blues. Three months later I was pregnant and scared, but this one felt different right from the beginning—somehow stronger."

Susan had enjoyed her job a great deal right from the start, while Peter had been meeting further frustration. During the middle of the pregnancy, when Susan discovered that she did not have to quit her job but could take a six-week, no-pay maternity leave, the couple decided that Mr. Blue would stay home with the baby and leave his part-time sales job, "which I did not care much for anyway," he said. "Besides, I'd always been the one pushing to have kids. I was curious to see how it would go. Susan said that after Henry was born, she realized that she 'sort of always had assumed that I would be a very involved father.' I also really wanted that, too."

They had kept their decision to themselves at first, although they could not explain why. They both agreed that it felt "quite private and that probably a lot of people would not really understand. Later we learned painfully that we were absolutely right."

This pregnancy had gone well from the beginning. Susan was an attractive, slightly built young woman with red hair, who described herself as "exploding" when she was pregnant. She gained thirty pounds with the pregnancy and found the breast enlargement particularly uncomfortable.

Peter, on the other hand, was fascinated. He was putting on his own weight and found that he could not keep his hands off his wife's body, especially her swollen abdomen. "She was so beautiful and so huge." Once Susan felt the quickening of life within her, Peter would spend "what seemed like hours" with his hands on Susan's belly just "waiting to feel something happen." He became convinced that his unborn child was "tapping back messages in code" when he tapped rhythmically on his wife's abdomen; "I could make him kick back, I really could." Susan meanwhile thought Peter was "nuts," although she greatly enjoyed his involvement. He even began singing to the fetus in the last trimester, because Susan thought his voice "calmed the baby down. Probably me, too," she added later.

The delivery was described by Peter as "tough," by Susan as "horrific." The labor had gone well, but the baby turned out to be breech. According to Peter, "the obstetrician—and this was a guy we both picked because he was supposed to be good about including fathers—turned to me when he was having a hard time turning the baby and said, 'Are you sure you want to stay? This is going to be a tough one.'" Peter said, "Of *course* I wanted to stay. God, I felt so sorry for her—she was trying so hard, and there was nothing I could do but stand by her.

"Finally it was over. I told her it was a boy, and that felt tremendous. We both wanted one because our own families were full of girls. They cleaned him off and handed him to me because Susan had to have a whopping episiotomy. I was just elated about his being okay. Everything was there. I remember when he kicked his brand new little feet against me as I held him in my arms that it felt almost familiar, like when we were tapping out code back and forth while he was still inside Susan."

After the episiotomy was finished, Peter had handed Henry to Susan and she held him. Peter: "I got my camera and took some pictures. I didn't realize until later that I'd shot the whole 36-exposure roll while he was lying in Susan's arms, still on the delivery table!"

Susan was later to describe her six-week maternity leave this way: "As new parents, we '50-50'ed the work. Peter was always picking him up and carrying him around and wanting to feed him. I really thought he needed more quiet and rest. I loved to be with him, too, and the nursing began beautifully. He was so easy compared to what I heard about other babies. I was very torn about going back to work. I couldn't imagine how women do this whose husbands don't stay home. At least my babysitter was in love with my son, and I am in love with them both. I'd be pulled apart to have to leave him with a stranger just so I could get on with my career. I liked my work, the money, the friends, and it felt important for me to try to do it. If Henry hadn't been in good shape, I don't know what I would have done. Neither one of our families was overjoyed with this plan, and that made the decision even harder, and definitely more lonely."

Families. What about Peter and Susan's families? Were they unique breeding grounds for such an unusual parental choice? Would they not rally more to this young couple's decision than had Helen's grandparents?

Grandparents Blue had had their first child late, by their generation's standards—she was 34, he 36. They had been married for eight years before Peter was born. They had a daughter five years later, also carefully planned. This was Peter's nineteen-year-old sister, who suffered a severe learning disability. Nevertheless, she was now attending college, thanks to what the family called her "guts." Peter was quite close to and fond of her, and because of her learning troubles, had always been "fiercely protective" of her.

The Grandparents Blue were "your average hard-working Yankee father, liberal mother marriage." Peter's mother was "in charge of the house, hearth, and kids," and the father was the breadwinner. He worked as a rural mail carrier in their hometown in Vermont. He retired on disability when Peter was an adolescent, having nearly died from a dog attack while delivering the mail. He then began to raise sheep and became a "gentleman farmer without the money." He was also a ham radio enthusiast and local politician.

Peter's mother was "ideologically left, but a staunch conservative on family values." She was a painter herself, having earned her "pin money" by painting "anything and everything... those huge chewing tobacco ads on the sides of barns that you don't see around anymore, and faces on pumpkins." She had also spent some time studying portrait painting in high school and had painted oils of both of her children.

Peter described his growing up as "Yankee all the way." He had been a "good boy... kept a paper route... joined the Boy Scouts... had 4-H lambs, and raised a little hell." He had been a fair-to-good student and "successful" as a high school athlete. He "drank a little too much beer sometimes on the weekends but never got into really big trouble." He had restored an old Harley-Davidson motorcycle given him by an uncle, and it was "the pride and joy of my youth." It was not until he became a father that he gave it up, feeling suddenly that the nonexistent margin of safety was no longer "interesting." He felt, as he told his wife, "It's just too crazy to go out there now that I have a kid. It feels nuts to be bombing around the streets just asking people to bump you off like that."

His interest in art had been strongly supported by his mother, though his father felt that he should try to get into something "more predictable." He compromised on commercial art. He initially had a difficult time with the functional demands of his field because "creativity always seems to be secondary to usefulness."

He said that early in his marriage, although he was very happy with his wife, he also really longed for male companionship. He joined a group of young men who rode their dirt bikes on the weekend and had a "few beers together on Fridays." Shortly after his wife had returned to work, Peter began, over Susan's objections, to take Henry with him to meet this group on Fridays at the local pub. At first, he said, Henry had a very sobering effect on the gatherings. But to his amazement, some of the other men became quite interested in what Peter did with Henry and in how he played with his son. Soon, one or two asked to hold him. After a couple of weeks, Henry had become a fixture at the Friday men's group.

Susan's family was "very different from Peter's. First of all, we were city people." Her father was 25, and her mother 24 when she was born, fourteen months after her sister. Both her parents had been adopted, and when they married, making their own family was very important to them. Susan, the second of *six* children, felt they had "overdone it a little." She described her father as "hard-working upward-mobile working class." He worked two jobs during much of her growing up, days as part-owner/ driver of a small heating-oil company, and nights and weekends as manager of a security guard agency.

As more babies came along, "all six were born within eleven years," her mother's health began to fade. Her memories of her mother now are of a chronically ill woman (presently age 47) "who really could not do much for us...except love us." Consequently, Mrs. Blue had taken much responsibility for rearing her brothers and sisters. As a result, she made a promise to herself not to have so many children: "Having seen how much mothering had depleted my mother, I was not going to follow in the same footsteps." She also knew that her parents' marriage had not been a happy one, with an overworked father and a chronically ill, depressed mother. She felt fewer kids would have helped: "Then they might have felt freer to divorce."

It was in Susan's role as "little mother" that she first encountered the legal world. Her older brother had been arrested as an accessory in a violent robbery of a store in which he was in fact an innocent bystander and customer. In meeting his lawyer and helping in any way she could, she became interested in the workings of the law and how it initially abused but ultimately protected her brother and family.

She had been an excellent student in school, a member of the National Honor Society and the debating club, but "not especially popular." She was "too interested in doing the right and best things. Consequently, I don't think I was much fun to be with...too straight.... I only dated a little bit."

She skipped a grade in elementary school and went to college young. "I lived at home until junior year, when Dad really forced me to live on campus because he thought it would be better for me there. I felt very guilty about leaving Mom and him, but it was such a relief. Then, I began to enjoy myself. I really wanted a good life, some money, a good job, and a boyfriend. Then I remet Peter and the fun started."

Both Peter and Susan's families had strongly supported their marriage plans. But when their parenting plans came to light, a chill wind came from both quarters. Peter's family, especially his father, worried that he would "ruin his career." His mother fretted that "it won't be good for your marriage." Susan's father asked, "What are you trying to prove?" Her mother said, "Do what you want, but I don't think it's particularly good for the baby." Siblings seemed dismayed. Susan's closest sister's response was especially rejecting: "How could you leave your baby, your *own* baby?"

Needless to say, this was painful and confusing for Peter and Susan, as it was for all the young couples in this study. Sometimes the couples reasoned themselves through to an understanding of a particular objection, but they all felt hurt.

At the time I first met the Blue family, Henry was eight months old. His father was 24, and his mother 23. Mr. Blue had taken over one of the back, well-lighted west rooms of their apartment as his studio, and Susan used a corner of the living room as her study, which was cordoned off by a meandering collapsible gate. Peter had invited me to see his studio at the time of the first home visit. He drew my attention to two large oils he called "Genesis I" and "Genesis II," a pair of abstract collages of warm colors and heavily textured cloth (I later discovered the cloth textures were actually Henry's old diapers and nursing blankets). He explained, "Since Henry's birth I've felt more creative energy than I've ever felt before. It's like I *need* to paint. I just think about him, and it flows out of the brush and onto the canvas."

When I interviewed them together later on, the couple explained their child-care arrangements: Peter was in charge of Henry Monday through Friday; Susan took Saturday, leaving Peter to work and run errands. Evenings and Sundays were "50-50 time."

The Blues were still feeling quite isolated from friends and family, and a little strain was obvious in their relationship at the time of our first interview, especially in the way they competed over the role of "best baby-understander." On the occasion of the first home visit, Henry got his fingers a bit far down his throat as he steered a Zwieback into his mouth and toward his tummy. He gagged momentarily and coughed. Susan winced noticeably and started to grab his hand away from his mouth. Peter calmly stopped her in midflight saying, "He knows when to pull his hand out. He's okay." Henry had in fact already renewed his play and looked back over his shoulder at his parents, seemingly wondering what all the fuss was about.

This father did seem to be in good contact with his son. Another feeding scene gave us even more evidence of the reciprocity most of the father/infant pairs had achieved quite early. Henry was seated next to his father in a high chair proudly, if exhibitionistically, feeding himself with his fingers from the high-chair tray. A game evolved in which Henry would wait for his father to raise food to his own mouth before he followed suit with his food. He stayed in touch with his father vocally as well by humming as he chewed, pausing only when his father conversed with him. Henry would respond with a "Da Da" when his father would "chitchat" during the meal. When he was finished with his finger food, Henry held his arms up in anticipation of being picked up by his father and held for the bottle portion of the feeding.

He nestled quickly against his father's chest and sucked vigorously on the bottle, maintaining an intense, almost longing eye contact with his father for a few moments. He then felt for his father's hand, transferred the bottle into it, and began looking about the room while exploring his father's shirt or face. His father followed his gaze and spontaneously labeled and named the objects at which he assumed Henry was looking. Henry would "coo" responsively between swallows until sated. He ended the feeding himself by pushing the bottle away and struggling to sit up. His father agreed that dinner was now concluded and put Henry down to crawl off to investigate the observer.

When Henry was given the Yale Developmental Schedules, he was found to be doing well, scoring more like a twelve-month-old than an eight-month-old. He was especially competent in motor skills. He pulled himself vigorously to the standing position and was just on the verge of walking as he squealed vigorously while cruising around the testing room. His balance was quite good and he seemed to tolerate, indeed enjoy, the vigorous jostling about by his father without becoming distressed or overstimulated. He liked to position himself with both feet and his head on the floor, with his hind end sticking up in the air in the position of a tripod chanting "Da Da," as though he were inviting his father to join him in this topsy-turvy world view. His language, too, was ahead of schedule. He could call both of the family cats by name, and knew the landlady as "Bot" (translation—Dot).

As I took leave of the Blue family on the occasion of the first evaluation, I reassured them that Henry was doing beautifully and that I would be in touch. They asked if they could call me if they had any questions or new "insights" to tell me about. I pondered whether I should give them the name of another family in the study; they seemed so alone. In the end I decided against it, choosing instead to try to stick to my protocol to protect the validity of the study. I reminded myself that this was not an intervention study.

A year and a half passed before I saw Henry and his family again. I had not heard from the Blues in the interim, though their pediatrician told me they were well. When I recontacted them for the follow-up interview, I found that the family had just moved to a new two-family house, and the child-care arrangements were essentially the same. The mother was considering taking some training as a paralegal; the father's work had stabilized and was more successful financially.

Mrs. Blue began by describing Henry as growing up "much too fast." He was no longer being breast-fed. Henry had weaned himself at ten months when Susan "had shrieked when he bit down hard on my nipple. We both sat there looking at each other, stunned and horrified, but that was the last time he would ever take the breast."

When I saw Henry again, his vigorous, captivating personality was still much in evidence. He was carrying a stuffed kangaroo under one arm and a fluffy elephant under the other as he toddled animatedly about his new home. The kangaroo was cuddly in texture and had a baby stuffed upside down in the pouch. Its feet and tail flopped as it bounced along under Henry's arm. The stuffed elephant was gray and fluffy, with a long nose that had seen better days. Peter informed me that these were his son's constant companions since the summer vacation had ended a month previously. The animals were less in evidence on the weekends when both parents were home together.

On such weekends, Henry tended to wander around

the house in his father's shadow and would ask "Mommy —whazzat?" whenever he heard a noise in another part of the house obviously made by his mother. When he was in his mother's company, he would not ask about his father's presence in the reverse circumstance.

Henry and his father had anticipated the move with pleasure. His mother described herself as adapting less well to the change, feeling depressed about leaving their old home.

Just prior to the move it seemed that, although Henry spent the bulk of the time with his father, he had begun to prefer his mother, and more or less to disregard his father unless distressed. At those harder moments, he would climb into his father's lap, rest quietly against him, and then, when satisfied, toddle off in an exploring fashion to do something with his mother.

Henry had meanwhile continued to develop vigorously (as seen in the developmental testing) and in the same precocious pattern that was obvious in his previous assessment, except that now his language was even more highly developed. His parents described him as using his father as the primary source of nurturance and "battery-charging," turning exclusively to his father when he was tired or distressed. Henry had managed the move, frequently a quite upsetting and perturbing event for a child his age, quite well.

Especially interesting was Henry's differential use of his mother and father during his struggle for autonomy and independence, the main developmental preoccupation of this era of life. At about eighteen months, mother had assumed the job of putting Henry to bed, as the father had taken to sneaking out of the bedroom because his son had become so upset at separations from him either day or night. The couple theorized that Henry was more accustomed to his mother's comings and goings (as had the Mellows before them).

Shortly thereafter, Henry had his first bona fide temper tantrum when he saw his father holding another infant at the family holiday gathering. This appears to be the father/infant counterpart of psychoanalyst Ernst Abelin's interesting description of the "Madonna constellation" conflict, a term initially used to describe the toddler's distress at seeing his mother hold another infant.

Meanwhile Henry's mother was emerging as an important figure in helping lead her son out of the intimate, symbiotic tie with his father. As we've seen previously, this certainly has been a classic "father's job" in the traditional family—namely, helping dilute the intensity of the exclusive mother/infant tie so crucial to the healthy evolution of autonomy and separateness as a person.

This is also a time of life when stuffed animals, "softies" or "blankees," symbols of a child's capacity to soothe himself when distressed, can also be much in evidence. Such objects are often called transitional objects because they help ease the transition from needing the comforting parent to acquiring the ability to comfort oneself. Did Henry's possession of *two* transitional objects, a kangaroo and an elephant, indicate the blessing or the curse of having two parents so committed to his well-being? Probably the blessing.

Although Henry was clearly thriving, the couple continued their struggle over "best understander." Susan had to point out to Peter that Henry needed some time to be alone. Peter seemed more interested in maximizing every moment. They turned to me to solve the dilemma.

Interestingly, as Henry was so obviously thriving,

both sets of grandparents had begun to close the gaps they had placed between themselves and the young couple. Henry could now dial the telephone (with some help) and say "Hi, Gamma [or Gwappa]—Come here, Come here." They were being slowly but surely hooked.

Henry was two years three months old when I saw him next. He opened the door himself this time and announced "Doker Pru here," turned on his heels, and ran to get his father, who was in the kitchen preparing dinner. Like many of the working- and middle-class families in the study, Peter was househusband and child rearer. These tasks were Siamese twins for these families, joined in different ways and places, but joined nonetheless. He returned to take me by the hand to come see his father in the kitchen. "Makin' zgetti—mommy home yet" (the "not" inadvertently deleted).

They still lived in the same two-family house, but things appeared less cluttered. Henry was anxious for me to "see somepin' [something]...fast!" He grabbed my pant leg and pulled me down the hall to the bathroom. There, next to the toilet bowl sat the object of our forced march, Henry's potty chair. This is a cherished yet fearsome possession for many toddlers. I learned later that Henry had recently half-mastered its use.

A few other things had been added to the Blues' family life. Henry was now attending family day care at a neighbor's home, three doors down the street. He was there a half day, three mornings a week. Susan, now 25, was working full time as a paralegal in a large downtown law firm and "loved it." Her salary had increased by about half, and she was considering going to law school "some day." Peter, now 26, had started his own business painting large delivery trucks with advertising logos and was working more hours during the week, having acquired a partner.

Henry had protested initially when he began attending family day care. Peter said, "He kicked up just enough of a fuss to let us know he loved us. What if he had not protested at all? We both felt bad, but we were glad to see that he cared. Now they are all in love with one another down there. He can't wait to go. There are other kids there that he loves to be with."

About fifteen minutes later, Susan arrived and Henry greeted her warmly, if theatrically, at the door. The current evening ritual was for her to give him a bath while Peter finished dinner preparations.

Their respective chores completed, the family chatted animatedly during dinner. The couple began bringing me up to date by reporting that Henry seemed to be coming out of a period of being more compliant with mother than with father, making her authority seem more effective than his. Peter: "It was like I meant *entertainment*, and she meant *business*—but we're over that now." They also explained that Henry had been quite aggressive with his mother after she had returned from a four-day business trip. Henry had impulsively hit her in the face several times during the bath ritual the day after her return, while they were "playing rough." His mother responded equivocally, out of surprise and uncertainty, but told him firmly not to do it again. He thereafter called the incident "playing bops." She later reflected that "maybe [she] had it coming because [she] felt so guilty about going away." She'd "broken the day-care rules, and sneaked out without saying goodbye" the day she left for the trip because she was afraid she would cry and make it worse. The family day-care mother had told Peter that Henry was upset for the rest of the day.

At the time of the home visit, Henry seemed to be making quite different use of his parents. He brought dolls, stuffed animals, and clothes to his mother, who then became actively engaged in helping him clothe his "babies." The baby bottle he carried to his father after the babies were clothed. He always *walked* to his mother but *ran* excitedly to his father, initiating a tickling game while crawling up on his lap.

Susan made several attempts to pick Henry up to cuddle him, but he squirmed out of her grasp. At one such time, his father commented, "I think he really prefers to get around by himself these days." The mother responded, "I really do think he knows Henry better than I do at times. That takes some getting used to, but now it just seems right. He was the one who heard Henry crying at night, not me. In fact, Henry and I really only began doing better *together* when, after he started walking (at ten months) I felt like he *required* less of me, and so I could *give* him more. We've been doing better ever since."

The Blues were roughly typical of those families who had achieved an increasing stability and adaptation to this nontraditional parenting arrangement over time. All three family members were thriving and progressing according to their own developmental tasks and stages within the life cycle.

At 27 months of age, Henry took much pleasure in the developmental assessment. His language and problem-solving skills based at the 30-month level, with some successes in each part of the developmental profile at 36 months. His personal-social skills were now especially prominent, and his capacity to play in a reciprocating complex fashion was more typical of a three- to three-and-one-half-year-old child. He was already riding a tricycle and could ascend and descend stairs with the skill of a three-year-old.

Peter was still spending an occasional Friday night "tossing down a few beers with the buddies." Because of

Henry's increasing activity and curiosity, he was taking him less frequently. One evening when he did take him along, an older man new to the group of "old jocks" had made a somewhat challenging inquiry about some doubts he had about Henry's "growing up to be a man when your dad is your mother." Peter responded with his own philosophical preference for an androgynous sexual identification clearly evident: "Any kid who bombs around the neighborhood in his Big Wheel with his baby doll tucked into the jump seat is probably going to make out just fine."

8

Henry at Four and Mr. Blue: Use It or Lose It

A few weeks after Henry's fourth birthday, I called Peter and Susan to arrange for our next visit. Henry answered the phone. "This is Henry—who wants to talk to me?" (I thought, yes—that's definitely Henry.) I identified myself, and we chatted about his topic of choice, his recent birthday party. When I asked if his mother or father were there, he said "Just Dad—Mom lives downtown." In the background, I heard Peter walking toward the phone and asking who Henry was "jawing away with." Henry said "Doc Pru" and gave the phone to his father. We exchanged pleasantries and Peter confirmed Henry's story. Susan had in fact moved out of the house six months ago, and they were pursuing a divorce.

This was not wholly unexpected, as some ten months earlier I had received a joint telephone call from Peter and Susan telling me that they were "having a lot of marital difficulty" and asking if I could recommend someone for them to see in "couples therapy." They were both quite upset, as their troubles "seemed quite serious." I sent them to someone I respected, and they had gone to work quickly and seriously. But the marriage apparently was not to be preserved. What had happened? Had we seen this coming?

Susan had been the one to leave, as she had been the more unhappy. She'd only discovered *how* unhappy when she had become involved with a fellow paralegal in her office whose attentions and pursuit of her made her feel "loved in a way Peter didn't."

The previous eighteen months had been quite difficult for her, and she felt quite alone. This period of loneliness began when her mother died quite suddenly at the age of 51, after a massive heart attack that came without warning. Susan was deeply troubled by not having been able to say goodbye to her. She was "on the outs" with her mother at the time, as she had been quite critical of Susan's lenient handling of Henry during the most recent summer visit home.

Meanwhile, Susan's law firm had merged with another, and she did not feel as happy or as confident in her work because she felt she had "slipped a few rungs on the promotion ladder." She felt Peter had become increasingly distant from her, and too involved with Henry. Their sexual activity decreased significantly during the same time period. Susan talked about feeling "kind of strangled, not by any one thing or even by Peter, just *things*, and I wanted out."

Peter was devastated. He knew Susan was not always happy and that she had become increasingly intrusive in his relationship with Henry ever since his mother-in-law died. He did back off, but that didn't change much. He had become quietly angry with her, feeling that she was becoming self-indulgent and sorry for herself. These were most unwelcome feelings, because he admired and loved Susan deeply.

At the same time, Peter's erotic interest in Susan had been declining as she became more depressed and irritable. He tried humoring, teasing, cajoling—even confrontation, but to no avail. Henry had come to him one evening just prior to the separation and asked, "Why doesn't Mommy laugh at you any more, Daddy?"

It was clear that both Peter and Susan were feeling guilty about the fracture of their marriage: Susan because she had involved herself with another man and Peter because he'd let her get away. They had become quietly furious with each other.

The couples therapy had been a determined effort, but its yield was a civilized, minimally destructive divorce. They had been assiduous in avoiding fighting too frequently in front of Henry. They worked hard to keep from ensnaring him in their mutual disappointment. The couples therapist had rightly pointed out that if they walked about grinding their teeth, never allowing any contentious words, Henry was going to be mighty confused if and when they did separate.

Peter meanwhile had become a changed man. He was a more somber person than the one I'd encountered three years before. He was deeply saddened and hurt. He had longed to make "his" family work, and he thought he had. His own family had come to his support, especially his newly married sister, who now lived near enough to come to help care for Henry on occasion.

Peter and Susan agreed that Henry would thrive best at home and that Susan would take an apartment nearby.

The child-care arrangements were easily established. Custody was not a battleground either, despite the legal counsel Peter initially retained. The first attorney he'd consulted about the divorce had urged him to give custody of Henry to Susan: "What do you want to look after your son for? You have *got* to make some money. Besides, most judges don't look approvingly on men who want to keep custody of their children. They think they are troublemakers, who aren't thinking of their children's best interests... only wanting to make things hard for their wives. I advise you either to give Henry up or seek joint custody with Henry's living with Susan. You'll be in a lot better financial position in the long run." Peter told the attorney that it was unlikely they were going to work well together, and he changed counsel the next day.

As for Henry, he was now in family day care, the same family as previously, five mornings a week. He stayed with Susan all day either Saturday or Sunday every weekend, and one night during the week. On that prearranged night, Susan would come back to Peter's home, Peter would leave, and Henry and his mother would have the evening together at "Henry's house," as he'd begun to call it.

Peter was now working half time in his marine hardware sales venture and half time as a commercial artist. He was home four afternoons a week with Henry, and his sister helped out on the fifth.

When his mother first left, Henry had been bewildered. No explanation, no matter how accurate, loving, or authoritative could satisfy him that this plan made any sense whatsoever. He enjoyed visiting his mother's apartment but could not for the life of him figure out why she needed "two sleeper places." It was very painful for Susan and Peter to be unable to help their son understand.

After Susan moved out, Henry began to lose some of his sparkle. He also lost his appetite and stopped eating much of anything for a while, although he did not suffer a weight loss. He made up a story, which he told repeatedly to both Peter and Susan, that he wanted both of their houses to "burn up," and they could "all stand outside *together* and watch." For the first two months, he had implored his mother repeatedly to "stay at Henry's house," but his entreaty had since waned in intensity.

Now, six months after the separation, the Blues were just beginning to settle down. Although everyone was behaving better as time passed, I had the sense that all three were still feeling pretty raw. The visitation schedule had been respected and was flexibly followed. Henry's incessant pleading had eased. Peter had begun to date now that the divorce was imminent and was feeling a little more lovable himself.

Susan, meanwhile, was still with her "other man,"

and Henry was gradually getting some of the facts straight about this bizarre adult behavior. He was puzzled that Peter needed a girlfriend to dine with and "kissy with" when he already had Henry to "eat dinner with and kissy with."

Henry had also figured out some ways to deal with his mother's absence. They sometimes went for walks together on the weekend on a nearby beach to collect shells. One Monday morning, the day after Henry had been to his mother's, Peter went in to wake up his son and sat down on the edge of his bed. He noted some lumps that felt like rocks under the bedcovers. Henry awakened suddenly and said, "Daddy, don't squish my shells!" He'd taken the bulk of his large (and sandy) shell collection into his bed with him the night before. One or two shells followed him to sleep nightly for the next several weeks.

As I interviewed both Peter and Susan, I gradually became aware of the fact that I was more preoccupied with the divorce than they were. It was newer to me and felt more immediate. They, however, were getting on with their lives, and Henry seemed to be doing okay, better than they'd both expected, in fact. Susan said that in her time alone with Henry, they were "closer" than they'd ever been before. She wondered if she wasn't feeling some relief from the parental competition she had always felt with Peter.

But how was Henry *really* doing? In a word, he simply devoured the Yale Developmental Schedules when I gave them to him again. He relished his each and every success, of which there were many. He was 49 months old at the time of the retesting, and his performance was above the average expected norms across the board. In fact, only his small size suggested his real chronologic markings. He could throw a ball overhand like a five-year-old and make it go where he wanted it to go. He could draw a person with a recognizable head, body, and appendages, while most four-year-olds draw a person with only two parts, usually a face and arms.

Henry's play was remarkably elaborate for his age, as we shall see later. His language was disarmingly articulate, so much so that it was easy for adults to overestimate his usable vocabulary. He also had a clear idea of right versus wrong, fair versus unfair, whereas most four-year-olds are just beginning to honor simple bargains.

It seemed that, though the divorce was an important and powerful event in his life, he had not been permanently derailed by it, and his developmental capacities and maturation were marching confidently onward. Growing up was still his main job, and it had most of his attention.

But what was really on his mind these days about his life, his family, his self, his feelings? As with Helen, we turned to his play for the answers to such questions, and we found them.

Henry came for his diagnostic play interview with a knapsack stuffed full of books and some favorite "softies." The kangaroo had been summarily abandoned after Susan had washed it one weekend, feeling that it had become a health hazard. The elephant was, however, still a trusted, if weathered, fellow traveler.

As I rounded the corner into the waiting room, I saw Henry lying comfortably with his back against his father's chest, devouring a Dr. Seuss "I-Can-Read" reader for his father's admiration. On my entry into the waiting area, Henry scrambled down from his father's lap, stuffed the books into his knapsack, and took an evasive tour through the clothes closet of the waiting room, emerging from the far end with a "bet-you-can't-get-me" laugh. When I explained that he would be coming to my "play office" with me while his father waited in the waiting room, he sobered rather quickly but agreed to go. From this cue, I invited his father to come see the play room with us both. As soon as the choreography was clear to Henry, he suggested, "Let's go, Doc. We've got playing to do." After his father had seen the play room, Henry closed the door on him, as though he was determined to be in charge of the leavetaking. He then took a rather rapid "hot-potato tour" of the play room.

Henry was still a rather small child for his age, well dressed in designer bib overall jeans, sneakers, and a Harvard sweatshirt. His curiosity about the play room and me seemed to be running neck-to-neck with his worry about being separated from his father. He began his play by picking up a small bear hand puppet, examining it, and then giving it to me. Meanwhile, he donned the goose hand puppet after admiring the "bird head's big mouth."

The "bird head" immediately informed the bear that he meant business. He placed his puppet eyeball-to-eyeball with mine and heartily announced: "I am the birdhead with a *big, big, big* beaker." Animating the bear puppet, I replied, "What do you like to do with your big beak?" Henry replied, animating his puppet, "I like to bite noses!" I responded, "Oh, dear, and I have such a fine, nice, round black nose!" Henry quickly reassured the bear puppet, "No, I only like to bite *people's* noses."

Henry then turned away from the bear and instead systematically "bited the noses" of all the members of the human puppet family. He saved the father puppet until last and took special pleasure in biting the father puppet's nose. He giggled sardonically and gleefully as the whole head of the father puppet found its way into the goose's mouth. This led, not surprisingly, to a rather abrupt change or disruption of this play sequence, as though Henry had scared himself with his own fierceness, not an unusual occurrence for children this age.

Henry next turned to more comfortable play themes. He seemed more at ease now and began by demonstrating his general field of knowledge. He proudly named all of the miniature rubber barnyard animals and collected them into a pile in the middle of the floor. He arranged a landscape around the pile of animals, consisting of a doll house, a family of puppets, two toy trucks, and a pair of plastic guns. He excitedly clapped his hands together, looked at me, and announced, "We're going to have a city, right here!"

Throughout these early moments of play, Henry's speech gradually became more articulate and less immature. Finally, these opening gambits came to a close when he invited me to sit down on the floor with him. He then clutched the small gun in both hands, sprayed the entire room with imaginary bullets of power or competence, and settled into his play.

Henry next turned to the doctor's kit and began a sequence of examinations, first on his own chest and belly, then my chest, and eventually the baby and father puppets. The father apparently had been laid low by a "piece of meat in his blood." The father was restored to health by repeated injections to the stomach and crotch, carefully administered by this attentive, if overeager, young physician. The father suddenly jumped to his feet and announced that he was "all better."

Henry then rushed excitedly to the far side of the play room, grabbed his guns again, and began "blasting away" indiscriminately. This was the first of what was to be a dozen or so rather brief, unique play "disruptions." They were not really disruptions in the classic sense, because the story line was always restored. Instead, it was as though Henry found himself suddenly overstimulated by the thematic content of his own play and responded with a brief flurry of semidistracted and excited discharge that enabled him to return to his pleasurable play.

Now that the father was restored to health, Henry decided to "get the family all together and run a zoo." He began his zookeeping by carefully categorizing animals according to who "was nice and who was not." He got the large block box out and used the blocks to build a series of fences and pens for his zoo animals.

I inquired, "Now, who goes where?" Henry explained, "All the animals that don't bite get to be together here. The lion and the bear have to be in their own cages." I then inquired of this young storyteller, "How did the good animals get to be so good?" Henry patiently explained, "They took swimming lessons." Somewhat confused, I asked, "And that made them good?" Henry: "You bet!" (Henry had recently begun to take swimming lessons at a local high school pool on Saturday mornings, sometimes with his father and sometimes with his mother. It had become a special, meaningful enterprise for them all.)

Henry then placed the mother puppet in charge of the animals as "the boss zookeeper." She had been originally placed in the cages with the good animals but then was brought back outside the gates, "where she won't get so yuckied up. She's not scared. She is a *mommy!*"

He momentarily considered whether to give the mother a companion "because she probably needed helping— this is a really big zoo." His plan foundered, however, when he could not decide which sex to assign a somewhat unisex doll. The doll was first called a "little boy," but then the physiognomy did not seem to match. He then changed it to a "bad little girl," then back to a boy, and then finally abandoned the idea altogether.

He next found a toy milk bottle and poured the imaginary contents of the bottle all over the "good animals." He then handed me the bottle and instructed me to pour the imaginary contents over the lion. The "milk" turned the lion into a "statue," apparently neutralizing his aggressive potential.

Suddenly it began to "rain," and all the family life

dolls retreated to the house, where Henry discovered that the father had "a problem—he can't stand up." He decided to take the father to the doctor, who then examined him and found "carrots in his blood."

I next introduced a small male child doll who came to the doctor's office to express some concern about the father's well-being. Doctor Henry announced that the father would have to "stay in the hostibal for seven days." The little boy reported that he "could not stay at home alone, because his mommy and daddy didn't live together any more." (This, of course, was the situation Henry had been facing for the past six months.)

Henry would have none of my invitations to talk about the parallel in his own life, however, and instead plied the young boy with promises of going to the zoo or even having his own zoo. When I inquired about the absence of the mother on the subsequent trip to the zoo, he replied, "Mommy doesn't come to the zoo." (The Mommy he was talking about seemed more his actual mother than some generic Mom.) I asked, "How come the Mommy doesn't come to the zoo?" Henry patiently explained, "She doesn't come because she works." I asked simply, "What does Mommy do at her work?" Henry: "She does important things.... She gets money and gives it to Dad...and she spends a lot of time at work...that's why she can never come to the zoo."

This last statement was said with noticeable sadness. Henry sat back on his heels, his body slumped momentarily like a balloon with a slow leak. Suddenly, he reached out and grabbed the boy and father dolls and put them into a truck. The boy and father then drove recklessly to the zoo, careening about the play room and encountering a policeman, who arrested them for "speeding and driving crazy."

The father and son together joined forces to roundly

throw the policeman into the lion's den. At Henry's direction, the boy then jumped fearlessly into the lion's den and "kicked the lion out of the zoo." The father doll, played by me, came to admire the son for his "strength and fearlessness."

Henry then suggested the boy and father lie down together to take a rest. Again, Henry fell silent for a moment, but this time with less apparent sadness. The rest, however, was disrupted by Henry's taking up arms to go "kill a tiger" who had been "hiding in the closet." (He had discovered the rubber tiger puppet during the close of the previous play sequence when we were looking in the play closet for the play doctor kit.)

After this brief disruption, Henry returned to the theme of the excursion to the zoo. Now, however, the trip to the zoo involved increasing numbers of fellow travelers. All available zoo and farm animals were piled into the truck. The animal puppets and life dolls became involved in an increasingly stimulating, upward spiral of visits to the zoo, camping trips, boat rides, and going out to dinner at "fancy restaurants." In the midst of all these goings-on, two of the cows were examined and announced to "be pregnance [pregnant]."

I commented on the increasing excitement, noting that everybody seemed to be wanting to "go first." Henry quickly changed his tune from tour director to conflict resolver and began working skillfully to resolve conflicts over who got to do what "first." Finally, it was agreed that everyone would go for a boat ride out in the "*deepest* part of the water, where the whales are—everyone wants to do that!"

Henry invited everyone to the boat, which had been hastily constructed out of the old zoo fence. He then gave a description of how to use a gun safely so that "you don't have to have it scare you so much." (Guns would turn out to be an important part of this outing on the water.) Since Henry's final play sequence was a remarkable one thematically, I will describe it in some detail.

Henry walked to the top of a three-step stair in the play room and instructed me to bring all the animals and life dolls and puppets to him so that "they could all get ready to go swimming together." Henry, in the style of an ever-enthusiastic camp counselor, asked from his perch atop the stair, "Does everybody know how to swim?" To test the story line, I decided to introduce a little dissent. "No, the pig and the lion don't know how." Henry retorted angrily, "Yes, everybody does know how to swim. Come on, let's go. I'm going to shoot some fishes with this gun."

Still trying to get things straight, I asked, "Okay, who's going to go first?" Henry, after a large sigh, as though he were organizing the story line against some resistance from me, began again. "All right. The pig doesn't know how to swim, but I'm going to teach the pig. Now look, pig, you hold your breath, and you don't swallow water, and you kick your legs and pull your hands through the water like gloves. Okay, now, are you ready? In you go." (He throws the pig into the "water" and makes a struggling sound, but then finally allows the pig its success.)

"Okay, Dad, you're next. You know how to swim very, very, *very* well, don't you? I'm going to let you go in the deep part. Watch. You can take off like a bullet!" He then threw the father with all his might, headlong into the wall at the far end of the play room. I admired his prowess as a storyteller: "He really *is* a good swimmer." Henry, with a satisfied declaration, "Yes, he is *the* best!"

The remainder of the collection of dolls and animals were then thrown, one by one, into the "deep water." Henry: "Did everyone have a good time?" Speaking for the assembled multitude scattered about on the floor, I loudly replied, "Yeah!"

Henry noticed at this point that the bull had been overlooked. He leaned over to pick the bull up and asked the bull if he wanted to go swimming. Animating the bull, I spoke: "No, I don't want to go swimming. I'm so big and strong I don't have to go near the water if I don't want to." Henry, seeing through the ruse, "Oh, no, you're just being a big shot 'cause you're scared. Here, I'll help you learn how to swim. Do you need a gun? Here, use this gun. You need a gun to help you learn how to swim. Just put it between your legs and be sure to use it. Don't let it drop out!"

Henry then completed this play sequence by throwing *himself* headlong onto the floor and making swimming motions while belly crawling from one end of the play room to the other. He then rescued the goose (with which he had begun the play session), who had mysteriously forgotten how to swim. He placed the gun in the goose's mouth, and instructed the goose to "hold onto the gun" and then he'd be able to swim. He exhorted the goose, "Be sure to shoot the gun off; don't just let it sit there. And then you'll learn how to swim real fast."

For many young boys this age, and also a goodly number of girls, guns serve not so much as weapons of destruction or mutilation as symbols of external genital equipment usually, though not always, male. Little boys enjoy using their "genital equipment" exhibitionistically in a number of normal settings. It was not unusual for Henry, for example, when he was out in the family yard, to decide to "take a pee in the garden," as he was proud to announce. He sometimes called this activity "shooting on the garden." It was clear from this sequence that Henry felt it was not only important to *have* genital equipment, but that it was also important to *use* it. If the goose did not shoot off his gun, he would never learn how to swim. Hence, Henry's philosophy of athletic endeavor, and perhaps masculine expression, was "Use it or lose it."

As the session had come to a close, Henry, good manners in evidence, assisted in cleaning up the play room and asked if he could go show his father the guns, which he did with great gusto.

Henry was an intact four-year-old little boy with clear and articulate speech. He was highly animated and personable, warm and curious. He demonstrated a broad, rich range of age-appropriate emotions and an almost precocious capacity to move comfortably between modulated and overstimulating interchanges in his play.

Strains of parental loss or loss of a sense of "family" (shown when he slumped back on his heels in the play sequence, telling me that "Mommies don't come to zoos") were also heard when he struggled to deal with Peter and Susan's separation. His defensive and adaptive repertoire and coping skills, though not quite as varied as Helen's, were nonetheless very rich. Identification with the important adult figures in his life, the formation of a reliable conscience, reproductive curiosity, and interest in body contents were all present, as were certain powerful feelings.

The longing for intimacy with his father and sadness over his mother's distance were obvious throughout his play. His gender identity and "masculinity" seemed obvious and secure, as did his gender identity and "femininity." But, very significantly, Henry's masculine style has a *nurturing* tinge to it.

As with Helen, we had the clear impression that there were no signs of trouble either intellectually or emotionally. There now seemed to be substantial evidence to strengthen my initial speculation that having a father as a primary nurturing figure may well stimulate more curiosity and interest in father as a *procreator* than is the case for more traditionally raised children. Helen's interest in the loose particle inside the male doll and Henry's fascination with "meat and carrots" inside the father who could not walk raise the prospect that these are going to be much more active issues for these children than they are for their more conventionally raised peers.

Such body content interest focused on males is unusual in most children's play. Henry and Helen both enjoyed exploring themes of "inside things," often symbols of pregnancy or pregnancy-making (procreation) potential in their play with the father dolls. Henry had, in fact, suffered a brief period of constipation when he was 40 months old during his father's cousin's Christmas visit with him in the eighth month of her pregnancy. (Stool retention sometimes serves as a frequent, if transient, symbolization or substitute for pregnancy in young children.)

Possibly more interesting than the questions raised and addressed by this focus on gender identity are those broader questions of style we also saw in Helen. Henry, too, played in ways that were remarkably similar to the descriptions of father/infant play we've seen before.

I had a final conference with both Peter and Susan after giving them the choice of either coming alone or together. They both said that they were now able to be together when dealing with issues of Henry's well-being and wanted to come together. Peter and Susan were quite pleased to hear that Henry was doing well and a little surprised that he wasn't reeling more from the divorce.

"Why?" they wondered. I told them that it was clear that Henry felt deeply loved by both of them and that their efforts at keeping Susan actively and realistically involved in his life were paying off.

Finally, just before our time together was up, they both said that they had a question to ask which, Peter said, "We've saved until last because we're afraid of the answer." They bickered momentarily over who would actually *ask* the question, and finally Susan began: "We've both been plagued by worries that our decision for Peter to raise

Henry had something to do with our marriage coming apart. We never brought it up when we were in couples treatment because we felt the therapist wouldn't even begin to understand the question as well as you, and might not even take it seriously. She was good, but this question we wanted to save for you."

The question momentarily numbed me. I *had* wondered about this myself but had never asked it of myself as clearly as Susan did of me now. It was clearly not just her question, as Peter was watching me just as intently. I wondered if Henry was somehow in on this too, if not grandparents and friends.*

After much mulling over, I began. There was most probably no way to answer their question and hardly any way even to approach it. There was no other Peter and Susan Blue whom we could study who'd had a Henry and had done it the "other way," without divorcing. They had done what they believed in and what they had felt was right for them at that point in their lives. Yes, they had competed about parenting of Henry, but so do countless couples who raise their children traditionally. Furthermore, there is no evidence that expressing parenting-role competition shortens marriages any more than does stifling such competition. Furthermore, Peter and Susan had competed in a number of areas of their lives—cooking, and occasionally breadwinning, and their year-long gin rummy

---

*Divorce had a surprising impact on a recent National Institutes of Mental Health Conference I attended with a dozen other colleagues, all of us having been invited by the government to come together to discuss our various research on fatherhood. We had been studying a wide range of questions related to child development and fatherhood which seemed rather remote from the question of divorce. Some of the studies were prospective, i.e., planned to study questions over time (future time), and some were retrospective looks backward at recorded events. Sadly, we came to understand that any prospective study of family life these days would also occasionally become a "prospective" study of divorce, regardless of the questions being addressed.

tournaments were family legend. Although I had no proof, my hunch was that their choice about raising Henry had not dealt a fatal blow to their marriage. It was in fact one of the chief reasons that permitted them still to care for each other.

9

Father Young and and Daughter Nancy: The Morning People

You've already met Nancy and Allen Young in the introduction of this book: the nine-teen-year-old father who had papered the walls of his photographic studio with huge Polaroid enlargements of his daughter's faint ultrasound-outlined profile while still in utero. You have also heard the story of the beginning of their life together. Let's reconnect with them halfway through my first home visit, just after Allen had told me the story of his elation when attending Nancy's birth.

Allen stopped his story of Nancy's beginnings and leaned forward to put some cheese on the tray of her walker. He'd been putting her lunch together at the same time we'd been talking. He explained that he had to feed her "on the run these days" and not in her high chair because "she loves moving around so much. She'll only sit still for her bottle. Then she likes to cuddle and be still—me, too, Pumpkin," he said as he tousled her hair in response to one of her transfixing smiles.

Mr. Young was describing another classic trait of his daughter's age (nine months), the joy in motility and inde-pendent movement for its own sake. The body and mind are priming themselves for walking, an extremely complex and powerful event in the life of the child and the family. The child will then be able to move away from the physical boundaries of the parental landscape and begin to explore its own new worlds, whether the family is ready or not.

It is probably no accident that stranger awareness and the drive to independent motility are coupled develop-mental landmarks. Such pairing equips the child with the capacity to distinguish between home and uncharted waters while returning to safety whenever necessary.

Mr. Young returned to his story, prompted by my few nondirective questions. He explained that his decision to stay home "just happened. We were running out of money, and I was trying to find another job. Barbara didn't want to ask her mother to help because she really wasn't feeling good after the surgery. Barbara's boss called to ask her to come back to work as a head waitress just part time. She's really good, and they know it. They offered her bonuses. I worked pumping gas for a couple of weeks and hated it so much. Finally, Barbara asked me how I'd feel about looking after the baby 'till I went back to work. I was getting pretty good at it, and Nancy didn't seem to mind."

Nancy didn't seem to mind: Here it is again. How often I heard the fathers comment, subtly at first, on how their baby's *response* to them had played such a pivotal role in their feelings about themselves as fathers and in supporting their faith in themselves as nurturing parents. Not that the babies didn't scream and yell sometimes or occasionally arch themselves away from their fathers' arms. That certainly happened. But it was the sense that important, meaningful, real, and intimate things were happening and growing *between* the father and his child that was so often the *hook*. "We are affecting each other." Something was growing, sending down taproots, here, now, for tomorrow.

"I was nervous as hell when Barbara went back to work that first afternoon. Nancy was about eight weeks old. I had this awful feeling that when Nancy looked at me she didn't recognize me. Then, after her nap on the second afternoon after Barbara had returned to work, she gave me this mammoth grin. I can still remember the feeling. And that was it—right, sweetness?—we never looked back."

Allen had been warming a bottle as he talked, and now he squatted down to lift Nancy out of her walker as he called her "sweetness." He asked if I would follow them into the nursery where "Nancy liked getting her bottle." He sat down in a lovely armless bentwood nursing rocker. Allen noticed my admiration of its quality and asked, "Like it? It's the best piece of furniture in the house. My mother gave it to us when Nancy was born. She used to rock me in it when I was this size."

When Nancy saw the rocking chair, she started squealing and pumped herself up and down on Allen's arm. She was so stimulated she couldn't really start sucking on the nipple of the bottle, though she obviously wanted to feed. Allen skillfully settled Nancy down by talking softly and rhythmically to her and *then* introduced the bottle. Good technique, I thought to myself—I wondered where he learned that, and asked. "I saw Barbara's mother do that once, and it works pretty good, doesn't it?" he answered.

Allen returned to talking about his early days with Nancy. He described a period of two weeks when she was four months old when he was afraid to be away from her. He'd seen a "Donahue Show" on Sudden Infant Death Syndrome (SIDS) and it left him with two weeks of nightmares and "a bad case of overprotection. To this day I'm nuts about her health."

How had it come to pass that Mr. Young was "still at it"? Allen: "I never thought about it till my stepsister asked me how long I was going to 'fill in' for Barbara. Her question made me realize that I wasn't feeling like I was 'filling in' for *anyone*. The junkyard was still shut down, and I'd never really looked for another job. Barbara asked me about three weeks after I started with Nancy if I wanted to keep doing it. Her boss had asked her to come back full time, and she said she wanted to, but only if I felt okay about it. I said, 'why not?' And since then the time has just gone by."

The overtly casual, informal character of this child-care decision was typical of the families who had decided after the birth of the babies to have the father take over as the primary caregiver. It was in bold contrast to the carefully planned and orchestrated style of the earliest-deciding families. Yet as seen earlier, their children could not be distinguished from one another on developmental testing. So much for linear causality in child development.

How did Allen feel his parenting style resembled or contrasted with Barbara's? Allen: "When a friend of ours or a relative she hasn't seen for a long time picks her up, Nancy will look at me and not at Barbara. That worried me at first. I kind of wished she would've. I felt kind of nervous that I'm *that* important to her. I think it hurts Barbara's feelings a little, and I ask her, but she always says no. I care for Nancy in my way, and Barbara does in hers. Can't say how, but it's just different. When Nancy's upset, and you go in to pick her up, you have to talk her down first, get her attention, look her in the eyes, and *then* you pick her up. It just works better that way. Maybe I've got more patience than Barbara has with her right now. But I know I'm going to be a sucker later. Barbara might be better for her then than me."

This complementary view of parenting that Mr. Young espouses, where one parent excels in one area and the other elsewhere—the sort of "Jack Sprat" philosophy of parental union—*is* probably a better, more enduring model than the "Ken and Barbie marriage." Trying to perform identically as parents is less useful than the capacity to respond flexibly and empathically, if differently, to the variable developmental needs of one's children. For decades child development experts have erroneously directed parents to sing with one voice, a unison chorus of values, politics, disciplinary and loving styles. But duets have greater harmonic possibilities and are more interesting to listen to, so long as the cacophony or dissonance remains at acceptable levels.

Nancy had finished her bottle and was sleepily rubbing her eyes. Allen put her quietly into her crib, and tucked her in "in her favorite position"—buttocks up in the air, knees drawn up to her chest. Allen: "She always crashes right away after this noon bottle."

As we returned to the kitchen, Allen continued, "It never occurred to me that I might have a choice in life about whether or not to work. All guys work—that's it—those are the rules. So right now, I'm feeling pretty damn lucky. Barb makes pretty good money. Things are tight, but my family's business is such a mess, I'd rather not work. Who knows how long that'll last?

"It ain't all roses, though. We've had some tough times. The breast-feeding didn't go so well. Barb really wanted to do it. She came home on breaks to nurse Nancy, but she always worried that her milk wasn't enough. To make matters worse, she got some nipple infections. She had to express milk for feedings, and it was tough on both of them, especially Barb, 'cause it was their special thing. She finally gave it up and we were all relieved.

"It's also tough not being able to go anywhere. We go out a little. But I've lost half my friends, 'cause I can't go anywhere or do anything without the kid. At first that drove me nuts—the loss of freedom. That's the only thing I've resented about the kid, trapped here at home watching the soap operas. The only people around with kids are women, and I'll be damned if I'm going to 'have the girls over for tea!' I don't know any guys who're doing with their kids what I'm doing."

Were the troubles worth it? Were there things in his present role that Allen valued or felt proud of? "You bet. I'm proud of what a beautiful child I've got. I'm proud of how she gets around, moves around all over the place—

she's a mover. And I'm always proud when people think she's older than she is because they hear her talking and making words. Yeah, it's worth it."

As the interview came to a close, we arranged to meet again with Barbara at my office, as she worked nearby, and Allen "wanted an excuse to get out of the house." As I turned to leave, I commented on Nancy's enjoyment of his photographic equipment. "You know, it's really weird; my mother used to weave, and she wove me this scarf when I was about ten. I still carry it around my neck, sometimes even when it's not that cold. I guess it's nice to have a piece of these people around."

Our next meeting was the first opportunity I'd had to meet Barbara. She had to come attired in her crisp, formal waitress uniform. She apologized for being "overdressed" as she firmly shook my hand in greeting. She had jet-black hair, dark brown eyes, smiled warmly, and gave the impression of being older and somehow less casual than Allen.

Barbara told me that she "only had about fifty minutes to talk," and so she wondered if she could start by telling me "some things you might want to know. I hear you're interested in us as well as Nancy. So I'll start with what I think's important about us."

She began by telling me that she, like her daughter, had been a premature infant. Her parents, now both 45, married early, too, each twenty at the time. Her mother, unlike her, had waited five years to have Barbara. "As you've probably figured out, Nancy was already on her way when Allen and I married. Neither set of parents was especially thrilled that we were getting married so young. They wanted us to wait till we were ready—but who *ever* knows when they're ready? I wasn't sure I was pregnant at the time, but Allen and I had been joking right along about having a child, and the wedding had been planned for about six months. I knew that the diaphragm didn't fit very well, but I didn't bother to get it changed. So I can't say she was a *total* surprise."

She had told Allen at the time she knew she'd conceived that she was anxious about being a mother. She'd never really liked to babysit as a young teenager and feared she might not be "as good at it as my mother was." Nevertheless they comforted each other through the pregnancy.

Nancy was born three weeks early and weighed three pounds, eight ounces. Barbara corroborated Allen's depiction of her difficult last trimester, marked by weight gain and toxemia. Barbara reported that she'd had repetitive "bad dreams about losing the baby somewhere—leaving it someplace and not being able to remember where."

Allen, upon hearing his wife's story of the dream, said that he had dreams about babies during the pregnancy, too, but that he didn't say anything to his wife because his dreams were "pleasant." Barbara reminded him that he had gained weight as well, because he started drinking so much milk! (In the final tally of the whole study population, eight of the seventeen fathers consumed uncharacteristically large quantities of milk during "their pregnancies." Were they just beating the baby to the starting line, or were nurturing preparations so thick in the air that even the fathers' nutrition was being affected?)

Barbara described Nancy as "funny looking at first. Her head was molded from crowning, and she was a little jaundiced" (not unusual for a preemie). This was some contrast to Allen's depiction that she was "perfect in every way."

During the five weeks before Barbara returned to work, she had begun to feel that "Allen was the 'play machine,' and I was the 'milk machine.' I tried breast-feeding a short time, but it was hard right from the beginning. I started expressing milk for night-time bottles so Allen could feed Nancy. I noticed that she seemed to work harder at feeding from the bottle with him. I really wanted it to go better. But since I had one inverted nipple and an infection in the other one, my pediatrician gave me permission to stop, so I did. I felt sad but relieved.

"Right from the beginning, Allen was so gentle with her, and that just amazed me. My father's an egg farmer with thousands of laying hens. He's gentle with eggs but not with children. So Allen's calm and easy style really surprised me."

After she'd begun returning to work more and more, Barbara and Allen worked out a plan for her to be with Nancy completely on weekends and in the mornings before she went to work. During such times, Allen tried to distance himself. This didn't work too well, because Nancy was an early riser like her father while Barbara, who had to work late often, slept in. This was one of the more obvious temperamental qualities Nancy and her father shared, according to Barbara. Hence, she called them "the morning people."

Barbara also noticed other similar characteristics. They enjoyed similar "musical styles, had the same taste in food, and even had certain facial expressions and body movements that looked alike." Did this mean that father's body, and its movements, could be used in the same comforting, familiar, repetitive ways that infant researchers have seen in mother/infant pairs? A surprising but reasonable assumption, suggesting that it was not just the fetal environment but the postbirth nurturing environment with the father that was responsible for promoting the self-regulatory behavior in the infant and young child.

Barbara then changed the focus of the interview, saying, "I want to tell you where I came from. You probably are interested in that. Besides, becoming a mother has made me think of my growing up more than I usually do."

Mrs. Young's mother was from a Swiss background, and her father a second-generation immigrant from the "hills of Tuscany," in Italy. Her mother had worked before Barbara's birth as a school nurse and had returned to work full time when Barbara entered school herself. She remembers her mother as "good, strict, and kind. But, she was distant, too, you know—Swiss."

Barbara could remember feeling jealous as a child that her mother spent all day caring for *other* children. In her leisure time, her mother was a skilled dressmaker and seamstress, and Barbara had spent many hours with her mother learning the "needle arts." The mastectomy had slowed her mother down some, but she was "totally devoted to Nancy—she's one of those women who's a better grandmother than mother."

Barbara's father's family had come to America in the previous generation to help start a vineyard in New England. But it was not to be, so her father borrowed some money to start a small chicken and egg farm. He'd worked hard and done well, and he now had 10,000 chickens and a secure life. She described him as "pleasant, loving, very passionate and opinionated in a charming and affectionate way—you know, Italian." She had felt close to her father all her life, and, unlike her mother, had learned to converse with him in simple Italian.

She also reported being spoiled. "They had a miscarriage before I was born, so I was always treated like fine crystal. It got a little stifling after a while. That's why Allen was such a treat for me. He treated me like a real person."

Barbara, having completed her family history to her satisfaction, began talking about her marriage. The couple had met in high school and dated "on and off" since they were fifteen and sixteen. She was drawn to him because he was "cute, funny, and a little wild." Allen reciprocated; he was drawn to her "because she was beautiful and mysterious. All the other girls I knew were on the make—but not her."

After graduation, they went their separate ways for a while and then reconnected through mutual friends. They fell "madly in love" this time and decided to get married six months after they'd started dating again.

Later, Barbara and Allen were to tell me that their sexual attraction to one another had been "magnetic." In fact, they had both resented Nancy's birth and early sleep problems because of how it disrupted their sexual routines.

Speaking of sexual matters, having Nancy and choosing this unique child-care plan had affected Allen's erotic attraction to his wife in an interesting way. For some reason he chose this point in the interview to talk about it. When Nancy was seven months old, Barbara's restaurant closed for renovations. For two weeks she was home full time, and Allen "backed off" for a while. Interestingly, he found his sexual attraction to his wife waning when he withdrew to the position of secondary parent. When she returned to work, he reported, "It was like she became her sexy old self to me."

This same incident struck Barbara powerfully as well, but in a different, nonsexual context. The day after the restaurant reopened and Barbara returned to work, Nancy started clutching one of her mother's hair curlers in her hand as she crawled about the house. It was her constant possession day and night for several days.

The transition back to her father's care was not exactly seamless, but within a day or two Nancy had returned to her usual routines and attachments. Barbara was briefly upset by the force and clarity of this return to the father, but she was also comforted by the ease with which her husband and child reattached, as it evoked pleasant memories of her close relationship with her own father.

Barbara ended her part of the interview with the following vignette. "Sometimes I think he's gone too far as a mother. Did he tell you that he sometimes sits *down* on the toilet to pee now?" Allen rushed to his own defense. "You can't see the damned bowl when you're holding a baby on your chest. It's just easier—besides, who cares." They both laughed warmly.

Allen was not the only father who had become a transient squatter. Three other fathers, once I began to ask, admitted—after their amazement at my question subsided—that they too had taken up the habit.*

Primed and intrigued by his wife's disclosures, Allen decided to talk about himself and his own origins. As a couple, the Youngs were to prove quite open. They were not unique in this aspect among the families in the study. Something about the telling of it seemed to ease and validate this often lonely venture.

Allen began by describing his family "as one of your typical American composites." Each of his parents was still in a nearby community and still quite involved in his life, although each had remarried after having divorced when he was sixteen. "My mother had a great business sense and her judgments were usually right. That's what they always fought about. I always thought she was a frustrated businesswoman."

Allen had one older brother and two younger step-sisters. "My big brother is so wild, I hope he never has kids." He reported that his experience with his parents'

---

*Boston child psychiatrist James Herzog, who has been involved in a number of clinical investigations of traditional fathers and young infants, has reported a similar finding.

---

marriage had been quite an unhappy one, and that during his first intense relationship with a girl, he felt himself panicked when she asked him for another date. "I always thought I'd rather die than marry, and she was moving too fast for me."

Although he still had strong and positive relationships with both of his parents separately, Allen reported initially that he "felt funny and kind of odd when I fed Nancy in front of my mother or my father. I don't think Nancy liked it very much either. We just learned not to do it if possible, whenever they were around.

"My father told me last month he was 'astounded' by my choice. He asked me, 'How do you do it?' I feel a little misunderstood by him, but I also feel his respect. When I became a father I stopped feeling like a punk. It was like I was more my own father's equal."

Mr. Young had moved out of his home when he was fifteen, after a "real bad scene with my father." He had gone to live with a married uncle, his mother's brother, who lived two miles away from his parents' home. The couple was childless and enjoyed Allen's company greatly. His uncle was a successful photographer, and his wife was a "homebody." Allen reported that his relationship with his mother and father got better "instantly," and he was able to be of some support to each of them when they divorced a year later. He stayed in high school after leaving home, and his grades and social status improved significantly.

Living next door to his aunt and uncle was a family whose home and farm served as a temporary shelter for battered and abused children. Mr. Young found himself spending long periods of time in that home, being drawn to the young children and their riveting life stories, by their friendliness and neediness.

By eighteen, Allen had finished high school and started to work in his father's family junk-car business. He was also hired, with the help of his uncle, to do part-time freelance photography for a small advertising firm. Allen's father, who had once worked as a successful advertising promoter, had taken an early interest in his son's talent for drawing and sketching and, over his wife's objections, had supported Allen's interest in the graphic arts.

Allen Young reported that his favorite subjects for photography were children. "I took lots of pictures of kids for their parents, for family albums and Christmas presents. I couldn't stand seeing the parents push their kids around during shootings. Soon, I realized I could handle some of the kids better than the parents could in my own studio, and I got much better pictures in the bargain."

Though Allen felt Nancy was "the most important thing" in his life, he sometimes felt distressed at the envy he felt over the attention and affection his daughter received from family members and friends. It was as though this nineteen-year-old felt in competition with the importance of his own child, indicating that his own adolescent development may not yet have been fully complete.

As this particular interview was concluded, Mr. Young commented that "our marriage seemed to be off to a good start. That's really important to me. My parents had such an horrendous marriage; they fought like George and Martha in this movie I saw called *Who's Afraid of Virginia Woolf?* I guess I was kind of lucky to find my aunt and uncle. I got a chance to move out while I could still keep a good relationship going with both my parents. I'm not sure it would've lasted much longer if I'd stayed."

It was then Nancy's turn. When she came for "her" appointment, as the father called it, I was struck again by how much she resembled her father physically, although she had her mother's pretty coal-black hair and dark eyes. There were none of the facial features, such as high foreheads or small eyes, that sometimes mark premature infants. In fact, her face was somehow both complex and open.

She was well scrubbed, with every hair in place. Allen explained that Barbara had dressed her this morning in "her mother's favorite outfit." She wore a yellow pinafore and a cardigan sweater "popcorn-stitched by my mother," said Barbara. "Picture perfect," her father said, as he placed his daughter in the high chair at the testing table.

Nancy had not taken her eyes off my face since she had entered the testing room. Though I had been in her home twice, I was still getting "checked out." Her eyes were so wide and intent that I, an experienced child watcher, felt *so* watched I almost had to avert my own gaze! When I started to look away, she squealed loudly, as if to restore the staring contest! I had to agree with Allen; I did feel "looked through."

When young children with a history of prematurity are tested, the examiner usually takes into consideration the normal gestation period of nine months actually finished sometime after the delivery, depending on the degree of prematurity. As a consequence, the child's chronologic age is "adjusted" to reflect some built-in catching-up time, in the first year at least.

Nancy's age on the developmental assessment needed no such adjusting. Though she was only nine months old, her manipulation of the test items as a whole looked more like the work of a twelve-month-old. She was nearly walking, having begun in the last two weeks to pull herself up on the furniture and cruise around. She was also a tenaciously curious child, especially when exploring more novel testing materials.

But above all, Nancy was a "looker." She was capable of attending to and remembering the visual details of her environment at a level well beyond her nine months. When I had first met her in the garage, she had leaned forward from her father's arms to pull a pen from my shirt pocket. She proceeded to pass it back and forth from hand to hand, feeling its texture and looking at its details, pausing occasionally to taste it. Then she handed it back to me.

Now three weeks later, her first official act at the testing table was to look for the pen in my pocket. Eventually she reached up to pull at my shirt pocket to examine its contents, since the pen was not in its expected place! I asked Allen if he kept his pens in his shirt pocket and was told, "None of us do that; I think she's actually remembering." For a child of this age to remember such a detail from a previous encounter with a stranger was quite noteworthy.

When the testing had come to an end, the Youngs were sitting there beaming, obviously aware that Nancy was doing well. They both commented that they'd seen her do things they didn't know she could do. Barbara asked as they walked down the hall, "So, she's doing okay? We think so too. But it's that remembering that gets me. Almost makes me nervous, she's so good at it. But it's really a good thing to have. Allen and I are always having remembering contests—you know—do you remember when...?" It was obvious this was a quality of Nancy's that the Youngs enjoyed and valued highly. Little wonder Nancy enjoyed it too.

10

Nancy at Five: A Duet for Three

My next meeting with the Youngs was a chance encounter nine months later at an annual local handcraft fair, where Barbara was exhibiting some of her needlework. My own wife is a weaver, and she has patiently taught me to appreciate this functional and exquisite craft. We were in the Needle and Fabric Arts tent when Allen came up to say hello. Then he took me by the arm and said, "Come here, quick." He assured my wife, "We'll be right back."

Nancy, now eighteen months old, was with him, but not at his side. She was a short way off, standing in front of a long mirror for use by potential patrons of the shawlmaker. Nancy was playing a raucous game of peek-a-boo with her father's reflection in the mirror. There were gales of laughter whenever she took her hands away from her face to squeal "pee-boo" for the benefit of the assembled admirers. I thought to myself that she obviously knew how to play to a crowd.

Allen reintroduced Nancy to me and then to my wife. She repeated her name after she'd heard it, saying "Ahzee, Ahzee." Allen: "That's what she's started calling herself these days." (An unusual capacity at this age.) Allen and daughter then took both of us to the end of the tent where the soft-sculptured dolls sat on tables and shelves in various poses. Nancy reached up, extending herself to full, tiptoe height, and pulled one down by a dangling foot. She dealt with it as though it were hers. It was almost her height, and she hugged it tightly to herself while smiling broadly. Allen explained: "This is Barbara's booth. She started making these on commission after she'd competed at these fairs and won a mess of ribbons. Pretty good, huh?" I remember thinking as my wife and I admired the doll's features, textures, and charm that Nancy was not the only one who liked the details. We said our farewells and arranged our next meeting some months hence.

Nancy was twenty-two months old when I visited her family next for the first follow-up home visit. The jolly-jump-ups and walkers were gone now, and a brightly painted rocking horse sat in the center of the living room. The entire wall of one side of the spacious living room was covered—no, papered—with black-and-white photographs of Nancy. Nancy alone, Nancy with Barbara, Nancy with Allen, Nancy with grandparents, Nancy in the bath, in her father's shoes, her mother's uniform, Nancy laughing, crying, sleeping, or chasing her grandfather's chickens.

Nancy came toddling animatedly into the room, sporting a pacifier and "feet gommies" (her recently acquired phrase for footed, zip-up-the-front sleeper pajamas), having just finished a bath. In a few seconds she was on her rocking horse, talking and rocking away. It was immediately clear that Nancy was her same warm, up-front, vigorous old self. She had now added a pointing finger to her "checking out" look, which had its usual riveting effect on me.

Allen said, "Watch this." He asked Nancy to turn on the music so we could "see her dance." She dismounted and ran over to the stereo system. She carefully threw the power switch and pushed the mode selector button, and the music began. She turned around and smiled so broadly her pacifier fell out on the floor. Nancy: "Uh-oh, pacy-duwhty." She squatted down, picked it up, and ran with it to Allen, who stuffed it in a pants pocket.

Barbara: "He loves to show her off." Allen: "What do you mean *I* love to show her off? Who's modeling mommy's new sweaters for the next craft fair pictures? Huh? Huh?"

He quickly grabbed his daughter and tickled her so

that she collapsed in breathless laughter onto the floor. Allen: "We had to teach her how to do that with the stereo because she was getting into a lot of hot water messing with it. She thinks a lot about being naughty these days— huh, Tiger?" (More tickling and peals of laughter.) "But she tries to stop herself. She'll go to the TV or stove, or Barbara's needlework stuff, stand in front of it, clap her hands and say 'no no Ahzee.' She understands enough so you can sometimes teach her beforehand to stay out of trouble. It works better that way because she's so stubborn after she gets into something."

Barbara laughed. "She's so independent these days she goes around saying 'be-a-help, be-a-help' when she really means 'do-self, do-self.' *Just* like her father—stuhbbornn! I don't really like to tell her 'no' all the time, because I don't get to see her that much, you know. I want quality time, not just 'telling her "no" time.' Besides, Allen's better at discipline than I am. His 'no' seems to stick better than mine."

The child-care arrangements for Nancy had changed little over the last year. Barbara was still a waitress, working forty hours a week, mostly evenings. Allen was still freelancing, contributing about one-fourth of the family budget by working some weekends. Allen's family business was still dormant, so he was feeling no pressure from his father to come back to work.

Barbara, however, was feeling that "sooner or later" she would do something else. "I look at the women who have been waitresses for a long time, and it's scary how tired they look and how many of them hate their jobs. My dad wants me to start thinking about coming to work for him. He's been sick a lot and could use the help. But not yet." Barbara then changed the topic and said she'd been noticing some things she wanted to tell me about.

She described a recent family visit to a neighbor's

house where she'd been struck by how jealous Nancy seemed to be of Allen's holding other children. Allen had picked up one of the neighbor's three-month-old twins, and Nancy had started whining and pulling at his arms. At first, they both thought she wanted to hold the *baby*, but then Barbara realized Nancy wanted Allen to hold *her*, and not the infant. (Another example of the "Madonna constellation" conflict, a toddler's negative response to its parent holding another child, described earlier? Probably.)

The incident had stuck in her mind, because she had started thinking about having another baby herself. She said she was a little more enthusiastic about this than Allen was. "I remember feeling hurt that Nancy called Allen 'Dadduh' for so long before she called me 'Momma,' that maybe I'd let them kind of shut me out. If we do have another one, I think I'll do it different."

More recently, Barbara had been feeling more important to Nancy. *She'd* been the one able to get her daughter back to sleep over the past several weeks, during the course of a difficult sleep disturbance. Nancy had been awakening and crying "Daddy, Daddy, Daddy." Allen would get up and go in to try to comfort her, but when he'd leave, Nancy became even more upset. So, Barbara went in to try. Her presence seemed more calming, and Nancy could get back to sleep quickly and stay asleep.*

Overall, Barbara seemed to be increasingly enjoying

---

*Babies are struggling, during their daytime lives, with increasing independence from their primary caregivers, in our case here, the fathers. The freedom feels good and powerful while it's being acted out. But the other, fearful side of independence is loneliness. That feeling makes itself felt during the night, when the conscious mind is no longer on duty. The reappearance and disappearance of the primary nurturing figure during a night-time visit to an upset toddler is consequently all the more frightening and regressive for the child. The other, secondary caretaking parent's comforting (in this case, the mother's), however, is already understood as the coming-and-going kind. Barbara felt good as she could intuit the right technique to easing the expected, normal sleep disturbances of the second year of life (as many fathers have done before her).

her role as "the uncontaminated other" (see Chapter 3), and her success felt very good to her. She had been teasing Allen lately about his complaints about the drudgery, loneliness, and boredom, saying, "Mothers have been saying that for years. Stop complaining and go watch some soap operas!"

Allen then said that things *had* been bothering him more lately, especially the loneliness. He really missed "the guys," his old high-school friends of whom he saw less and less as time passed. He was now largely dependent on Barbara's friends for his meager social life. "Not that this one isn't fun enough," he said, tousling Nancy's hair.

Allen changed from self-reflection to Nancy talk. "She's a lover—she loves her bath, she loves her crib, loves to ride in the car, she loves to talk—you know—she's Italian. She just loves everything. And doesn't miss a trick. She saw a Budweiser beer can in the fridge one day. She pulled it out to look at it and said 'horsey.' You know, the horses that pull the beer wagon on the TV commercial? That even took me a while to figure out!"

Nancy, as though on cue, had run out of the room just as the focus of the interview moved back to her. She reentered the living room towing behind her a large doll. Nancy said simply and plainly, "Mommy," and hugged the doll tight against her cheek. It slowly dawned on me that the doll bore a striking resemblance to her mother—same color and style of hair, same color eyes, glasses—and it was clad in a scaled-down copy of her mother's waitress uniform. Barbara explained, "I just made that for her, and she loves it. She calls it 'Mommy' and takes it with her everywhere. I hope that it holds up; it gets a real workout."

Nancy suddenly stopped, squatted down and dropped her doll to examine something on the floor that had caught her eye. She had found a dark spot or stain mark on the rug. She rubbed it with the palms of both hands, stood up and said excitedly, "Pee-pee." Both parents laughed as Barbara said, "Guess what we've started doing—or maybe I should say *she's* started doing?"

Barbara explained that a few days before, Nancy had put her stuffed doggy on a small potty that was accidentally left behind at the house by a family after a recent weekend visit. Nancy would put the dog on the potty and say "Doggy pee, doggy pee." Allen and Barbara had quite different versions of the exact meaning of this event. Allen: "She's really ready to start toilet training." Barbara: "You're nuts—she's thinking of a real doggy peeing on the rug. That happens all the time at my folks' house and she sees the dog get into big trouble for it. She's not really ready for toilet training."

Because of summer scheduling difficulties, our year-long interval between visits was cut to eight months, and I next saw Nancy when she was two-and-a-half. This visit occurred at my office when both Youngs brought Nancy for the follow-up developmental assessment. Not much had changed since the last visit, the child-care arrangements remaining stable.

Barbara, however, was finding increasing fault with her employment. Her father continued to encourage her to join him in his business. Barbara: "I like the *idea* of working a lot—you know, getting up, dressing in something different, going out in the world, driving a car, making money, being with people, and getting something done...like that. It's a private thought, but I think my temperament is better suited to working than just staying at home and being a mother. I'm just real lucky that Allen's [temperament] is so suited to being a parent. I don't feel as jealous of that, or as guilty about it as I used to. So, I notice that, well, he's more patient with her than I am, and he knows when to leave her alone. I'm always, like, *at* her when I'm alone with her.

"He can put up with the messiness, too, that seems to go along with having kids. I'm becoming even more a neat freak! The chaos and sloppiness just drives me nuts, but it's, like, he doesn't even notice till we have to clean the house on weekends."

Allen brought me up to date, as always, on Nancy's latest repertoire. She was now toilet trained, as of three months prior, having spent only a matter of weeks convincing her mother that her father had been right: She *was* ready. She talked incessantly of "potties, doggy pee," and "big girl-mommy pants." She could now get her shoes on the correct feet (most but not all of the time). She also loved pouring the milk from the pitcher for her parents' coffee or breakfast cereal.

Nancy had recently mastered the fact that she was a girl. Having gotten that clear, she was endlessly curious about the genital equipment of the dogs and cats in her neighborhood. She had in fact sustained a small scratch from a neighborhood puppy, who took offense at Nancy's examination technique of turning over the smaller animals to look for a "peenie or a hole."

Even though she needed it less and less, she liked her parents' help getting dressed and choosing her clothes. Allen reported that he was less interested in dressing her up than Barbara was, preferring the child's version of his own casual at-home workclothes. "But it's not *how* you dress them that makes them boys or girls—right, Pumpkin?"

Nancy's developmental testing was again strong and competent. Her vocabulary had jumped even farther ahead of the levels for her expected chronologic age; she knew and used some words that were more typical of three-and-a-half-year-olds. The *rate* of her excellent, even precocious, performance had slowed somewhat, but the overall profile was more even. (Many of the children in the study were to exhibit this same leveling off over time.) Nancy seemed to be doing well across the board: in motor skills, intellectually, emotionally, and socially.

Ten months passed before I saw the Youngs again. By then, they were a different family. To begin with, there were now four of them. Three months earlier, when Nancy was 37 months old, a sister, Naomi, was born. She was a large, healthy baby, and full term. But Barbara had had a rough pregnancy. Her obstetrician had told her she was a prediabetic halfway through the pregnancy and that she'd have to "watch it carefully" after the birth.

Allen, meanwhile, had added yet more sonograms to the garage wall, but he personally gained less weight. "Instead," Allen said, "I had some toothaches—can you believe that?"—laughing at the obviousness of his involvement. (Not an unusual occurrence in the pregnant father as we saw in Chapter 2.)

The Youngs had decided after their last visit with me to "start" on a second baby. Barbara had conceived on the first ovulation cycle. She was delighted from the beginning. "Now I could have a real good excuse to quit my job. Besides, I really wanted another one. Maybe a boy for me, I thought, because Allen's already got his girl."

Midway through the pregnancy, Barbara's father sustained a serious heart attack. He recovered, but Barbara became quite anxious and depressed. The life inside her began to feel even more precious as she saw her father's threatened.

In the final trimester Barbara gained 25 pounds. She had to quit her job earlier than she had intended and go to bed. Being home with Allen and Nancy helped ease her depression.

About the same time, Allen's family of origin was

also stirring. The suit against the junkyard had been settled, and the business started up again. Now there was much pressure from Allen's father for him to come back to work.

With Naomi's birth, the geography of Nancy's world changed radically. Her father had for the last two months been working about twenty hours a week in the afternoons in his family junk business, not "enjoying it especially but making real money." He looked after Naomi and Nancy in the mornings. Barbara had just started the previous week to work about fifteen hours a week for *her* family's business, starting to learn "the details," and looking after the girls in the afternoons. Both Allen and Barbara felt very lucky to have the opportunity of such flexible schedules. They split the cooking half and half and "simply stopped seeing very much of each other," according to Allen.

Barbara was quite happy. Allen was grumbling. Nancy was adapting in her own unique fashion. At the end of Allen's first week of work, Nancy asked her mother to make her a "daddy doll—like mommy doll—but with a bearded." At the same time, Nancy was not sleeping well and had become uncharacteristically cranky and irritable.

During the first few weeks of Naomi's life, Nancy had reattached herself tenaciously to her father, reversing a trend toward increasing independence that had been obvious for some time. But Allen's return to work had interrupted this reattachment, which seemed to have the primary purpose for Nancy of eclipsing Allen's attachment to Naomi. She had also begun carrying around one of her new sister's empty baby bottles. Allen interpreted: "She seemed to be saying—look guys, this is a bit much. A new baby is one thing, changing parents on me is another!"

One could not be sure if that was what *Nancy*

thought, but it certainly was what Allen thought. He felt as though *he* were letting Nancy down by "changing parents."

The Youngs were considering putting Nancy into a preschool program because she "seemed so ready and interested in learning." But, after seeing Nancy work so hard to keep her balance after her sister's birth, they decided against it.

Allen was also quite concerned that he was not feeling the special attachment to Naomi that he had felt toward Nancy. He commented to his wife, "It's probably impossible to do it twice."

In retrospect, Mr. Young reported that the first week of caring for Nancy had been "the most powerful learning experience of my life. Nobody had ever influenced me that much in such a short time. My relationship with Naomi seemed to be a more typical father/daughter one at first. Now we're doing better." (As if "better" were only marginally acceptable to him.)

Barbara was feeling much more "with it" as Naomi's mother than she had as Nancy's. "I realized that I'd learned a lot from Allen, and just felt more confident as a mom. Although my mom was a nurse, I'd never *seen* her really look after another child, and I'd never learned much from babysitting. A lot of things a mother was 'supposed to know,' I didn't, and I was too embarrassed about asking to learn. So, watching Allen helped a lot. But, everyone says the second one's always easier than the first."

This couple was typical of a small but homogeneous group in which some dilution of the father's dominance of the parenting role occurred through the mother's increased involvement with the second child. This was true regardless of the sex of the first or second child. In the particular case of Mrs. Young, she had used her husband's successful nurturing of Nancy as a role model for her increasingly nurturant presence in Naomi's life, because her identification with her own mother had been so ambivalent and conflicted.

Nancy at 40 months was a larger, more sophisticated version of the verbal and social little girl I'd seen before. Her speech now was wholly intelligible, and her vocabulary was more typical of a four- to four-and-a-half-year-old. She and her father had always been especially fond of word games, and she even had a rudimentary understanding of punning. She was now able to dress herself completely. Barbara reported that Nancy loved dramatic play and was usually assigned the roles in the neighborhood "pretend" play. Such skills were much more typical of four-year-old behavior.

I had brought along on this home visit a medical student who was working as my research assistant for the summer. Nancy seemed intrigued with him and repeatedly invited him into play situations with her. Consequently, his efforts to take running notes on the observation were unsuccessful. Nancy was also especially active and skillful in her (eventually) successful attempts to find accommodations for her infant sister *other* than on her father's lap.

Throughout the visit, Nancy demonstrated her competence in myriad ways. She proudly "read" to Naomi, threw a ball expertly, and sang songs of her own unique design.

Near the end of the visit, she invited me to play "Supergirl" with her. She became "Supergirl" by wearing an old Super*man* cape. Her father chuckled as she "flew through" the living room, cape flowing behind in the breeze, and said, "I suppose we really *ought* to put a dress on her someday. She seems so fearless in the neighborhood, it's hard to think of her as a *girl* girl." It had occurred to them only with the birth of Naomi that maybe they should be making a more sincere effort to "feminize their daughters."

A year and a half later, one month before Nancy would turn five, I saw the Youngs for the last time. During the intervening months, their life had changed so radically that, judging by appearances, they were now a pretty traditional family, doing pretty traditional things. Allen was now working full time at the family salvage yard, "making bucks, but not especially thrilled." Allen, who was always given to teasing and satire, gave a kind of forced chuckle. "It's about time I made an honest living, huh?" he said, teasing Barbara. "You can't just hang out at home, playing with the kids, forever, now, can you? People would think I was queer."

No one was fooled.

Allen was not a terribly happy man these days. He had even stopped finding time for his photography. However, he said two things had definitely improved since he had returned to work full time; their financial status was getting better, and he was seeing much more of his family and friends. Nevertheless, he missed his children terribly, especially Nancy, and apparently it was mutual. Barbara: "They talk on the phone—more than Allen and *I* do!"

Barbara was now the primary nurturing parent in the family. She had become, in her words, "housewife and housemother." She continued to work, however, three mornings a week for a total of twelve to thirteen hours a week in the family egg business, which she greatly enjoyed. Her father had sustained a second heart attack a year before, and was working less and less, so Barbara and her mother were making more of the business decisions. Barbara: "Besides, I have practically no experience doing this. But I figure my dad didn't either at the beginning. I'm blessed with plenty of his common sense. Mom and I are doing okay so far."

Nancy was attending a preschool program three mornings a week and was about to start going five mornings. Allen: "She loves going and seems ready. They think she's terrific, so we're going to try it. It'll be good for her anyway. She feels grown-up over there."

Naomi, now 22 months old, was in the day-care section of the same preschool two mornings a week while Barbara worked. On the third morning, Allen stayed home to be with Naomi. "Nancy's not thrilled, but it's my only special time with number two. I really dig it. My dad, who still can't believe I raised Nancy, bitched a little when I asked for the morning off, but it was part of the deal for my coming back. I have to watch him like a hawk. He's always trying to schedule me to work Naomi's morning. It makes me feel sorry for the women who get harassed by their bosses about the same thing—you know—trying to be a good mother *and* a good worker? It's hard enough to keep it straight in your *own* head, even without the boss bitching at you."

Given such far-reaching changes in the Young family system, the evaluation of Nancy's development seemed especially valuable. What sort of shape would she be in, and what would be on her mind after "changing parents in midstream," as Barbara called the family transition?

Her developmental profile on the Yale schedules revealed a very competent abstract thinker and problem solver. Her vocabulary was typical of a five-and-a-half-year-old child, and as before her visual and spatial skills were even more advanced; Nancy remained "the looker." But, once again, it was in her play that she revealed the most about her life.

Nancy was one of eight children in the study whom I had an opportunity to observe in day-care or preschool settings. Children play quite differently with their peers than they do with an interested adult like me. But their group play still reflects the power of the same personality, its inner workings, and its emotional supplies and repertoire. I considered such play a valid source of data about how Nancy felt about her life, her world, and her family.

Nancy was, according to her preschool teacher, a "legendary player" (a reference to her excellent play skills), and I was invited to come observe her in action. The preschool that Nancy attended was equipped with a small observation booth in one corner of the playroom for parents (and associated other watchers) who wanted to see without being seen.

First, a word about play in prekindergarten children. Most day-care centers and pre-K's (as the older nursery school or prekindergarten groups are called) allow periods of extended free play in their schedules. These periods often precede the more organized table activities such as painting, cutting, or coloring, and group experiences like storytelling, "show-and-tell," or listening to books being read. Play is encouraged or facilitated by carefully chosen materials such as blocks, dress-up clothes, puppets, or play spaces such as a doll corner or a kitchen equipped with domestic utensils. All types of "superhero" adventures and dramas of domestic bliss or turmoil are seriously portrayed in such places. (Remember Mrs. Kits' kindergarten in Chapter 3?) Life is being explored here in all its shapes, sizes, colors, and turns and tricks of fate.

As we saw in Chapter 3, male and female roles are assumed and interchanged, turned upside down, and clarified in such places. By the time children reach kindergarten, their roles are irrevocably fixed in the doll corner. The vast majority of six-year-old boys would sooner die than spend the morning in the doll corner. The six-year-old girl, in turn, who enters the hallowed male bastion of the *Star Wars* heroes risks exile from her colleagues in the doll corner.

Four-year-old boys are just beginning to rebel in the doll corner. There, "mothers" usually reign supreme, designating the boys to portray fathers, babies, policemen, grandfathers, and the like. Boys, however, are beginning to feel the magnetic pull of the superhero gang. The doll corner is becoming "the woman's room."

Three-year-old girls and boys, on the other hand, play almost interchangeably in the doll corner, boys as mothers, girls as fathers, back and forth very comfortably. The differences we see in the older child are there, however, whether we want them to be or not. They are more part of the business of crafting a strong gender *identity* than they are of shaping a gender *role*. Chauvinism makes its appearance later on, and it is important not to confuse the two.

Seated in the booth with note pad on my knees, I spotted Nancy in the doll corner with three other girls "making breakfast for the babies." The girls were clad in various articles of attire from the dress-up rack of castoff adult clothes. Nancy had a Superman cape over her shoulders and a long, pink fake-feather boa around her neck. The others had various hat, purse, and glove combinations. The "babies" in the small cradle were "screaming for pancakes."

A small, blond-haired, fair-complexioned little boy named Bobby turned to look at the girls when he heard the word "pancakes." He then left the block corner where he and several boys were building a "space station." He came to the "kitchen," and one of the girls said to him, "Don't come in Bobby, we're busy." Bobby stopped dead in his tracks and didn't move. Nancy looked at him and said, "He's okay. He can come in and change the baby." That idea did not intrigue Bobby particularly, and he retired to the block corner to join the other boys.

A few moments later, Nancy seemed to tire of the

domestic play and went to the block corner to join in the building of the space station. She was readily accepted, and her ideas for structural adaptation and improvement were implemented eagerly by the male crew. One of the girls called to her from the doll corner to ask her to come back. She replied, "No, I'm busy." This was typical of several of Nancy's excursions back and forth between the newly forming stereotypic territories. I was struck with the ease with which she moved back and forth from the doll corner to the construction site or games of cops and robbers. She was apparently so comfortably identified with both her mother *and* father that the traditional boundaries bound her less.

Near the end of the play time Nancy, who had organized an excursion to the space station involving several girls *and* boys, was confronted with a mutiny. One of the class's "tough" boys, Sam, who had been especially active and aggressive throughout the morning (consequently often in trouble with the teacher), challenged her. He said that the cradle that Nancy had pressed into service as a "space shuttle" could only take "He-Man and Battle Cat" (superhero figurines from a popular Saturday morning cartoon series) to the space station. Nancy told him to "Cool it, Sam—we'll make two trips." Sam faced her down. "No—He-Man goes first. He always does. He's the strongest and the bravest." Nancy negotiated. "There's lots of room. Barbie and He-Man and Battle-Cat can all fit." Sam retorted: "You always want your way. I'm tellin'!" But Nancy's last word worked. "Don't tell or we'll have to stop. Then He-Man and Barbie and Battle-Cat will *never* get there."

This interchange was especially interesting because it showed Nancy in two different lights. She not only enjoyed and used play and its symbols in highly innovative ways, but she was confident and free to move back and forth among the expanding demilitarized zone of five-year-old sexual stereotyping. She was certainly not immune to the immense power of societal shaping of sexual roles and attributes, but she was skillful in using what she knew about what boys and girls liked or *had* to do. She seems comfortable with but not wholly convinced of or restrained by the evolving (new to her) "sugar and spice" view of girlhood, or the "snips and snails" view of boyhood, gender/role stereotypes so familiar to us adults.

As I talked with Allen and Barbara about this last formal evaluation of Nancy, Barbara said that she wanted to tell me about a feeling that she'd been having lately. "We've been going through a lot of changes—some good, some bad. One I don't like is not being with Allen as much, but I see the kids a lot more. When I have a few minutes alone with Nancy, like when Naomi's asleep, I notice a lot of things in her that are a lot like Allen—like she's funny and likes to tease. It's almost like I'm with *both of them*, even when he's not there." It was obvious that Barbara enjoyed and was comforted by Allen's "presence" in her interaction with Nancy. It was probably a pleasant harmony for Nancy as well: like a duet for three.

11

The Nurturing Father and the Privilege of the Long View

As you may have already noticed, the original research timetable was abandoned early in the project. The Helens, Henrys, and Nancys and their families were studied for five years, not one. Typically, one tries to stay within the guidelines of the protocol so as not to change or confuse the questions being explored, the researcher, or the subjects. But as the first year of the project drew to a close, I began to fathom the richness and complexity of the findings, and I felt compelled—even happily obligated—to continue. I now had even more questions than answers about the nurturing father and his child. The project design would simply have to yield.

But thanks to a unique feature of the Yale Developmental Schedule the protocol would not need to be hopelessly distorted. The schedules can be used to follow a child's development from birth to six years of age without having to change assessment instruments. I could simply reevaluate the children at two- and four-year intervals with a follow-up visit the fifth year. Home visits would continue as before. A diagnostic play interview could also be added as the children developed enough language and play skills. This would provide valuable data about the child's inner life and world view.

Thus, the project was easily converted to a longitudinal study, permitting us to follow the fathers, children, and families over time. If two looks were more than double the value of one in child development research, how many times more worthy were three? And so we went ahead, led on by the special privilege of the long view.

Although we have already carefully followed three families over that span of time, it is equally important to scrutinize the group portrait of all seventeen families in order to appreciate the breadth of the experience of the families committed to this natural experiment. Two years after entering the study, all the original families (save one which had left the area and could not be contacted) were studied again using the original investigation method.

The changes within these sixteen families over the two years were far-reaching when seen as a whole. Second children had been born into seven families. Fathers had continued to serve as the primary caregiving parent in eight families (including Helen's and Henry's), including four in which there were now siblings. Mothers had become the primary parent in three families (one of whom was Nancy's), all of which had second children. Fathers had returned to work or school in six families (three with second children). There had been one parental separation in which the father had retained custody (Henry).

All the children were tested again using the Yale Developmental Schedules. As a group the children, now toddlers and preschoolers, continued to perform well on these measurements, especially in the two areas seen before. Some individual children excelled at other levels as well. Three of the older children (two girls and one boy) also tested noticeably above the expected norms on language expression and comprehension. These three were all from the "early chooser" families and seemed to have been reared in quite fertile verbal environments. Two of the younger children from the "late chooser" families (one boy and one girl) were especially gifted in motor function and agility. It's noteworthy that they were both from families in which physical strength, coordination, and participation in sports were all highly valued and practiced by one or both parents. On the average, the entire group's capacity to use cognitive skills and intellect to solve novel or unique problems and their personal-social competence were again better than expected.

Primary Caregivers at 2–Year Follow–Up

	Fathers	*Mothers*	*Joint*
Number of families (total)	8	3	5
Percent	*50%*	*19%*	*31%*
Number of second children born	4	3	1
Percent	*25%*	*19%*	*6%*
Number of fathers returned to work or school	3	3	–
Percent	*19%*	*19%*	–
Number of marital separations	1	–	–
Percent	*6%*	–	–

Seeing this finding repeated two years later makes us turn once again to search for explanations.

I initially speculated that these babies may have performed especially well on certain developmental tasks as a result of a particularly stimulating, vigorous, and unpredictable handling style by fathers.* This quality was observed throughout the study and neither waned nor diminished over time, adding support for the idea that it may be a characteristic of the American father/infant pair.

Some researchers have speculated that this "hyped" style may result from infrequent interaction between the father and baby, the father choosing to make every second count by "turning the baby on as quickly as possible." The father walks in the door after work and immediately says (or acts), "Come on kids, let's wake up and get to it—what do you say! We've got thirty minutes before bedtime—let's party!"

Others have further speculated that this stimulating style is a result of lack of familiarity with the needs of the infant. This theory holds that the father assumes in his ignorance that babies always want to play when the father does. Conversely, if you know someone well, you don't always have to be "on" when you're together.

An intriguing study was recently done by University of Utah psychologist Michael Lamb, observing Swedish fathers who cared for babies for portions of the first year of life under the Parental Insurance Plan.[3] The Swedish fathers, who did not play with their babies as often as did American fathers even when they were primary caregivers, were less preferred by their infants than the mothers. Apparently these Swedish fathers, with their more phlegmatic style, were not getting through to their children in the same way as American fathers. Feeding and body care are important, but apparently so is the "big hello."

---

*Harvard pediatrician Michael Yogman has documented an especially heightened, arousing, and playful interactional style between fathers and infants.[1] Frank Pedersen, psychologist at the National Institute for Child Health and Human Development, further reported that fathers' handling styles may be "more novel and complex" than the more intimate style of maternal infant care.[2] Almost all the babies in the study seemed to have a heightened appetite for novel experience and stimuli.

Now, two years later, when neither the infrequent interaction nor lack of familiarity theories are remotely valid as explanations, we find the fathers and babies in our study still "carrying on" to some extent. Probably, most important, because they both love it. This quality may also be responsible for the strong performance on some of the developmental testing. So-called "father-released" behaviors, such as persistence and curiosity, are rewarded not necessarily because such qualities are more valuable but because they are more easily measured on testing.

We may point to yet another factor to explain why these babies are developing so vigorously. The children in this study were first-born. It has been shown repeatedly that fathers tend to be more involved with first-born babies, whether male or female, but especially male. Birth order must be acknowledged as a contributing factor here.

Furthermore, does the parenting in the hands of these fathers carry an extra charge because, unlike that of the mother, the father's life-long role identification has *not* been to nurture, raise, or take responsibility for his baby? Might these men enjoy primary caretaking more because it is a *choice*, not a fate, and could presumably be *un*chosen as well? For men, such an "unchoice" would not involve denial of a life-long role expectation such as a woman might suffer were *she* to unchose to mother. Obviously, this gives such men a certain *freedom* to parent not often enjoyed by women. We human beings tend to pursue the things we *choose* to do more joyfully and creatively than the things we feel we *must* do. *Ultimately these babies may be thriving because of the abiding commitment by two parents (instead of the traditional one and a half) to the infant's well-being and growth.* (This maternal commitment was demonstrated, for example, by the fact that the majority of these working mothers breast-fed, often at great inconvenience to themselves.)

Over the first two years, more than just the babies had changed. Pregnancies, as we saw in the first encounter, were experienced by both men and women as times of significant regression and growth, though the study fathers tended to gain less weight with the second pregnancy.

I continued to wonder what caused the father's physiologic response to his wife's pregnancy experience. Could it harbor some subtle awareness of masculine benefit? Although the fact that the mother values and incorporates her baby's existence long before it is born is well documented, her body is also changed and distorted in uncomfortable, sometimes painful ways certainly never experienced by her husband. Certain fathers might be more available to their newborns simply because they themselves had never been filled and then emptied of, or made ill by, their own baby. Might this obverse of what is usually seen as the special maternal benefit permit a less conflicted commitment by the father to fostering his child's separate identity because he himself had never experienced the discomforts and demands of physiologic symbiosis?

In those families where second children were born, the mothers tended to find themselves more deeply involved with their second children than their first, both in actual hours of care and in feeling more "attuned to their infants." Those women who assumed the primary caregiving role after the second pregnancy had described their own mothers (at the time of entry into the study) as being less available to them. These women were the ones who tended to credit their husbands as being nurturing role models for their *own* mothering of the second child.

This raised again the question of who actually acts or serves as the baby's primary caregiver. Over the five years of the study, parents offered some interesting descriptions of behaviors that in their view characterized or symbolized primary parenting, namely: "the person who wakes up at night when the baby cries...the person who decides when the baby is really sick...who calls the doctor...who decides to go home to take care of the baby when the day-care arrangements fall through." Usually, though not universally, these designations correlated with the overall time commitments to child care as well. Also, in the less economically stable families the primary caregiving fathers were also "househusbands" or housekeepers. This was less true for the upper economic strata of the study where some home care or housecleaning service was usually purchased.

Regardless of the socioeconomic status of the family, however, the mothers continued to report as high satisfaction in the workplace as they had at the time of the initial entry into the study. Many of them attributed some of their positive feelings about work in part to feeling free from worry about the quality of care their babies were receiving. One mother commented, "It's nice to have someone who loves you also looking after your baby."

The data from these observations that deal with parent and child gender role versus gender identity corroborate what we've already seen in Helen's, Henry's, and Nancy's families. The boys are boys, the girls are girls, the fathers are men, and the mothers are women. Although it was early to make predictions, an interesting quality was emerging two years into the study in the older children's expression of sexual identity. Two years into the study, I continued to find no evidence (though the majority of the children were still quite young psychosexually) that the gender identity of these children was in any way in jeopardy. Nor did I find any evidence to support any contention that the fathers' sexual identifications were compromised.

As we have seen in the families we came to know well, most of the parents had relatively unconflicted cross-gender identifications with their own parents. Consequently, they tended to differentiate less radically between sexual stereotypes in raising their children.

One of the questions that only a longitudinal study could answer was how long the role-reversed child-care patterns would last. Half of the fathers in the study retained the role of primary caregiver after two years. Of the original seventeen families, eight of the fathers still were the primary caretakers, although some were now supplementing the care of the children with various combinations of day care, babysitting, or family day care.

Ongoing familial development and role change seemed inevitable in these families. Exactly how many of these fathers would continue to forgo career advancement or fulfillment or how many mothers would continue primary child care was still a matter of conjecture.

Those children from the first group now old enough to be engaged in the struggles over independence (the "me do, me do" stage) of the second year of life evidenced some interesting patterns. As we've already seen, in the traditional family the typical breadwinning father has been shown to be most involved in two vital parenting tasks in his children's lives. One task is rendering his sons masculine and his daughters feminine—helping differentiate gender identifications clearly. The other is helping the child give up the exclusive tie to just one adult, the mother, and enter the outside world of other attachments and novel experiences. Who would fill these roles for the children in the study?

Mothers seemed to be beginning to fill the role of the supplemental parent, serving the critical role of sexual differentiation and dilutor of the early exclusive intimacy and unity with the father.

Now, two years into the study, it seemed even more important than when we began to avoid the simplistic seduction of "father versus mother" questions. They merely distract us from the more complex questions arising over the time of this investigation. The more important questions are these:

• Are these babies thriving because of an unusually rich, fertile mosaic of primary and secondary love objects?
• Does the human personality contain a kind of integrating mechanism that permits successful interweaving of the most important nurturing experiences from the most important caregivers, thereby enhancing the infant's overall competence?

We should probably be thinking much more in terms of the infant's *total parental experience,* rather than of its experiential relationship with one mother or one father.

Four years later we did another study of fifteen of the original seventeen families. One more family had departed, making direct evaluation of the child impossible, though the family remained in frequent touch by mail and provided a steady stream of snapshots.

It should be stated that by now no reasonable claim of objectivity could be made by this researcher. These families and I had come to know one another well over the four years. We had spent dozens of hours together, many of them in their homes or apartments, as they tolerated with affection my endless inquiries. Over the years, they had revealed much about themselves and their deep concern for their children as well as their aspirations and uncertainties.

The children now ranged in age from four to six, and the Yale Schedules were at the outer limit of their usefulness for the older children. Some supplemental testing, especially in the area of language competence, was required for them. Whenever possible, I now used other developmental examiners for the assessment of the children to try to protect the validity of the evaluation as the children were now so accustomed to me and my interest in them and their families that they could almost be considered collaborators.

As a group, the children continued to develop vigorously. Their problem-solving and social skills were still especially strong, though the degree of advanced functioning had waned somewhat. Now their scores were two to four months ahead of expected norms, instead of six to ten as they had been before. The test findings supported my clinical impression that the rate of precocious function had slowed for the whole population.

What had the families as a group been up to over the past two years? Eleven of the original children were now over the age of five. Of these children, four were still primarily in the care of their fathers and still in intact families. One child was in the custody of his father (Henry). The other six children in this older group were now mainly in the care of their mothers; all of these now had siblings (like Nancy). Two of the fathers in the younger, under-five group were serving as primary caregivers. This meant that four years after the study began, seven of the original sixteen families with whom I still had contact had fathers serving as primary caregivers. Of the remaining nine, six were families where the mother served as primary caregiver, five of these with second children. The last three all used supplemental day care, nursery school, or babysitting arrangements and described themselves as sharing child care "roughly" equally.

So after the hundreds of hours of testing, playing, interviewing, visiting, and watching, we came to an end after four years (five including the follow-up contact). What could we say about these men, their babies, and their families?

Primary Caregivers at 4–Year Follow–Up

	Fathers	Mothers	Joint
Number of families (total)	7	6	3
Percent	44%	38%	19%
Number of second children born since 2-year follow-up	–	3	1
Percent	–	19%	6%
Number of fathers returned to work/ school since 2-year follow-up	2	1	1
Percent	12%	6%	6%
Marital separations since 2-year follow-up	–	–	–

•First, there were as yet no signs of big trouble, either intellectually or emotionally, in this group of children, suggesting that men as primary nurturing caregivers could do a credible job with the species.

•Second, if these children were not troubled, were they different in some way? The answer is both yes and no. When one looks at the level and range of emotional maturity, the quality of the human relationships, and the ability to handle the stress of everyday life, there were no gross personality characteristics to differentiate reliably these children from their more traditionally mother-raised peers. Comfortable dependency, zest for life, assertiveness, a vigorous drive for mastery, and the usual childhood worries were all clearly present in both boys and girls.

•Third, there seemed to be no significant lack of emotional flexibility in any of these children. Nor could one call them as a group inhibited or constricted in the least. If anything, there were rudimentary signs that these children might be, in fact, developing more flexible personalities, particularly in the ease with which they moved back and forth between feminine and masculine identifications and roles, as was so vividly demonstrated by Helen, Henry, and Nancy.

If there is anything unique about their internal images of themselves or their parents, it may be the prevalence in their play of the father as a nurturing force. Over the entire study there was constant empirical evidence to strengthen the initial speculation that having a father as a primary nurturing figure stimulates more curiosity and interest in father as procreator than is found in more traditionally reared children. For the children in the study, father is seen as a *maker* of human beings along *with* mother, who makes *and* births them.

It was also clear by now that in these children's images of the world, men and women were not very interchangeable in their roles. The study children tended not to make a "big deal" about their families' differentness, sometimes to the point of portraying their parents' roles in their schools or day-care settings as quite traditional. Their family drawings depicted dad with a briefcase going to work, when he did not even own one, or mother cooking dinner when she had not done so for years.

Social anthropologists would not find this very surprising. They contend that socialization pressures in school and society as a whole are so powerful as to eclipse the portrayal of the real arrangements of these children's lives—a premise with which I agree, given the pervasive power of societal sex stereotyping.

An assistant district attorney mother was amazed on "back-to-school night" when her son's kindergarten teacher invited her *husband* to come talk about what lawyers do! This prevalent finding upset a number of the parents in the study. They felt that their children were ignoring how difficult it had been for them to bring off their kind of parenting in their neighborhoods, and sometimes in their families, and how hard they had worked to justify their nontraditional child-care decisions. If one just *listened* to what the children said, one would not think much out of the ordinary was going on. It was in the *play* of the Helens, Henrys, and Nancys that we found the intriguing differences and revelations.

As the only comprehensive view of human experience comes from watching a life cycle, the stories of these children are hardly finished. In fact, they may just be now coming into their own.

Though the men and women have principally told us their own stories, I would like to address some of the "developmental" progress of the adults as a group over the four years, too.

One experience reported to some extent by all the families was the sense of isolation they felt from friends and family early in the game, when it was clear they were "serious" about their atypical child-rearing plans. It was common to find friends distancing themselves. Families, both parental siblings and grandparents, cast doubtful glances and made dire predictions. This, too, seemed to run a natural course, easing significantly once it became clear that the babies were doing well. It was the thriving baby who first seemed to draw the parents' families back in.

The parents' friends often took a bit longer to return. By the fourth year, the families who chose to cultivate their friends and to whom friendships had always been important had repaired that deficit easily.

To the question "What do you imagine would be different about your marriage had you stuck to the traditional role models?" the most common response focused on this early isolation of the marital pair from social support. One mother articulated it this way. "When my sister first visited us and saw John bathing and feeding the baby, she said she 'learned something about me she'd never known before' and it upset her a lot; 'You don't like babies,' she told me. That hurt and angered me so much, but I kept trying to explain to her that I did, and so did John, and this was our choice."

The other clearest change over time had occurred in those fathers who'd been economically forced into the primary parent role, and who were often initially quite anxious, if not unhappy, with their lot. They thawed most slowly to their task, but as we've already seen, their children were indistinguishable from the "early choosers" by age two. Of the seven fathers still at it after four years, three were from this group of "last choosers," three were from the early choosers, and one was from the middle group.

There were some findings regarding all the families' functioning over time that were not especially beneficial. Two troublesome factors, one affecting the children, the other affecting the families, emerged which probably would not have burdened more traditional families.

Those study children whose fathers were still their main caretakers after 24 months (fifteen of the seventeen families) seemed to be more distressed than traditionally reared toddlers when the primary parent (the father) "backed off" to allow the secondary parent to "take over" temporary care, such as in the evenings or on weekends. It is well known that this is a particularly sensitive age for the development of independence in the toddler, so adapting to such "backing off," though not always easy, is a normal stress of growing up. Though far from pathological, this difference in adaptation seemed noteworthy. What did it mean? One speculation is that the traditional fathers' novel and stimulating style may briefly compensate the typically reared toddler for the transient loss of the mother when she "backs off." The study mothers, however, already so involved, may seem less "novel" than the traditional father, therefore compensating the toddler less dramatically, leaving a temporarily more distressed two-year-old.

The second factor that burdened the families, negative societal reaction to their nontraditional child-care arrangements, has been alluded to already but deserves emphasis here. This particularly poignant anecdote illustrates how intrusive that negative reaction could be. Amos King, one of the two "welfare fathers" in the study, answered the knock on his apartment door early one Monday morning, just after his wife had left for work as a licensed practical nurse. With his four-month-old son in his arms, he opened the door to find a uniformed police officer standing next to a woman who identified herself as a Department of Children and Youth Services social worker. Somewhat confused, he invited them in. How could he help them? The DCYS worker replied that they had come to investigate a complaint by a neighbor that he was "keeping" a young child in the apartment. "Keeping?" he asked. "Yes, keeping," she replied. Stifling both laughter and outrage, Mr. King carefully and calmly explained that, yes—he was keeping a child in his apartment, and it was *his*! (At that moment, his son began to fuss, undoubtedly sensing his father's tense mood and body.)

Next question: Could he *prove* the child was his? He diverted his visitors' attention to a birth certificate, several baby pictures, and a baptismal record, all proudly displayed on the wall near the front door.

Embarrassed and chagrined, his would-be accusers bid him goodbye with apologies (after two cups of coffee).

Though this is an extreme and invasive example, negative societal reaction was repeated to some degree in every family's circle of friends, extended families, neighborhoods (especially landlords), and workplace. Very few people from such groups came forward immediately with unambivalent support and respect for these study families' child-rearing decisions. A tough beginning indeed.

The study fathers, despite these handicaps, were all doing well with their babies, but not identically well. Unquestionably, it could be said that these men have all raised, in their unique style, interesting questions about an exclusory female ownership of the nurturing capacity. Looking back over the five years with the privilege of the long view, I wondered whether there had been any identifying characteristic present at the outset of this study that would have helped me distinguish those men who still served as primary nurturers from those who had given up the role. I still could find nothing predictive.

It seems that efforts to find some special predictor, quality, experience, or portent that sets these men and their kin apart from the rest of us are so far unsuccessful. Would it not be a most profound finding for these men *not* to be so different from the rest of their species in substance or experience? Such a conclusion would build a firm foundation indeed under the assumption of the primary nurturing function by any father who sought it.

12

Gender Versus Role and the Incomplete Self

Having met and lived among these intriguing families for a time and seen how beautifully, powerfully, and intricately paternal nurturing can work, we turn to the question of how the phenomenon is understandable emotionally. The place to start is with the impact of primary paternal nurturance on the child's sense of himself as male or herself as female, especially when that sense is compared with the parent's *own* sense of gender identity. It's here that we enter that quagmire we glimpsed while following Adam and Sarah through their struggles with the rules of roles. This quagmire's name on the map of development is the "confusion of gender identity and role."

Children first acquire the concept of being either male or female in interaction with the important people about them. The child learns as his experiences interact with the evolution of his own body and language that he belongs in one category or the other. This is the child's *gender identity* or what some researchers call "core gender identity." It is the deep, unshakable inner conviction that one is biologically male or female. It is also the sum of privately held ideas or thoughts about one's psychological identity, which obviously can vary from individual to individual. That's the easy part.

Defining gender *role*, however, is the hard part. It is less a biological than a *behavioral* concept. It is composed of everything that a person may do or say to the outside world (or even to himself) which he feels designates the self as male or female in the public eye. Sarah, from Mrs. Kit's kindergarten, knew that Adam was male, but she felt he was not *behaving* as a male should. (This attitude is not unlike the attitude of many friends and relations toward the fathers and mothers who have told their stories in this book.)

In keeping with the pattern of this book, let's begin at the beginning developmentally and follow the interaction between gender *role* and gender *identity* across a person's life cycle, from baby to baby maker.

At the beginnings of life, of course, there is no confusion, only biology. *The* sole condition of gender *identity* formation is the original chromosome assignment that occurs at the moment of conception, when the ovum is fertilized by the spermatozoon. This assignment is either male (XY chromosome pattern) or female (XX chromosome pattern). Once this biological choice is made, the gender identity case is by and large closed.

Gender *role*, however, is altogether a different story. Gender role is more the offspring of socialization and environmental influence than is gender identity. Unlike gender identity, it is subject to societal change and cultural influences to an astounding degree.

The power of the family to render a child typically boy or typically girl is undeniable, even after genetic gender assignment is set in the biological bedrock. Widely respected research has shown that in the extremely rare instance of children born with uncertain external genitalia (so-called hermaphroditic or "intersex" children), core gender identity follows the sex assigned at birth so long as the child is raised unambiguously as girl or boy.[1] If the parents decide to raise the child as a girl, *she* develops a female core gender identity. If the mother and father decide to raise the child as a boy, *he* develops a male core gender identity.

For the first year and a half of life, the nurturing environment holds sway in the realm of gender designation. It is not until around eighteen months that a child begins to identify itself as a girl or a boy, although unable to use the appropriate words for such designations. A child at this point distinguishes gender by the conventional dress or hairstyles of adults and children, even more than by external genitalia. At this stage of life, a change of clothes or hairstyle could change the apparent gender of a child or an adult easily, from the eighteen-month-old's point of view.

Something crucial happens between 24 and 30 months of age, however, which hardens a child's mental image of his own core identity, thereafter making it almost impervious to change. We suspect that both nature and nurture play vital roles here, but we do not yet know how such forces as parental handling style or sex hormones mingle to promote such solidification.

At around two-and-a-half or three years of age, both girls and boys are seen playing in the doll corner, happily passing babies, blocks, guns, baby bottles, and trucks back and forth without much ado. Seeing Adam in a dress or Sarah in a fedora and gun holster at that age would trouble few if any of their peers. Either of them could pretend to be Daddy one moment and Mommy the next without even changing costumes.

It is not until three, however, that the words "boy" and "girl" are used appropriately, and even then uncertainly. Physical size, hairstyles, and clothing are still more heavily relied upon to designate sex type than genitalia. How do children feel about their gender/role designations at this point?

Our older daughter, Lisa, had just turned three when, after all her birthday presents were opened and the cake consumed, she became involved in a serious dialogue with her grandmother about one of her grandmother's favorite subjects, destiny. What did Lisa want to be when she was all grown up? Lisa paused momentarily in her play and then climbed up into an overstuffed chair as though she needed to mount a throne to respond appropriately to this weighty question. "Well, Gamma, when I gwo up, I'm gonna be a mommy *and* a daddy—boths!" Her grandmother, mildly distressed, gently informed her that this wasn't an option. Lisa, undaunted and with great conviction, declared, "Yes, so, Gamma!"

Lisa certainly, and proudly, knew that she was a girl and that daddies were boys. But her wish to be both was stronger than her only recently acquired knowledge that boys actually grow up to be men and that gender identity does not change. Lisa would spend the next few years getting these facts straight.

From three to five, getting these facts straight is vital for personality and gender identity solidification. No matter how hard a parent may try to be "liberated" in handling children of this age, the inner drive to learn and apply the rules of girlhood and boyhood and to understand in the clearest, simplest way the differences between male and female gender roles is so powerful in children as to dominate most parental efforts at flexibly defining roles. That is why so many kindergartens (no matter how hard they may try not to) resemble bastions of chauvinism, both female and male. It's as if the children were saying, "Look, I've just got some of the facts straight, now don't confuse me. Boys are this, and girls are that. I know! I've now learned that I can't be both, so which one can I be?" Like Sarah, Adam feels he must choose sides, boys versus girls; he is *in* one group and *out* of the other. He can't, now that he knows the truth about sexual difference, have it both ways.

It is not until the fifth or sixth year of life that children have the categories down pat and cannot be talked out of the fact that boys have penises and grow up to be men and can't have babies and that girls have vaginas and grow up to be women and *can.*

All the while children are evolving more sophisticated discriminations, they are also interacting with adults. If the child is in day care or school, he or she will also have peers who may alternately reward, discourage, or ignore the sex-typical behavior. They are also watching a *lot* of TV. It is generally assumed that children come to value, emulate, and mimic same-sex behavior patterns as they increasingly recognize to which camp they belong.

By the age of six, all the facts are in as far as the children are concerned. On her sixth birthday, my daughter Lisa was embarrassed by (and quite angry with) her father when he told the story of her third birthday conversation regarding her life plans with her Grandma.

The next five years from six to eleven are then spent shaping and honing such male/female distinctions. Stereotypes evolve, and gender roles continue to be shaped but in an interesting order. Both boys and girls appear to fix the male stereotype in their minds earlier than the female one. Why, no one knows for certain. Undoubtedly, generations of unchallenged male chauvinism have marked males as somehow more "valuable" than females. But other forces are certainly at work, too. Could such early fixing be because, by this age, the still more biologically vulnerable male needs the stronger fantasied image to somehow stay even with the girls?

School-age children are very busy classifying activities and objects according to their evolving ideas of maleness and femaleness. Almost all children of this six-to-eleven age group are happy to demarcate any proffered item, animate or inanimate, as being "for boys" or "for girls." Gender neutrality is simply not a very useful concept during these years.

Then, like a rogue wave, hormones arrive to flood

the harbor that until now had been protecting gender identity and role alike from adult sexual behavior.

When puberty arrives, usually first in girls, gender identity begins its final evolution. Under the pressure of this profound change, sex stereotyping often becomes more rigid. The painful uncertainties in both sexes about physical appearance, sexual competence, desirability, intellectual capacity, and future destiny make gender distinctions all the more crucial. Even in our liberated times, there seems to have been little change over the generations about how girls, for example, feel about the beginning of their menses. Ultimately, variation from the central teenage (*not* adult) norms is a very risky business indeed.

Consequently, the young teenager can appear to be the most judgmental of all children, especially regarding acceptable standards of gender/role behavior. Meanwhile, feelings of previously unimagined intensity are experienced by the adolescent as part of normal development, although things don't feel "normal" to him or her. Erotic, loving, compassionate, aggressive, tender, competitive, jealous, dependent feelings (to name a few) sweep over them, leaving boys sometimes feeling "effeminate" and girls sometimes feeling "masculine."

Young male adolescents meanwhile hear from the world about them that they are supposed to "be male, strong, competitive, controlling," while they may actually be feeling more like little boys—insecure and needy. Young female adolescents hear "be nice, female, pretty, non-aggressive, alluring," while they often feel quite capable and competent. When boys are caught in the dilemma of trying to *be* more independent while *feeling* dependent, fathers become very important, complex figures. At those moments when the adolescent boy is feeling needy, his father seems to loom large as judge and jury. When he is feeling strong and capable, however, the father is often seen as a formidable opponent.

But one of the most profound capacities father and son now share is that of procreation. We now have come full circle on our living time-line of gender identity and role, the latter in large part the handiwork of the mothers and fathers and their society.

The message here isn't that grownups are fools for doing such obvious things to children. Cultural anthropologists have shown us repeatedly how important role assignment and division of labor within a culture or tribe is to the ultimate survival of that particular human group. It is not hard to imagine that uncertainty and bickering over who should keep the fires, hunt the game, feed the babies, plant the corn, tend the livestock, or dispose of the waste could get a species in big trouble in very short time, even in one or two generations.

Role assignment, historically linked, if not equated, to gender identity has been so important to survival in human history that newborn infants have often been assigned different symbols or colors to help the culture tell the players apart. Different woven patterns on infant blankets among Plains Indians, different head covers among the Mongols, or pink and blue wrappings more recently in Western culture, have been extensively used to keep handling styles and enculturation behavior consistent within the wider social unit.

But we are no longer there. Our late twentieth-century society is so complex, with backup mechanisms to provide individual and family sustenance and safety, that rigid role definition is no longer essential for species survival. Lots of other people grow our food, defend our boundaries, tend livestock, invest our capital, raise our children, and even decide what is "best for our families." Rigid gender separations cease to be directly or intimately linked to the biological survival of the species. No longer do we maintain our place on earth on the basis of muscle mass. Talent, wits, and the capacity to use technology are more important.

Gender/role delineations are not in themselves innately bad or inherently destructive. What is destructive is the archaic, one-to-one, fated relationship between gender *identity* and gender *role*, which assigns to a human being of the male gender exclusively masculine gender roles forever and to someone of the female gender exclusively feminine roles. No variations, no trespassing!

"Masculine," of course, does not mean male. It really means only the traits, behaviors, expectations, and appearances shaped by a society and its institutions that are *publicly* linked to maleness. "Masculinity" is a gender/role concept and one highly influenced by class and culture. "Feminine" has the same relationship to the word "female." The tenacity of this old confusion between gender identity and trait is what got Adam into trouble with Sarah and the fathers and mothers of this book into such trouble with their friends and relations.

Having made the effort to clarify this old conceptual mess, let's take a look at how male and female gender identities might be distinguishable. Apart from the obvious genital complementarity, there exist real biological (and possibly even a few psychological) differences and variations in the vulnerabilities and strengths of men and women. If we are to take seriously the notion that the nurturing capacity is an innate property of the *whole* species, as we have seen it expressed in the lives of the study families, these "facts" are worthy of our attention.

The differences that we discuss in no way render the genders as opposite, or oppositional, or designate one as innately "better" than the other any more than yellow is innately superior to blue. *Different*, yes; better, no. To acknowledge and appreciate the differences is to avoid the double jeopardy of hollow "unisex" child-rearing and the silly pedantry of "masculine versus feminine" child-rearing strategies.

The core irreducible difference between the sexes is of course the biological difference in genital and reproductive equipment. One X and one Y chromosome render an embryo male. Two X chromosomes render it female. The XX develops a clitoris, vagina, ovaries, and uterus and after puberty can conceive, gestate, and lactate for a baby. She retains that capacity for three to four decades. The XY develops a penis, scrotum, and testicles and (after puberty) can impregnate females. He will remain fertile for five to six decades. These are the only absolute, universal differences that categorize *all* females apart from *all* males. They are the prime numbers of gender identity. The further we float conceptually from this crystal clear premise of gender identity toward gender role, the murkier the waters become.

Still biologically grounded, but with shallower roots, are some areas of difference that can be used, *on the average* (and these are essential qualifying words) to differentiate the *majority* of females from the *majority* of males. Differentiation does *not* mean absolutely universal differences. Why these exist or *how* they are mediated, we by and large do not know. We begin with the physiologic list.

Male fetuses are *on average* more active in utero than females. More of them are born (105 for every 100 females), but more of them die in infancy. They are statistically more vulnerable to inherited metabolic and genetic disorders, such as hemophilias. Furthermore, when male children are born at risk, they survive less well, *on average*, than females born with the same disability or handicap.

Male babies, *on average*, consume more calories, breathe faster and more deeply, and have slower heart rates than females. Girls, *on average,* sit up, crawl, and walk sooner, while boys grow larger bones and muscles. Females, *on average,* teethe earlier and reach puberty first. Boys gain in physical height only after the age of puberty, usually reaching physical maturity and full adult physiology three to four years later than girls. By then, roughly around age 24, they average six inches taller. As adults, women, *on average,* live longer. These are physical measurements that distinguish *most* females from *most* males, but individual differences obviously vary enormously.

Once we move into the arena of psychological difference, we are on even thinner ice than when discussing physiologic differences. Here, fact about gender role shades into opinion. Much of the information now sounds like mythology and should be distrusted as such. It is important to remember that all the votes are not in. Again, *why* and *how* such differences might exist escapes us.

Prior to his death, the brilliant Harvard neurologist Norman Geschwind, along with a number of psychologists and neuroanatomists (experts on the shape and structure of the brain and central nervous system), had begun to explore differences in the way that adult male and female brains think about and organize certain kinds of information and experience. He felt there was growing evidence that, *on the average,* male brains have an ability to visualize and maneuver physical objects three-dimensionally "in the mind's eye" that differs from the female brain.[2] Geschwind was quick to point out that he himself was a "spatial Cretin, with no special skills in this area," just to document the vital point about individual differences.

Facility with language and verbal fluency, *on average,* may be more a characteristic of female than of male brains. Girls not only talk earlier than boys, but they also master foreign languages more easily. Speech and language disorders, such as stammering and stuttering or "dysphasia," all occur, *on average*, with much greater frequency in males.[3]

Geschwind and others speculated that mathematical competence, seen more frequently in males, may be a consequence of the male brain's facility with spatial tasks and manipulations. Females, *on average*, have superior penmanship and crayon and pencil control from earlier ages, probably because of their greater capacity to perform, *on average*, rapid sequential movements than boys.

It is extremely important to note, however, that such spatial and verbal differences in facility fade considerably when girls are given identical math curricula, expectations, and rewards and when boys are given identical language teaching and expectations and rewards from early in their education.

But we have no evidence of anatomical, structural differences in male and female brains. Geschwind favored the hypothesis that the variations in abilities were not attributable to structural differences but may be the result of chemical changes brought about by the presence or absence of the male hormone, testosterone, during fetal life. It is essential to remember, however, that no matter how elegant the research, none of these skills or weaknesses are *absolute* consequences of gender.

None.

It is equally important to recall that we are not just talking about testicles and ovaries here. Forces like nutrition, culture, adequate or inadequate nurturing, and socioeconomic status are probably of much greater significance than a child's gender in determining whether or not she or he exhibits these "on average" psychological characteristics.

We have seen so far that only a very few factors distinguish male from female absolutely in the gender versus role quagmire. Some physical predispositions distinguish one from the other, but not absolutely. Far less absolutely can a few still largely hypothetical psychological differences be used sometimes to demarcate male from female performance.

To date, this is the bottom line on the capacity of males or females to develop as *complete* people: *Although male and female gender differ fundamentally in genital equipment, each member of the species has such a rich repertoire of potential behavior that it is impossible to characterize any behavioral pattern as quintessentially male or female, including the capacity to nurture.*

As we conclude this odyssey of research and theory, we have not encountered a single finding that renders men inherently incapable of nurturing. Many adult feelings and societal attitudes make it *unlikely* that the capacity or wish to nurture will survive intact over the first two decades of an individual's life, but *nothing* says that it cannot happen.

But as we've seen so clearly, when men *are* able to use their nurturing impulses and capacities, they are very often profoundly moved by the experience. Why? Are there answers beyond the anecdotal or personal? I think so. What makes tending babies so powerful, moving, even healing is that it often allows men to attend to a gender-blind childlikeness in *themselves.* The abiding wish for intimacy, the capacity for unambivalent love, hope, and forgiveness, and the rewards of vulnerability and dependency are what make children so wonderfully human. These are the very traits that many men, unlike most women, have buried or banished to remote places in themselves as they were learning and being taught, like Adam, "not to cry," leaving them with a sense of being incomplete or unfinished as human beings.

In physically attending to his child, a man is reaching back into himself, into his own experience for something he cannot necessarily remember, in which he may have lost faith and trust, and for which he probably has no role models from his own childhood—an abiding, nurturing male presence. Here his baby has a very important impact. What his child actually provides is unforbidden access to the child*like* (not child*ish*) part of the father's unfinished incomplete, pre–gender/role self. The baby is not just progeny or immortality or fertility proven.

But, as we've seen elsewhere in this book, things may be slowly beginning to change, and access to this unfinished sense of a man's self seems to be becoming easier. Betty Friedan, in *The Second Stage*, entitled a chapter "The Quiet Movement of American Men" and reviewed a survey of college students done twelve years apart. She concludes, "A majority of adult American men no longer seek or are satisfied by conventional job success. For men self-fulfillment has become severed from success."[4]

If breadwinning, which has always been such a cornerstone for male self-esteem, is losing its status as the single clearest role-clarifier for men, then men as a group may be more ready for and capable of changing than the list makers we encountered in Chapter 3 presume. That feeling of having an incomplete self and having to settle for it may not be so easily ignored or fatalistically accepted.

Many analysts of the workplace and male adult development are increasingly aware of the toll exacted by the stress of playing competitive roles while stifling one's emotional self in order to be right, productive, affluent, assertive, responsible, clever, and tough, not to mention strong-willed. In a recent *Playboy* survey, Betty Friedan also noted the following trends: "The men from the most depressed backgrounds were the only group whose main concern was 'getting ahead, making more money.' The majority of the men polled, aged 18–49, valued 'personal growth,' 'self-fulfillment,' 'love,' and 'family life' more than making more money and getting ahead."[5]

Such changes are at work in profound ways in each one of the families we've studied in this book. The changes invite men to ask some vital but simple questions, such as "What kind of father or worker do I want to be? Where lies my primary satisfaction? Do I really want to spend my energy and time with my family and sacrifice my traditional 'run for the roses' in the workplace or vice versa? Maybe I *can't* have it all, as I've so long pretended."

Though there are many qualities men possess once they ease away from the constrictions of classical sexual stereotyping, the one that interests us here is the capacity to nurture one's children not only in a primary way, in the manner of the fathers I've studied, but in the more common way of direct, purposeful involvement in their lives.

Most men feel the nurturing capacity or remember its stirrings within them at some time in their lives. It may be so unfamiliar that to recall such stirrings may be uncomfortable or anxiety-provoking. That's why humor like the book *Real Men Don't Eat Quiche* seems so clever and funny. It addresses a conflict that all men feel about the conscious experience of their nurturing selves. The wit and humor of conflict is dealt with in satire that allows men to laugh at themselves because they *know* in their heart of hearts that the conventions are strangling them, just as women were feeling strangled by laundry and being housebound two decades before.

This discussion of how gender, roles, and expectations shape and limit fruition of the self would be incomplete without an examination of the powerful role that *non*familial institutions of our society play in promoting or discouraging the survival of nonrigid roles, such as nurturing capacities, in boys. Such institutions as schools, "parental guidance," or, as we've already discussed, the media can all serve to discourage nurturing impulses in males.

Schools have come a long way since the days of the late nineteenth century when higher education was not recommended for women because their smaller head size indicated they could neither use nor survive the rigors of higher learning. Now, some textbook publishers who court the vast California and Texas school-book markets compose "want lists" that reflect the current market demand for less sexist and racist textbooks. Such "lists" contain certain themes these markets want depicted by textbook writers and illustrators. A certain percentage of all text and illustrations must be devoted to the portrayal of, for example, Black or Hispanic children. Or when adults are depicted, a certain percentage of them must be portrayed in nonsexist stereotypic roles, such as men cooking and washing dishes or women driving trucks or working at construction jobs. (Although this is a good beginning, there is a mathematical rigidity in this "textbook view of everyday life" that is also worrisome.)

Though schools have begun to respond to the pleas to delete sexism from the curriculum and classroom, very few, if any, male teachers can be found below fifth grade in any school system, especially in the kindergarten and first grade. (Interestingly, probably about as few tenured women faculty can be found at the other end of the academic spectrum as there are male teachers to be found at the beginning.) Children almost never *see* men in the classroom during the critical early childhood education years, when, as we have seen, sex roles are beginning to take shape more clearly in their minds.

Years ago, when I needed to make some money between the end of medical school and the beginning of my internship, I applied for a substitute teaching job in the Newton, Massachusetts, public schools, a progressive suburban system near Boston. My wife had been teaching first grade there for years, and I had come to know the faculty and many of her pupils well. I asked her principal, who was generously supportive of my job search, whether I should indicate my preference to substitute in the early primary grades on the job application. She said she had "no hesitation as far as my school was concerned," but she had "reservations" about the other schools in the system. Consequently, she suggested I not indicate a preference. She explained, "A man in the kindergarten or first grade in other schools where they don't know you, might upset some people...not the children—they'd love it—but the grownups." "Which grownups?" I asked. "All of them," she replied.

When it comes to proffering "parental guidance" in our time (another powerful nonfamilial institution), there are few better known candidates than Benjamin Spock. But for parents, guidance can be fickle. Dr. Spock advised at the time of the first edition of *Baby and Child Care* (1946) that "it doesn't make much sense to have mothers go to work and have them pay other people to do a poorer job of bringing up their children." Then an interesting thing happened. In 1976, Spock reversed himself: "Both parents have an equal right to a career if they want one, and an equal obligation to share in the care of their children." (p. 13)[6]

The three decades that separate these two opinions by the foremost parental guide of our age saw an unprecedented move into the workplace by women, as well as increasing pressures on parenting such as upward mobility, both economic and social. This upward mobility is a trend that increasing numbers of families have found disappointingly hollow. Two-job marriages in 1985 struggle for the same standard of living as one-job marriages achieved in 1955.[7] More than one social commentator has noted that "Yuppies" may be more downwardly than upwardly mobile as the century closes.

During this same historical period, the possibility has emerged that men might assume more instrumental and expressive roles inside the family. This is a profound reversal of the pattern set by the stay-at-home mother and go-to-work father role segregation begun during the Industrial Revolution. It has also introduced the wholly unique idea in Western culture that paternal participation in child-rearing may actually represent a higher degree of differentiation and flexibility in family structure, rendering the family structure *more,* not less, secure and resilient. The experiences of the families in this study suggest that this certainly may be the case. It may make for both a stronger family, and a stronger sense of self, to refuse to accept the constricting old causality that leads like a conveyor belt from gender self to gender role.

We have seen repeatedly that the fathers and mothers in this study have gender identities that are secure and stable, allowing them to assume a broad repertoire of gender *roles,* often interchangeably. Consequently, strong, healthy, essential identifications by the children with the parent of the same sex were developing normally.

We also saw an interesting quality emerging in a number of the children's gender/role expressions. Henry, the baby-doll-toting, Big Wheel stunt driver we met, was more the rule than the exception among the children of our study group in his ability and comfort in stretching the adult gender identity-versus-role rules and expectations. Another boy in the study, whose father had set aside a $100,000-a-year job as a real estate broker to care for him while his mother pursued her own commercial real estate career, confidently labeled the sport jacket card on the Stanford-Binet Vocabulary Test as a "dress," in homage to his businesswoman mother's wardrobe.

In the end, it is probably irrelevant (to the children certainly) how closely a father conforms to the socially defined gender/role concepts of masculinity. From what we have seen in these families, there have been priceless rewards to the man, his child, and his mate in attending to his innate nurturing wishes and capacities. It *is* good for all of them—not simple and not easy but most certainly *good*. What is then ultimately allowed and experienced is a *real* masculinity that is nondefensive, creative, feeling, and unafraid of being full of care. In a new era for which these findings set the stage, a man never will be told, or expected, to stay out of the lives of his children.

13

Mothers and the Sharing of the Nurturing Domain

The subject of this chapter, women's responses to paternal competence in the nurturing domain, is simple enough to describe. But from early on in the public discussion of my work with varying groups of men and women, I often had the sense that I was ruffling feathers.

At first I was caught unaware. Then questions such as, "What makes you think that these fathers raise smarter kids than mothers would have?" or "Isn't this what men always say when they start doing the traditionally female things, that once they decide to do it, they think they can do it better?" or "Don't you think that it's really maternal deprivation that makes these kids work so hard to catch up and do well to get the world's attention?" revealed an adversarial attitude. There were comments, too, such as, "I think if you were to follow these kids for three or four years, you'd find them really falling apart."

Such was the audience response from my colleagues and students at the Child Study Center to the presentation of my first findings five years ago.

I was also keenly aware of other nonverbal responses within the group. Some heads nodded up and down vigorously, as if the results themselves were chalking up points in some invisible contest or debate. Many of the men were subdued and quietly anxious, looking down at their shoes, as if they had to work hard to sit still. Many of the women smiled and giggled a lot, leaving me with a sense that something was making them anxious, too.

I soon learned that this was just the beginning. The following summer, our family ended a pleasant two-week

idyll in Vermont with a stopover in the Berkshires, where I
was to give a lecture at Smith College. By now I knew that
the research sparked interest (as it often did), but I was
surprised by the bristling challenge I met. I had thought
that the news that men were *capable* of responding
competently and with an abiding commitment to the
raising of their children (whether they had to, or chose to)
would be of interest to this gathering. Many of the women
in the audience were of childbearing age, many had or
anticipated careers, and presumably a goodly number were
now or eventually would be planning to have children. But
it was a chilly, occasionally unfriendly night in Northampton,
Massachusetts. My daughters noticed, too. After the lecture ended and we walked back across the lovely, darkening
campus to our motel, Lisa asked why some of the questioners
seemed "so irritated." I felt I'd wandered into a mine field
peppered with pressure-sensitive detonators hidden just
beneath the surface. Instead of finding myself thinking
with my audiences about the *meaning* of these early
findings, I now felt that the findings themselves were
making for more trouble than headway in the study of
paternal nurturing capacities.

Such reaction was not wholly unexpected. The
nurturing domain has shrine status in most cultures. For
most of our history, and certainly since the Industrial
Revolution, nurturing has been regarded as a woman's
sacred calling, contributing to a feeling of worthiness and
self-esteem and evoking emotional power for many women
for many years. But when the women's movement focused
its searchlight with penetrating clarity on this holy voca-
tion, it saw that the shrine had also become for many
women a holding pen that stifled creativity, self-determination, and personal freedom while providing only mini-
mal security in exchange.

But time was supposedly marching on. It had been

over two decades since *The Feminine Mystique* had hit the streets in 1963. Fifteen years had passed since Phyllis Chesler put forward the idea in *Women and Madness* that motherhood was a burden from which women needed to be freed. The mid-1980s was considered to be the post-feminist era. I wondered what *was* troubling those bright women in Northampton? Were they not yet ready to look at the other possibilities for change their "revolution" had produced?

My grandfather Horace had patiently explained to me when I was a boy in Oklahoma, "Folks tend to get pretty worked up, son, when you start talking private business and they're not ready to hear it." More than a few questions at Smith revealed that many in the audience felt that the nurturing domain still deserved status as a woman's shrine. These women did not want to give up their preeminence in this vital area, for the nurturing domain is that psychological place in which our children are cared for, protected, and helped to grow into their own unique selves. Both noisy and silent, sustaining and frustrating, depleting and fulfilling, sensual and abstinent, it is confusing but never trivial in purpose or company. Lives come and go in the nurturing domain as does every conceivable shade of human feeling. Time never stops there. Ultimately it is our most intimate human residence.

Of late, a lot has been going on there; some good things are happening, some not so good. These happenings are affecting women and men both, although quite differently.

For women, the changes in the nurturing domain have been most profound. Changes here have been fueled by such forces as the women's movement, the exodus, both voluntary and forced, into the workplace, the decision to delay childbearing, the divorce epidemic of the late 1960s and 1970s, and what has recently been called "the feminization of poverty" (the increased number of single mothers and working women who yearly slip quietly below the poverty line). Simone de Beauvoir took articulate notice four decades ago of the "immunity" her sex was granted from certain responsibilities and risks in the external world in exchange for preeminence in the "protected" nurturing domain.[1] The women's movement has helped many women reflect on whether that immunity has been worth its very high price and has urged women instead to reach to become the sponsors of their own experience and self-determination. The women's movement has earned my enduring gratitude as the father of daughters.

But as the devotional, selfless mothering so characteristic of the pre–women's movement era seems to fade further from our view in many families, there seems to be no immediately obvious, universally satisfactory replacement. It is undeniable that a woman's ability to stretch and pursue her total competence outside the home and get paid what she's worth for it makes for happier and more fulfilled women. Such fulfillment in the workplace even seems to affect the way women see their children. Women who are happily working, especially if they are working as a matter of preference and not economic necessity, perceive their children as happier.[2] But such self-fulfillment comes with a price.

Often the price is confusion. Confusion about babies and business, and which comes first. How is a woman to decide in favor of the sensitivity, nurturing, availability, and tenderness that makes her motherhood so intimately powerful when competition, aggressiveness, creativity, and commitment to hard long hours of work make her life in the marketplace feel so wonderfully productive? Often, she feels she must choose which one is more valuable to her as a person, and that she's only got one chance to choose.

Very often the price for self-fulfillment is guilt. "Am I actually neglecting my children by not being with them while I'm out here chasing status and the almighty dollar? Or (much more often) making ends meet?"

Most often, women decide to try to take a nip here, a tuck there, and keep their balance as women *and* working mothers and somehow make the ends meet. Not so easy. They would be greatly helped in this effort if the workplace had a higher regard for their needs as parents, especially for things such as more flexible work schedules. They also would be helped by anything that made the nurturing domain more efficient.

One attempt at softening up the rigid schedule requirements of the workplace for mothers was the Pregnancy Discrimination Act of 1978, which required employers to treat pregnancy as they would any short-term disability. On paper it looked good, but in the trenches it's almost nowhere to be seen. Only five states have laws *requiring* disability leaves for pregnancy. At present, only a little over a third of working women are *entitled* to (but not mandated to receive) paid disability leave of six weeks or more when giving birth.[3] Not much flexibility here.

As for making the nurturing domain more efficient, it's hard to know what's happening here. One way to increase efficiency is to reduce the lifespan of parenthood and instead to plan more carefully *when* the work of child-rearing is to be done. American women are having fewer children: 1.79 per family in 1983, as opposed to 3.72 in 1957.[4] What's more they are having them later. The average age at which a woman has her first child has risen steadily and now stands at about 22.3. In 1970, it was 20.1. (The real average age may be considerably older. These statistics are skewed because they include the alarmingly destructive increase in adolescent pregnancy.) This is a dramatic upward shift in just thirteen years in the age at which women begin their families. Since menopausal age is not changing as rapidly, the time period in which women are actually having babies appears to be narrowing rapidly, especially when compared to the millennia our species has been procreating itself. The 30- to 35-year-olds are the fastest growing childbearing age group. Jobs first, babies second, seems to be the order of things. But there is a real limit to this efficiency drive—the limit imposed by the biological clock.

Mothers and babies are more and more at risk the closer most women get to 40; chances of infertility and complications of pregnancy increase for the women, as does the incidence of chromosomal damage and fetal abnormality in the babies. Thanks to genetic counseling and amniocentesis, these risks are being better managed.

But today's modern woman often feels conflicted about yielding her central place in the nurturing domain to anyone, whether husband or day-care worker. There is some proof that mothers fear loss of personal identity when they yield their control of the nurturing domain and surrounding territories. Joseph Pleck, the Associate Director of the Wellesley College Center for Research on Women, recently reviewed the results of a survey that indicated that only 42 percent of working women, despite their exhaustion and stress, wanted their husbands to help more with child care, and only 36 percent would like to have men do more of the housework.[5]

You may have noticed that I have not included day care as a way of making the nurturing domain more efficient, even though it's a fact of life for almost all families with working mothers. The reason I've deleted it is that as a society we have so far failed to meet the challenge of insisting upon good enough child care and day care. Standards for adequate day-care centers are uneven, unenforced, and often unenforceable. Until we as a society can straighten out this particular mess, each family is usually left to its own devices to try to decide which place is best for its child, budget, schedule, and convenience. With so many variables to be considered, day care is frequently so complex a choice it does not qualify as an efficient aid to nurturing.

Even if all the logistics of arranging care other than their own for their children are managed, women are not necessarily happy about their diminished preeminence in the nurturing domain even if it is exchanged for an increased sense of self-determination. Some women are pretty worried about this unhappiness. Betty Friedan is one of them. In a recent exhortation to men and women to get the women's movement going again, she notes:

> These new women, each thinking she is alone with her personal guilt and pressures, trying to "have it all," having second thoughts about her professional career, desperately trying to have a baby before it is too late, with or without a husband, and maybe secretly blaming the movement for getting her into this mess, are almost as isolated, and powerless in their isolation, as those suburban housewives afflicted by "the problem that had no name," whom I interviewed twenty years ago for *The Feminine Mystique*.[6]

If there is this much trouble for women in the nurturing domain, what about men—those men whom Simone de Beauvoir saw as bartering away influence in the nurturing domain, often even abandoning the desire for intimacy in exchange for the commitment to make and change history, to take risks, and to bear responsibility outside the nurturing domain? Do they sense much change with regard to their place inside the nurturing domain? Changes therein are not always met with open arms either.

My chance meeting with a recruiter for a large business machine corporation, who was headhunting for promising seniors on the Yale campus last spring, gave me some informal data about what's happening to some of the men out there. This impeccably attired man in his early sixties with white sideburns stood there shaking his head incredulously. "I just finished an interview with a guy who wanted to talk seriously to us about a good entry-level job. And he's hot.... Phi Beta Kappa and a varsity letter or two—great guy. And we want him. But you know what *he* wants? A decent, not outrageous, salary—that's not the problem. He wants flexible working hours, no travel unless it's an emergency, strict limitations on overtime requests, and get this—*paid* paternity leave if he decides to have a kid someday! I suppose we'll work something out if we really want him and he really wants us, but he doesn't sound like a fast-tracker to me."

The stirrings in the nurturing domain have also had another effect on men. Dr. Theodore Shapiro of Cornell, in discussing some of my research at the 1985 fall meetings of the American Psychoanalytic Association in Manhattan, said, "Well, gentlemen, Dr. Pruett's research has taken away a major male excuse for not being involved with our kids. We can now no longer say to our wives, 'Look, it's better for the kids if you do it, dear.'"

As we've already seen in the study families, many men don't *want* to invoke such excuses and can respond with flexibility, sensitivity, and attunement to their own and others' feelings, a capacity long considered a feminine province. But would most women openly embrace such change in the feminine province? Is the news of this book, that men can deeply involve themselves in raising their children without devastating effects to the offspring or the family, welcome to women?

Sometimes yes, sometimes no.

First—sometimes no. Last year, my experience at Smith (four years earlier) came to me with riveting clarity when I was invited to speak again, this time closer to home. A bright scholarly group of juniors and seniors at Yale, made up mostly but not exclusively of women, set up a successful symposium at the Yale Law School on "Women in the 80's and Beyond: Fulfillment in Work and Family." I was asked to address one of the many well-organized, thoughtfully planned workshops and seminars on some aspects of my fathering research. I was to share the dais with several other speakers, one a faculty member from the humanities who was to talk on the feminization of poverty. She sat down next to me, and we introduced ourselves and shook hands. After the pleasantries, she said somberly, "So, you're the competition." I found out later that she wasn't kidding, when she launched into a carefully if narrowly substantiated attack on men, especially fathers, who she felt were impoverishing women by "muscling in" on the nurturing domain "without paying for it."

Another group from whom I've heard frequently that also worries about men "muscling in" are the rightwing religious fundamentalists—some of them not so far from home.

A favorite cousin of mine called from Louisiana to chew me out in her lovely soft New Orleans accent after she'd heard a small piece on the radio about my research. Both of our fathers were Baptist ministers, although hers was much farther to the right than mine. (Mine has always been hard to pigeonhole, and this was not our first theological "discussion.") In a word, she was livid. "Kyle, you shouldn't be messing around with mothers this way. The Bible does not look upon it favorably. Women are chosen by God to raise children. I talked about it with my minister. Haven't you got anything better to do up there? Who do you think you are fooling? Men can't do what women do and the Scripture says they *shouldn't*! You've been hanging around those Commies too long [her favorite pejorative for the New England academic community]."

Letters have also found their way to me from similar quarters, warning me sometimes explicitly that this was "sacred ground" I was messing with. One of my favorites contains several scriptural passages from Bible translations I didn't recognize (and I know my share of Bible quotations, having apprenticed in my youth as a Bible quizzer in Youth for Christ). Like most such letters, it warned against trifling with the mother's preeminence (and oft-implied sole source of female worthiness) in the nurturing domain. It ended with a prayer for my mother, apparently based on the letter writer's speculation that I was a heavy burden of disappointment to her in concerning myself with such matters.

Many women of course *will* embrace the news of this book. The mothers of the children in this study came from many different starting points to do just that. As we saw in their stories, they almost all struggled at times with unwelcome envy of their husbands' competence and their shared intimacies with their children. But in the end all the women felt that their husbands' deep involvement with their children was part of something that was vitally important, often contributing ultimately to a validation of themselves as whole people and whole women. But they weren't the only ones who struggled with competitive feelings.

Occasionally, this study has been misunderstood as the pitting of males against females as primary nurturing parents. It is not. It *is* the study of families with children borne by mothers, raised by *fathers and mothers* where, during the early years, the father was on the front line. It presents evidence that the children are doing well not because the fathers do it better (they do it differently) but because these children were raised in families with two involved parents; fathers and mothers were deeply affected by their children and one another.

That this is so hard to clarify despite the simple words is evidence of the adversarial stances people assume when discussing access to the nurturing domain. In fact, this access is recognized as a precious privilege when marriages turn sour, a valuable bargaining chip, and an instrument of revenge when it is denied either mother or father. A National Institute of Mental Health study of the first two years of divorce in 560 parents documented that 40 percent of custodial mothers refused, at least once, to permit their ex-husbands to see their children.[7] Furthermore, the reason for such refusal had nothing to do with the children's wishes, safety, or health but instead appeared to be primarily punitive. The California Divorce Study by Judith Wallerstein of 114 families of divorce reported that "half of the custodial mothers were ambivalent or overtly negative about visitation."[8]

Some students of the divorcing family and others who study family law feel that such increasing father freeze-outs and denials of visitation have been on a steady rise since the advent of no-fault divorce laws, which many women feel have left them powerless in the face of the law, especially economically. Such feeling is not without cause. Sociologist Lenore Weitzman in her recent book *The Divorce Revolution: The Unexpected Social and Economic Consequences for Women and Children in America* states that in the late 1970s there was an astounding and immediate 73 percent drop in divorced women's standard of living while their ex-husbands saw an immediate 42 percent increase in theirs.[9] The long-term results show less radical differences but are nonetheless indicative of a dramatic change in most women's economic status after divorce. This was a wholly unexpected result of the no-fault laws originally supported by feminists, who initially saw them as treating both men and women "equally" in divorce settlements. Such laws have, in concert with the growing awareness among men of the meaning of fathering in their lives, certainly increased the tension over reasonable access to the nurturing domain in the case of divorce.

Most of the mothers we came to know in this study wrestled with these issues, some vigorously. But over time they discovered that it was the *sharing* of the nurturing domain, not preeminence there, that gave them pleasure. I don't feel that these women were unusual in that attitude.

We found repeatedly that when women saw their babies and husbands responding to one another, they did experience competitive feelings, but they also experienced relief and often joy over the validation of the family as a whole. Most of the time they did not regard the situation as armed conflict over parental honor on the field of battle. Mothers noted that there were ways in which their husbands dealt with their children differently than they did, but these differences rarely led to contention. They talked more of sharing than of yielding the old preeminence. Clearly, it is when parents can feel they are *making common cause* about kids or work that the empty malaise of the workplace or the tedious repetitions of the daily parenting become less onerous. The sharing of the nurturing domain is not an adversarial issue as far as kids are concerned. It need not be one for the parents, either.

If men and women are ready, as the signs seem to show they are, to scuttle the old bartered immunity of which de Beauvoir wrote in the 1950s, then we do stand on a threshold of parenthood as common cause. The cause we share is certainly not radically new in principle. We seek the creation of a place where children and adults are nurtured and valued for who they are as people, unique beings whose real worth need not be determined by the stereotype of gender/role. What is unique is the idea that parenthood may be owned jointly, not by just mother or father, but by both.

Such joint ownership creates a place where mothers can "father" and fathers can "mother." It does *not* encourage mothers and fathers to compete with one another for "first-place parent." Such competition is not especially good for a marriage and furthermore drives kids nuts. A seven-year-old first grader recently contributed this comment to a class discussion about fathers looking after children: "I have to love both my mom and dad just the same or they get jealous. It's so dumb." Sharing doesn't confuse children; competition does.

The common cause for which I speak here is one that demands dedication and purpose, not just changes in behavior. It involves men and women working and compromising together. Neither wives alone nor husbands alone can reshape or even control their lives, homes, or jobs (or the balance among the three) just by talking quietly (or loudly) among themselves. It is not easy to share this domain; compromise is required in areas of both male and female strength and vulnerability.

There is vulnerability aplenty for both men and women in this business of procreation.

Men and women risk a good deal of themselves when they make babies. Lots can go wrong. Betrayal is a possibility from either side. He could refuse to act as father to the child. She could deny that the child was his, deny him access, or even can carry the baby away, refuting both his paternity and his progeny. These are some of the shared private vulnerabilities.

Some of the public vulnerabilities are also shared, especially by dual-career or dual-job couples. For example: Until the marketplace is forced to adapt, delayed promotions and shrinking raises await both men *and* women who are committed to assuming day-to-day responsibility for the care of their children.

Men and women who have been able to embrace

mutual dependence free of the worry of being emasculated or exploited can and must struggle more effectively to protect and sustain their own unique nurturing domains. The choice to share this place is not merely a personal one. Working out the life or even daily schedule of work and child care to create a shared nurturing domain certainly requires a strong personal commitment. That the sharing itself be protected as a potential option in the first place is a much more fundamental task. If we want it badly enough it can be done, both personally and socially.

Couples can and should think together carefully about their work and family goals. It is permissible, even wise, to consider such questions as who *should* or who *wants* to be the front-liner for the children. Who is willing to serve as full-time or major-time homemaker? Whose career plans would be less damaged by retiring "for a while" (as so many of the study fathers said) from the workplace? Which job should be preserved because of its greater financial or long-term benefit and security?

In the social arena, a promising move in the struggle for the option to share the nurturing domain was the 1985 report of a national blue-ribbon commission called "The Infant Care Project" of the Yale-Bush Center for Child Development and Social Policy.[10] Its bold (some say brash) proposal was the establishment of a *national policy on infant care leave* (a.k.a. maternity or paternity leave), consisting of (1) mandatory availability of leaves for childbirth and infant care, (2) income replacement for wages that would have otherwise been earned, and (3) continuity of benefits and job security for *mothers and fathers*. The committee urged that the leave "be available for a minimum of six months and should include partial salary replacement (75 percent of salary) for three months, while job security and benefits are available throughout." The panel advised a nongovernment funding model, based on private insurance funds.

But unless mothers and fathers both want this option to share the nurturing domain and unless they make common cause for the vital parenthood of their children, it will never happen, no matter who else thinks it is a good idea. I've listened to the parents who have already made it work for themselves and their children and I am in awe of their capacity to pull together and to affect one another's lives deeply and meaningfully. No lack of conviction here.

It seems a fundamental error for the woman who shares the nurturing domain to think of her mothering as somehow diminished. It is possible, even probable, that such sharing can strengthen the nurturing domain as a caring place for everyone in the family, including the mother herself. It may in fact be a gift of special value to one's children as well, for they seem to thrive in this environment like plants in the whole light of a southern window.

Divorce and the Nurturing Father: The Dangerous Opportunity

Nearly half of all U.S. families are wracked by separation and divorce at some point. A few work things out, but most are torn apart. Divorce occurs so frequently, we prefer to numb ourselves to its lacerations of the spirit and, most particularly, of human relationships. When it does come, the family changes its complexion and integrity, never to be the same again.

One particular statistic bears stark witness to this change. The number of single fathers in American mushroomed by over 125 percent from 1970 to 1984 in homes that care for 1.5 million children. The reordering of this new life and its relationships constitutes a major crisis of our time. The word "crisis" evokes our attention and concern, but it need not imply hopeless destruction. Crisis, as defined by *I Ching*, is a "dangerous opportunity." I think many fathers and mothers would agree.

Most fathers who divorce lose custody of their children, but some share it. Depending upon the divorce decree or agreement, they may have ongoing contact with their children through "visitation" (a most unsatisfactory word). The time a father spends with his children in such arrangements may not be much less than he had before. It may even be experienced by both father and child, after the initial shock of the "moveout" has eased, as "better" time, since it is usually less constricted by the depleting, conflicted misery of a painful marriage. Thus freed, father and children may embark on new explorations of the territory of their lives and relationship. This is the opportunity part.

The dangerous part comes later, especially for the father who loses custody. Most major studies of divorced families conducted over time show that after five years, fewer than half of noncustodial fathers still maintain "actively nurturing roles" in the lives of their children.[1] The rest either have been actively excluded from their children's lives by courts or mothers or have slowly suffered a kind of paternal erosion or drift, slipping inexorably out of the main current of their children's lives.

This loss of contact with one's children is a huge loss, whether sudden or by slow degree, that wreaks much profound devastation upon both fatherhood and childhood. Since the majority of custody arrangements favor mothers, this situation clearly qualifies as a major problem for fathers. One father likened the loss of his children from his daily life to being "slowly disemboweled." Not surprisingly, many men are radicalized by such experiences.

Here at the threshold of this chapter, I want to clarify that I shall be dealing for the most part with divorced men who want to be involved in the lives of their children. The thousands of men who choose to leave their children's lives after divorce, for whatever reasons, have forfeited their option on the dangerous opportunity and are no longer within the interactional nurturing domain that is the focus of this book.

Over the past few years, I have collaborated with a highly successful, respected Connecticut attorney in giving testimony as expert witness in several intensely contested child custody disputes. We have spoken often about the price exacted from all parties during such bitter conflicts.

Given what many men feel are the judicial odds against them in such circumstances, I asked the attorney why she felt her male clients tried to retain all or partial custody of their children. She responded, "I see only the ones who are so angry or so scared about losing their kids, that they kind of 'damn the torpedoes' and go ahead anyway. For every man who musters his courage and resources to enter the fray to protect his relationship with his children, there've got to be six or eight who don't even try because they feel, and justifiably so statistically, that the odds are so heavily stacked against them that it's not worth the effort emotionally or financially."

I have encountered many men who are plagued by guilt years after such potential battles because they "didn't try harder for my kids." Yet those who do try often watch in pain as their finances, property, and emotional lives are devastated by interminable legal maneuverings, when the odds are they will lose anyway.

On the other side of my courtroom experience, I have encountered judge after judge who has shown interest in the new fatherhood research, as it reassures the system of justice that "father care" is not inherently incompatible with the "best interest of the child" or "tender years" doctrine.

Shortly after I began to speak and write on the subject of primary nurturing fathers, I was contacted by several groups of divorced men, describing themselves as "radical divorced men's groups." They sought my aid and/ or consultation to assist them in their struggles to protect their rights to father their children.

I quickly came to the realization that many of these men were willing to do whatever they could to keep from being evicted from the lives of their children, a happening that one man called "a very totalitarian experience." I shuddered occasionally as I heard of the rare but dramatic tactics sometimes employed without much regard for the well-being of the children. I was told that their loose consortium of regional groups of similar conviction had newsletters and nationwide mailing lists containing 50,000 names! It's easy for me to imagine that for every man actually on the list, there may be at least three or four more who feel just as strongly. And this is only the tip of a still-growing iceberg.

Given these large numbers of affected fathers, it is absolutely amazing that we know so little about how divorced men actually feel about losing their children from their daily lives and the havoc that it wreaks on their sense of fatherliness.

We do know that divorced fathering starts very painfully much of the time.[2] It begins with a period of numbing, often bitter, shock and sadness for both father and child that can "feel like death," as one 25-year-old accountant described it. The sadness may vary in intensity for the father whether he feels he "won or lost." It is more uniformly painful and sad for the children, as they feel they've usually lost either part or all of a father. It is painful for the father because he's just experienced a lengthy, depleting emotional battle that often leaves his self-esteem in shreds.

Such hurt is rarely short-lived. It often forces competent, well-functioning, caring parents into atypical, obstructive roles vis-à-vis their children and each other. Intimacy, affection, self-esteem, and communication are frequent casualties during this early period. Fathers take flight into the Santa Claus stance, becoming givers of *presents* in lieu of their frightened, uncertain *selves*.

As men become increasingly aware of the enormous damage that divorce (whether they sought it or not) can inflict on their fatherhood and their children, a growing number are seeking sole custody. However, the single father, not unlike the single mother, once embarked can expect heavy weather. Exhaustion, boredom, worry, confusion, and disappointment are all fellow travelers. So are exhilaration, emotional rewards, and pleasures unique to this experience never before felt or thought possible.

Career advancement is often put in cold storage

while adjusting to the enormity of the new responsibilities and drudgeries. Women, because of sexist role expectations, are *expected* to put children first; but when a man does, balancing career and parenthood can feel very precarious indeed. Although the single father, because he's still a rare (supposedly even heroic) species, is more likely to receive offers of community or family help than the single mother, his independent—even antidependent—nature will usually cause him to shun help more often than he probably should, making things harder for him and his children.

As we saw in the previous chapter, some courts may see today's single custodial fathers as slightly more likely than single mothers to succeed in their difficult task, especially if financial resources are given undue weight. As a group, single fathers are often motivated people who have chosen to be parents, while many single mothers, particularly those deserted by their husbands, are not in their situation by choice. Many men are also likely to draw higher salaries than single mothers because of decades of unequal wages in the workplace. Such men therefore suffer less frequently from the double jeopardy of lower pay and sole parenting that faces single custodial mothers.

Some important questions are beginning to be answered as we begin to study and understand such men and their life situations. In 1983, more than 1,000 single men with custody of their children responded to an interesting Parents Without Partners survey about single parenting.[3] Their biggest worries were not about their competence in child care or homemaking responsibilities. Their largest concerns were about the juggling of careers and parenthood. When asked what they felt would help them resolve their real-life difficulties, they gave the following solutions: (1) more time flexibility in the workplace, (2) more legal and mental health support for themselves and their children, and (3) wider, less stigmatizing acceptance of men as sole parents. (TAKE NOTE: Such solutions also appeal to a lot of single mothers.)

I was recently asked to advise a New Haven court on a custody battle between a third-year medical student and his wife, a respected emergency room nurse, over their two-year-old twin sons. Initially, the father felt joint custody was best and had not sought sole custody of the boys. His wife, who had been married once previously and was eight years older than he, had calmly told him the first time they'd discussed custody, "Hell will freeze over first before you find a judge to let you have custody, even part of it." He realized then he would have to fight for a place in his children's lives. He managed to find an attorney who thought the odds were better than his wife did.

To many men, the judicial system often seems to be guided by some ancient, timeless commandment when granting maternal custody in divorce. In 1985, 90 percent of the 12 million American children of divorce were in the custody of their mothers. Yet for most of Western history, the reverse was true. British law, which served as the template for early American law, routinely awarded custody of children to fathers because the children (and the mother) were treated as his property. Late in the 1880s, the radical concept of the "doctrine of tender years" emerged, shaped by the "new scientific view" of maternal preference—namely, that mothers were uniquely and exclusively suited, biologically and psychologically, to raise children under seven.[4] This overturned the old precedent of the child as "father's property." From that moment on, giving custody to mothers was presumed to be "in the best interest of the child."

A less rigid wisdom is now making itself felt, as seen in the adoption of a number of new custody statutes across the land. To wit: In Section 240 of the New York State Domestic Relations Law, neither mother nor father is given automatic preference in custody conflicts. Here is an example of how one New York judge applied this statute:

> The simple fact of being a mother does not by itself indicate a capacity or willingness to render a quality of care different from that which the father can provide. The traditional and romantic view, at least since the turn of the century, has been that nothing can be adequate as a substitute for mother love... later decisions have recognized that this view is inconsistent with informed application of the Best Interest of the Child Doctrine and out of touch with contemporary thought about child development and male and female stereotypes.[5]

But many attorneys in family law will tell you that although this is the new principle, in the trenches it's still another story. I have encountered several attorneys who encourage men involved in especially bitter divorce contests to seek sole custody as a strategy even if they don't intend to take it in order to have something to "give away" in compromise (the civil law equivalent of plea bargaining). Fathers are then, supposedly, in a better position strategically to get what they really want—a legal, protected *place* in their children's lives.

Many judges are probably trying to grapple fairly with the application of some of the new statutes, largely enacted (like most laws) to reflect changes in public opinion. Joint custody legislation now stands in 30 states, thanks in large part to lobbying by men's groups occasionally in coalition with certain women's groups. Judges are leaning increasingly toward awarding joint legal custody to mother and father while assigning primary residence or physical custody to the mother.

A number of jurists, however, cling to the view of fathers as "troublemakers." I cite remarks by Judge Richard

Huttner, quoted in the November 18, 1985, *New York* magazine article, "The Father Also Rises."

> You have never seen a bigger pain in the ass than the father who wants to get involved; he can be repulsive. He wants to meet the kid after school at three o'clock, take the kid out to dinner during the week, have the kid on his own birthday, talk to the kid on the phone every evening, go to every open school night, take the kid away for a whole weekend so they can be alone together. This type of involved father is pathological.[6]

Pathological? Far from it. There are tens of thousands of children (at least), and probably as many single mothers, who would clearly love to have a father so involved. But, despite such unenlightened views as those expressed above, a growing number of men really do want custody and a few are getting it. They tend to achieve this mostly if the mother does not want custody or if the court finds the mother incapable of parenting her children in a manner that meets its standards.

What are such men like? Psychologist Kelin Gersick recently studied a group of newly divorced fathers, comparing the half who "won" custody with the half who didn't.[7] The half who won were not unconventional, radical, young "troublemakers." They were in fact, on average, older, more stable men of somewhat more secure socioeconomic status. They were also indistinguishable from the noncustodial group in the degree of family cohesion in their backgrounds.

But for each such father, there are ten who lose the irreplaceable dailiness of life with their children. Some are granted joint custody, which permits them some say in important life decisions such as schooling and medical care (access to which often comes with a high price tag in terms of child support payments).

But many fathers have only "visitation." Not unlike the concept of "babysitter," "visitation" is a bizarre term that consigns the parent to the designation of remote relative or circuit rider who comes into the child's life not to "father" (or to "mother") but merely to "visit."

Making "visitation" work as an ongoing arrangement for a life with one's child is very difficult indeed. One young journalist father of two daughters described it this way. "At first the relationship is so vastly affected, it's like nothing mattered from before. It's a grotesque artifact of what used to be. It's like death, and this is some sort of afterlife or painful 'out-of-body' experience."

Such men find themselves scrambling, overreaching, maneuvering, and manipulating to find what the young journalist called a "strong second place" in the life of their children.

Competition with the ex-wife over importance as an abiding, effective presence in the child's life is nearly universal and almost as universally damaging to the relationship with the child. The children, depending upon their age and level of sophistication, may be initially titillated by the competition, which involves the giving and denying of affection as well as material goods and services. But eventually the children are less and less impressed. One eleven-year-old boy "divorced" for three years said, "It's not that I don't *want* an all-terrain cycle—I do! Who wouldn't? But what I *need* is for my dad and mom to stop the silly Santa Claus stuff. It's like a dumb TV game show. It just doesn't mean anything after you watch it for a while."

Eventually, many a man comes to realize that part of the competition does not come from his ex but comes instead from another part of himself—that part that clings tenaciously to the image of the full and perfect father, the giver of life, goodies, wisdom, protection, and happiness.

But the fight for *importance*, no matter what its individual source, is ongoing, and many men feel it is never confidently "won." The young journalist: "It's really like a guerrilla action aimed not at a complete overthrow of the regime but just to win a presence in the governance of the life of my child. I am secondary and I'll never be primary—I know that. But goddamn it, I still want to be *important*! And I'm not just fighting my ex in the jungle, I'm fighting the inevitable drift out of my growing child's life. Her independence from me, no matter how much I want to make it happen well for her, seems like an enemy, too."

The guerrilla action is a heavy drain on resources, mental and economic. Of course, some men, those who leave or quit their children's lives, never start, or eventually stop trying. They just stop fighting. No one knows how much that costs them, but it usually costs the children plenty.

But what happens to the "visitors" who *do* visit?

One of the longest running myths about divorced fathers is this: A father may be a good protector or breadwinner, but his innate (stereotyped) inability to respond to his child emotionally leaves him to feel little, if anything, of depth about the impact of divorce on his fathering. His role as husband and provider certainly is affected but *not* his fathering.

How wrong, how wrong. This witless view has made it much easier over the years for attorneys and judges to dispense wisdom and justice in contested divorces.

Staying involved as the "visitor" is a job that usually changes with time, although more radically for the noncustodial than the shared custodial father. E. Mavis Hetherington of the University of Virginia found that noncustodial fathers were in progressively less and less contact with their children as time passed.[8] Of the 48 fathers in her study, she found that after two years, 19 men saw their children once a week, 21 saw them every two or three weeks, and 8 saw them once a month or less. Remarriage, resistance on the part of the custodial parent, and child drift were all variably responsible.

For the joint-custody father, things are quite different. Los Angeles psychologist Ann D'Andrea found that joint-custody fathers stayed actively involved well beyond this two-year dropoff point.[9] Fathers on such regular visitation schedules not only kept more current with child support payments, but they expressed greater satisfaction and self-esteem as fathers than did those who did not keep to a schedule. This of course could be a cart-before-the-horse finding, but the fact remains that the men who stay involved *are* more involved.

Such involvement may not be without its price. David Chambers of the University of Michigan Law School has found that men who wished to "visit regularly" with their children paid court-ordered child support payments that were significantly higher than the average: the "put up or shut up" visitation/child support syndrome.[10] The lowest payments were made by those men who had no contact. He concluded that money and involvement seem to come from the same source—"affection and devotion" to one's children.

But the investment is hardly risk free.

One 42-year-old father, a successful commercial real estate broker who had joint custody of his twin twelve-year-old sons, had "suffered a lot since the divorce of six years ago. Every time I come to pick the boys up, it's like running the gauntlet with my ex. She just never lets go of the opportunity to be mad at me. I think of visitation rights sort of like beach rights. When you get down to the water it's great. But if the neighbors don't like you, and they make it plain they don't like you over and over again, pretty soon you start thinking about not going. That's why I hate calling it visitation *rights*. It's God given that I ought to be in their lives. Hell, I helped to make 'em! Why do I have to pay over and over again for it? Once she offered me back half of my child support check if I'd cut down on 'visitation.' That would have made my cash flow problems disappear, but it would've wrecked me in my kid's eyes, in my own eyes, and in the long run, made things even worse for the kids."

Making things worse for the kids.

That happens most of the time in divorce. I have never known a young child to say or feel, "Well, thank God that's over" as his family disintegrates.

One of the most respected ongoing studies of the children of divorce, *Surviving the Breakup* by Judith Wallerstein and J. B. Kelly, shows us repeatedly that the absence of the father is a serious, sometimes dangerous condition.[11] They found that most of the children in the study missed their fathers painfully. "Two-thirds yearned for the absent parent, one-half of those with an intensity we found profoundly moving." Depending on the sex and developmental stage of the child at the time of the break-up, children who never saw their fathers again, *regardless* of the reason, frequently developed emotional and behavioral difficulties. Such difficulties were very often quite serious and emerged immediately, but some appeared and reappeared later on as well.

One of the few things on which students of divorce and child development agree, even across disciplinary lines, is that father absence makes for a lot of potential trouble in the evolution of the child's personality and sense of self.[12] Poor control of aggressive behavior in boys and girls, difficulties in establishing unconflicted gender identities and roles, impaired intellectual and school functioning, depression, and troubles in the regulation of self-esteem are all more common in children from divorced families than from intact families, even unhappy ones. Although most responsible researchers stop short of attributing such problems to linear cause and effect, their prevalence among the children of divorce is very sobering indeed. If the child, however, is guaranteed an open, continuous relationship that stays essentially protected and unchanged over time, the *probability* of such unhappy results is greatly reduced.

Now that we have begun to pay attention, we have found that fathers who want to be involved after the divorce have their own list of vulnerabilities. These may be especially obvious during the early months of the breakup (and may be shared with the children). Such things as depression, troubles in the maintenance of self-esteem, impaired work function (impaired school performance for kids), occasionally even poor control of behavior show up early. Fathers often have feelings that are much more than they bargained for.

Some of what fathers feel so intensely is certainly linked to the end of the marriage. These strong emotions are also often related to the threatened termination of the effect their children have on their lives, and vice versa. Much of this feeling is based on the fear, hardly irrational, that the power of the father to affect his child's life and to "feel affected" by the child's life is slipping out of his grasp.

This capacity to be affected by the life of the child is what divorced men discover painfully is so seriously threatened by the event of divorce. This same capacity, however, is shared by the fathers studied in this book.

Ultimately, that's what this book is about—*the capacity of men to be profoundly affected by their children, and consequently to profoundly affect their children's lives.*

Let's examine *how* this interaction pervades the lives of fathers and children by listening to the stories of divorced fathers.

David Lambert, a successful 38-year-old attorney, was divorced early in the second year of his daughter Lauren's life. "My first powerful feelings were great sadness and fear that she wasn't going to *be* there—out the bedroom door and down the hall twelve paces. I'd always had a kind of primordial feeling, something chemical, that I was to protect her. And for the first time in her life I couldn't do that. It was an awesome feeling that shocked me and left me with a lot of remorse."

Over and over again, divorced men speak of the shock they feel when the realization hits them that the dailiness of their lives with their children is gone. The gap left behind can be bottomless, and it's not easy to bridge.

David continued, "Once the early shock settled, I had to get to know her all over again. It happened slowly, through regular contact—plain, conventional everyday stuff—like getting her up on the weekends, feeding her, changing her diapers, giving her a bath, buying her clothes. The old protective 'man the barricades' view of fathering is pretty empty. It's doing that regular boring stuff that makes the relationship real. The special trips to Boston and fancy restaurants are nice, but it's the mundane I miss most of all.

"The biggest monkey on my back at first, and it took me a long time to realize it, was my plan to be *the* perfect father. But I overdid it. I was 'macho father.' I slept at the hospital till Lauren came home from the hospital, redid her room, bought the furniture. I was so intent on being involved and so afraid of being left out that I fought for a role in her life—I made it like boot camp. I'm sure it was overbearing.

"I took pictures of her right at her birth, and looked

long and hard at her face and body because I had this paranoid fantasy that the hospital would mix up the babies. I was a father junkie. I was not going to be like most fathers."

"Most fathers," according to a 32-year-old post office worker (and amateur poet), who had recently divorced and was sharing custody of his three daughters, "are like my dad. He'd come home like a breeze that blew in the window, frisked you, and then moved on. But I just can't afford to be like that any more, not if I want them to keep coming over for visitation. You have to actually *be* there emotionally—*all* of you, not just the exhausted hulk at the end of the day."

A 40-year-old minister, divorced for eight years and sharing physical custody of his two young teenage sons, seemed to caution himself and me as we talked of his fathering.

"You've got to be careful here. There's a strong urge to put myself up as a good father. But I really don't know if I am. There's a certain comfort or confidence I get occasionally in my professional life sometimes that convinces me that I'm really good at what I've chosen to do for a living. But I don't think you ever get that as a father for very long. I'm never really sure—really *certain* that I'm doing okay."

Sooner or later, most divorced fathers are presented with the "opportunity" to explain to their kids their view of the divorce. It's generally a pretty difficult moment if the father tries to be honest. The words are often hard to come by, but the children usually appreciate the effort. Here was David's moment. "Once Lauren nailed me on a Sunday afternoon visitation. I had to leave her with someone to go into my office on urgent business. She stood on the front step, she was about seven years old at the time, and said quite matter-of-factly to me as I walked toward my car, 'That's why my mom divorced you—'cause you always go to the office.' I stopped dead in my tracks, collected myself, and decided that this was the moment of truth. I told her that she was pretty right, that I hadn't been such a great husband." As much as David may have wanted to defend himself to his young accuser, being honest and real in his response to her had become important enough to override self-defense.

For many divorced fathers, fatherhood itself is something that they learn never to take for granted again. That causes one kind of problem, a kind of constant vigilance of fatherly performance, explained by a young author, the father of two girls: "One of my ongoing problems is that I don't want to give up the idea of still being the ideal father. When I want to talk with one of the girls about the divorce or any feelings they're having about it, I come to realize *I'm* the one looking for reassurance—reassurance of how *I'm* doing. They don't like to talk about the divorce directly...both of them shut down. They have this kind of strength and acceptance about the divorce that's both wise and innocent at the same time."

Mr. Lambert ended his soliloquy with a description of a new threat he may soon face in his ongoing relationship with Lauren. Though it's hardly a unique dilemma, his analysis of his own response reveals the father problem in yet another guise.

"Right now I'm pretty frightened. Lauren's mother is in love with someone, a guy I've met and like. They may move to Florida. I just don't know what to do. I can't imagine losing Lauren like that. I worry about her too. She says over and over again, how much she 'hates change.' She doesn't even like it when I buy a new car!"

A long pause...

"Something happened about this that really bothered me. Lauren and I were talking about Florida and that she might move there with her mother and this guy she likes, too. She was just talking quietly about it, but she was obviously upset and feeling a lot that she wouldn't say. Finally she just said, very calmly and matter-of-fact, 'Dad, life is not a fairytale.'

"It hit me so hard I started crying. I just couldn't help it. And I kept on crying. I'd never done that before in front of her—never. I felt quite bad about it—real ashamed. I worried that I had made things harder for her. But there she was, understanding and accepting reality better than her father! Me—I'm still busy trying to change it."

I saw David Lambert's tears differently, but of course it wasn't *my* heart that was hurting. I saw his tears as a gift to his daughter, a gift woven of the deep empathy of which parents and children are capable—that feeling of "you are not alone in what you feel, whether it's good or bad, and neither am I. I share those feelings, and the vulnerability that goes along with them, painful as they are."

This gift of feeling in this man at this time in his daughter's presence bears witness to the enduring capacity of men to be affected by their children. David's guilt about such a revelation of feeling, though obviously highly personal to him, is resoundingly familiar in the vast majority of men, who as boys were taught not to cry. That a man can reveal such sadness may hint that things might be changing. That he feels *ashamed* may reveal how far young Adam in Mrs. Kits' kindergarten still has to go.

Given all these thoughts about the dangerous opportunity that is divorce, how is the divorced father to make his presence best felt, and usefully so, in the life of his child?

First, custody, however it's carved up judicially, is largely an internal, emotional commitment. Children *feel* that sense of "belonging" to a father and mother, not as property but as beloved kin. They watch carefully, no matter what the State says, to see if their fathers *act* as though they feel that sense of belonging, too. So here's some advice I shall address to divorced men to preserve that sense of mutual belonging.

The first and foremost guiding principle regarding any decisions about visitation or changes in your life that might affect your child should be made with what is best for your child, not just you, in mind. David Lambert bit the bullet and stayed with Lauren in his wife's home once when, at the age of two-and-a-half, she was too worried about separation to leave her mother. He visited her at her mother's home until she was able to return to the routine. It was not especially good for him, but it certainly was for her.

Second, be guided by your child's developmental needs, and especially his or her different sense of time. Frequent brief visits are a lot better for toddlers with short memories than are long visits at greater intervals. Older children with successful social or school lives (about which you would feel understandably proud) need more flexibility about visits with you.

Third, live close to your children if you can, especially when they are younger, for obvious reasons.

Fourth, honor your "visitation" rights. "Bite the bullet," run the gauntlet, but don't give up and stop seeing your children, no matter who tests you, your ex or the kids. Your life together is preserved in and by the mundane tasks, such as changing diapers, blowing noses, helping with homework. Be with them whenever you can. The door may close if you don't keep going through it.

Fifth, pay your child support. If you don't, you are the real loser. Skipping may deprive your kids of something, but it deprives you of much more—your self-respect as a father.

Sixth, do not overindulge your children. No matter

how many "I wants" you hear, children of *all* ages inherently *want* you to define, guard, and keep the limits for them. That's how they learn what to expect from life, and they see you as one of the experts, whether or not you think you are.

Seventh, don't press for talk about the divorce. Your job is to figure out how you and your kids can fit into one another's lives, not cross and recross-examination. All your kids want to know is that you are not going to quit on them. The details are usually not as interesting to them as they may think they are, anyway.

Finally, crisis need *not* spawn failure. Though divorce can be dangerous to the leaving father, and to his staying child, some opportunity lies in the shadows of all that sadness. A man may define his fatherhood to himself for the first time in honest and intimate terms. He and his children may also struggle to shape together in some way a vision and understanding of what they have taken for granted in one another's lives and then to decide whether or not to protect it. When accomplished by both father and child, the rewards can sometimes reach beyond words. When our whole society learns to understand and value these relationships, that part of the father problem which plagues divorced men and their children can fade quietly, namelessly away. Solving the *rest* of the father problem will require a longer journey—further even than we've already come.

15

Solving the Father Problem

Mr. Greer sat forward on the edge of the bench outside the courtroom, head down, wringing his hands, and slowly shaking his head. His young face was tightly drawn, and his eyes were fixed on the floor. His wife sat next to him anxiously conferring with their attorney. I had come because the Greers sought my help in a most unusual legal struggle.

As the father rose stiffly to greet me, he spoke in a pressured voice, "I can't believe I caused all this trouble. I'm beginning to wonder if it's worth this hassle. Thanks for coming. God, I hope it's worth it."

Already in the judge's chambers were another attorney representing the couple, the director of a large urban adoption agency, and that agency's counsel. Here was the problem: Mrs. Greer wished to continue working and to support the family. This venerable, respected adoption agency had revoked its promise to place a child with this young couple because the father announced his plan to be the primary parent for the adopted baby.

Mr. and Mrs. Greer's salaries were equivalent, but they felt that career continuity was more important at present to her life goals than his. So they made what they thought would be a private, simple decision that was best for their young family.

Enter the father problem in yet another guise.

Once the agency social worker heard that Mr. Greer was to be the child-rearing parent, the infant whom the couple had already met suddenly became "unavailable." After much frustration and many tears, they decided to seek legal advice to solve their dilemma. Such stories stun but do not surprise.

And so, here it is. How *does* the father problem get solved? Alvin Toffler tells us that change is not random, episodic, or haphazard but is a commodity that can be measured and observed.[1] And fatherhood *is* changing, with fastball speed, especially compared with the languid pace of social evolution.

We have seen that men are learning that work, productivity, and marriage may be very important parts of life, but they are not its whole cloth. The rest of the fabric is made of nurturing relationships, especially those with children—relationships which are intimate, trusting, humane, complex, and full of care.

Though we've covered plenty of ground just to get here in our understanding, the father problem must ultimately be solved through means that are productive and responsible in themselves, not insidious devaluations of women, work, or even success. There are many ways in which this can happen without shattering sacrifice or wrenching confrontation. An awareness and a vision that are both sensitive and conscious but nonetheless intensely purposeful are required. What is needed is a call to men to reach out and claim their *own* fatherhood.

It is time to stop giving lip service to the idea of "family development" as a concept that automatically includes fathers. It doesn't. And it most emphatically should include them. The truth is leaking out through the real lives of men and their children that the uninvited, uninvolved, unwelcomed, inept father is moving toward obsolescence.

But let's not delude ourselves. Such change is frequently unwelcome, highly suspect, and often seen as "unnatural." Aided by stories of the families in this book, we can say with much conviction that it can be enormously

rewarding for a man to attend to his nurturing capabilities
and wishes. It is good for him, for his children, and for his
spouse.

Despite dire, impassioned warnings and even some
threats about "man's place" and "woman's place," the
Greers ultimately won their case against the venerable
adoption agency—not easily, quickly, or cheaply, but they
won. They won because we *do* know enough. After my
testimony on their behalf concerning my research on the
primary nurturing father and his effect on babies, the agency withdrew its objections forthwith.

The only way for many men to find the nurturing
quality in themselves is to stop restricting and strangling
it—to allow it to come forward. Once a man experiences
it, he can often use it with unimagined rewards. A father
may embrace his children, but until he embraces his own
unique, irreplaceable value to them as a parent, he does
not have as much in his arms as he thinks.

As we've already seen, there are forces at work in
men that have brought many of them into the nursery, not
just out of need, but out of a desire, even the conviction
that they should be there. But, as many women proceed to
define themselves less in terms of child-rearing and go
outside the home to work, there is a real danger that some
fathers will see the child-care gap as a vacuum into which
they are reluctantly, inevitably sucked. When the family
cannot afford or find quality infant day care (not an unusual problem), it may seem to the father that he's being
forced to fill this vacuum, and resentment can take root. A
few such men refuse, telling their wives they won't or
can't care for their children. A particularly troubled few
even abandon their families. This tragically myopic "entrapment view" of fathering, when combined with the
long-standing admonitions to men that they couldn't, even

shouldn't, be involved with their children, often fuels a powerful flight from fathering itself.

To assist men in freeing themselves from this entrapment view, our first job is to help them to see fathering for what it truly is. Fatherhood is not a milestone to be marked by running out to "get a piece of the Rock," or as partial fruition of the Calvinistic work ethic, or as the genital expression of immortality. Nor is it endless drain, misery, and sacrifice. Rather it is the single most creative, complicated, fulfilling, frustrating, engrossing, enriching, depleting endeavor of a man's adult life. So often, as the septuagenarian reflects on life's rewards, we hear that "in the final analysis" of money, power, prestige, and marriage, fathering alone was what "mattered."

The body of knowledge that we have studied in this book shows us beyond question that men can and most often should be involved in nurturing their children. In the second half of the twentieth century we have embraced the idea, thanks to Spock and Freud among others, that human beings should be allowed to unfold in a guided way, rather than be sculpted or molded. This revised concept of human destiny has compelling implications for the contention that men have innate nurturing qualities. It means that it's a big mistake to associate the ability to comfort, protect, accept, be close, and feel empathy exclusively with femininity.

Reviewing the stories of these men and their children, it becomes clear that their experience matters little if we fail to understand what it means for all men and do not use what we have learned to envision, even plan, for a different new involvement for men as fathers.

There are no simple universal answers to be found to the father problem, and it is a confusing, often painful struggle for many men, and often for women. What's most needed is a fundamentally new scheme for a man's life and especially the use of his time—a scheme that enhances the quality of life more than it centers on work and that doesn't conflict with one's worth as a working, successful, even powerful man. When a man can truly and honestly examine fatherhood in this way, he is well on his way to solving the private dilemmas of the father problem.

Next comes the hard part: getting involved. This step is farther-reaching in its implication than is the decision to become a father. It means getting educated, taking decisive action, doing it early, and then staying there—right there in the life of his child, firmly fixed.

So where to begin?

We begin where a man needs to start thinking of himself as father: when he and his mate are making ready for the birth of progeny.

The obstetrician, clinic, or health care system chosen for the mother's prenatal care should be chosen by both mother *and* father, if they're lucky enough to have a choice. Questions will come throughout the pregnancy, and the father should have access to answers, just as the mother does, especially if trouble appears. He also must make certain early on that he can attend the birth, even if it's a cesarean section. He must be able to ask about the growth and health of "his" fetus too, not to mention what is happening to his wife's body. The father can play a critical role in support of his wife if he's allowed to and has enough of the facts.

Just as important as the physical change and growth, however, is the evolution of an image of the child in the father's own mind and heart. Fantasies, daydreams, random thoughts, preoccupations are important in this early attachment, whether positive or negative. Far too many fathers concern themselves only about the gender of their unborn child, with a heavy preference for male offspring.

The mother also contributes, often unwittingly, to

limitations in the way a man thinks about himself as father. She may define his fathering in terms of her own needs and perceptions, delineating her mate as someone to "father" her, or be the security force, master repairman, or financial center. The widespread, unthinking acceptance of such "father defining" makes it critical that men get involved immediately.

It is vital that the pregnant father get himself educated in the physical care and feeding of his coming baby. This is so fundamental because men don't often think of themselves as "pregnant" and consequently don't prepare themselves for the arrival of a *body* that will need care and attention. Most need all the education they can get, and a lot of it is available. Many hospitals offer such group experiences, and the better ones are run by women and men, with real live babies. (Some fathers worry that they don't feel immediate attraction to such infants in the education process. The real attraction, however, usually occurs with one's own child.) The prepared birth movement has been a strong incentive for father involvement in the actual birth of the baby. Lamaze classes are widespread and offer fathers an active role in the birthing process.

The birthing of the baby affords the father his first direct physical experience of his child. For most men it's one of the single most moving moments of their lives. But men shouldn't assume automatically that attending the birth will be available to them as an option. It's still far from a universal practice in the United States. But there will be no other event in the life of the father that will so profoundly affect his early attachment to his child, not to mention his wife. Therefore, it's crucial that he be there at the beginning, otherwise he may have the feeling that he has been left at the starting gate.

Some hospitals permit only those fathers who have attended prebirth classes to watch. Our research shows that men should be there regardless of whether or not they have had preparation. All fathers should be allowed to be there—it's that important, period. Father presence means laboring mothers need less medication, thereby lowering the prevalence of birth complications. It means that babies go home from the hospital sooner. It means the father develops an attachment and understanding of his baby as a person more quickly, is more likely to be involved in the baby's care, and is far less likely to be abusive. The list of benefits goes on. (They were detailed in Chapter 2.)

Once the baby is out, the father should be permitted, encouraged, and helped by the obstetrician, midwife, or maternity nursing staff to touch, look at, or hold his baby. This is what happens in the ideal situation, but often the father himself must insist on doing these things rather than just letting the "pros" take over. These first few moments of intimate contact will make the baby real and alive for the father, often for the first time in a truly physical, sensual sense. Since he did not, nor ever can, feel his baby inside his own body, he has had to hold another place open, perhaps in his mind or soul, for this child. Such an open space is a fertile garden indeed, in which to grow attachments and feelings for babies.

If the father has had the advantage of child-handling instruction or experience, or feels strongly committed to trying, he might even bathe his newborn baby in the delivery room (albeit with help nearby if needed). If not, diapering, bathing, and bottle-feeding must be in the father's repertoire before his baby leaves the hospital.

The importance of this early contact with the baby cannot be overemphasized. The father should plan somehow to spend a few hours directly with his baby as soon as it's born.

A young Black father had the last word on why. "I stood there a long time just staring at her in that little plastic bed. The nurse said I could pick her up. I said, 'Are you kidding? She's only two hours old.' She looked like a little puppy to me. I did pick her up with my hand under her head like they showed me, and then I held her in close—just pulled her in—kind of like a magnet. And then you know what she did—all by herself? She turned her head toward my chest like she was looking to suck on something that sure wasn't there! But you know she didn't look too disappointed when she didn't find much. She opened her eyes and we just looked at each other. She's the greatest, Doc, and I'm not kidding! I'm going back there later to get some more of that!"

"*That*" is the beginning of an attachment that no adult can give or teach to a father. He must be there to have it happen with his baby. Once it does happen, he will never be "a babysitter" again.

One way of helping fathers and babies have this essential early experience is for the hospital to provide, even encourage, rooming-in for fathers in the hospital wards. At the very least, their unrestricted visiting must be permitted. Employers can also help by giving fathers the time to be there and take advantage of such opportunities.

As the next step in getting involved the father should continue his presence and his own commitment to his child's well-being in concrete ways. For example, he should actively share with the mother the choosing of the pediatrician, just as they selected their obstetrician. Men have their own questions, and they differ from those of mothers. New mothers are more interested in nutrition and vulnerability to illness while fathers tend to ask about when they can take their babies out of the house or how much sleep babies really need.

As we've seen time and time again, a father is a parent in his own right, not a substitute mother, and as such must have the information he needs to parent freely and usefully. Good pediatricians encourage father visits and father presence in their offices because the doctors are then capable of understanding the familial and nurturing context of the baby's life and world.

Using a pediatrician who appreciates father care is especially important if there are parental worries about a child. The baby with a difficult temperament (and they are not unusual or rare) or extended, protracted colic is a hard child to "read," because there are so few understandable cues other than diffuse distress. Both parents can feel rejected by such children.

Parents of babies who have difficulties often blame themselves, and the home environment can become strained and tense. The father's availability to such a baby is all the more important, both as nurturer and as sharer of the distress. Therefore, the family must choose its helpers from pediatricians to babysitters especially carefully.

Another situation in which father care is of even greater significance is when an infant is born at risk. As mentioned before, both Yogman's study of middle-class infants in Boston[2] and psychologist Juarlyn Gaiter's studies of inner-city families in Washington, D.C.,[3] found repeatedly, even in such economically divergent families, that fathers had a profound and positive effect on babies and their mothers in the frightening, uncertain, risky business of the seriously ill infant. Here the solution to the father problem seems almost easy by contrast, because the need is so obvious and great.

An early, preterm, small, sick baby pulls the father into its life early and decisively. Dozens of decisions have to be made quickly yet carefully. For example, should the baby be transferred to a more specialized care facility? If the birth has been complicated for the mother, she may be too ill to begin the all-important attachment or bonding with her baby, and the father must step in.

This is also true for babies born by cesarean section. Fathers of such babies are often more involved in their lives and care, even a year after the birth. The father's early direct contact with the baby during the mother's surgical convalescence has a dramatic and enduring effect on both father and child.

Whether he is allowed in or drawn in, the father's involvement is powerful and positive for the sick baby and family. Gaiter found that if the fathers of critically ill inner-city babies touched their children's fragile, often bruised little bodies, talked to them, and stayed by the incubators for more than fifteen minutes per visit (often with the encouragement from newborn ICU nursing staff), they were much more involved fathers after discharge. There is also some early evidence to support the theory that these babies may recover better and even leave the hospital sooner than if the father is not so involved.

Certainly such babies need more gentle, slower-paced care because so many of them are so quickly overwhelmed by excitement or stimulation. This is something that fathers especially must be told, because their innate handling style tends to be more stimulating than may be good for such babies. Because fathers are *needed* more with such babies, this is an example of how they must also *learn* more. Therefore, physicians and program designers for high-risk infants *must* include fathers if lasting benefits are to be realized.

Wondrous though it may be, this early involvement is just the beginning of solving the father problem. Once the babe is in arms, the fathering instinct becomes an active nurturing instinct; but because most fathers are inexperienced, untaught, often isolated from the needs of their children, they have a lot to learn.

The most dangerous period in the new father's direct relationship to his child is the first three months of his baby's life. As we've seen before, this period is sometimes known as the "fourth trimester" because the baby is so often treated and experienced as still being part of the mother's body. But given a chance, the baby can help pull the father through this risky time in their relationship. Babies are unusually responsive soon after birth, given the right rhythm of handling and feeding.

The fathers should take time with their infants, especially after feedings, to get to know them. They should talk to their babies, watch them, take them out of the house if necessary, show them off. Father and child must be *together*, even if it's just to hang out.

This hanging out, merely "being together" business is a special weakness of fathers. The natural tendency of fathers is always to be *doing* something to or with his baby, especially in the arena of play. But hanging out is equally important. Moreover, this time alone together should start early and should last if possible throughout the life cycle. There is probably no better way for a relationship to stay in tune.

Fathers must struggle with other learned patterns, too. The playful, stimulating robust handling style so typical of father care is usually interesting and invigorating for his child but not for the tired, irritable infant who needs to get some sleep. Older children can usually manage their own settling down better, but fathers must be especially aware of this tendency in handling their infants.

There is another common fathering trait that bears scrutiny if the father problem is not to continue unchanged into the next generation. Fathers must become more aware of their tendency to treat their sons so differently from daughters. As we have already seen, this is less of a problem for full-time nurturing fathers, but it requires vigilance for the traditional working father if we aim to soften the constricting aspects of gender/role stereotyping.

Clearly boys and girls have differences that matter and must be acknowledged. Completely sex-blind relationships and education would be ridiculous. But there are gross differences in the ways fathers handle their sons and daughters that may be less than helpful.

As we saw in Chapter 4, discriminatory treatment of boys and girls begins early, even in the ways fathers talk to their male or female infants, and certainly in the way they handle them. The special propensity for wishing for a first-born son, shared by both men and women, and being overly attentive to one's male offspring, especially at the expense of one's female children (as it usually is), is an ancient pattern with religious and cultural roots extending throughout history. But it is probably much less instinctual than it seems. Primary caretaking fathers feel and express sex discrimination less acutely than do traditional fathers. If men want their sons to feel less conflicted about their nurturing capacities, then they must treat them with open, tender nurturance from the beginning, not solely with aggressive, assertive handling and communications styles. If men want to help their daughters feel comfortably assertive, competitive, happily curious and competent, then they must begin early not to rely wholly on passive, protective, nonemotional interactional styles.

Tenderness in sons and achievement in daughters should be valued and actively supported. Society will certainly continue to pull in other directions, but fathers and mothers must support less rigid views of gender roles in their children. It is easily done, and promotes the overall personality growth and emotional flexibility that can help children resist the stresses they will encounter later in everyday life.

This flexibility can be supported at many levels throughout the life of the child. Sons can be encouraged to babysit. Daughters can be brought along when the father is involved with other children, such as in coaching, or teaching in the community. A father can give his young son dolls and even play with them. He can tell them how important being a father is in his own life. He can unabashedly show off his offspring. He must read to his sons as well as to his daughters, teach his sons to cook and his daughters to play baseball. If the father begins this involvement early, the rhythm of attachment takes on a self-sustaining cadence that will continue to nurture his child's development over time.

The other arena into which solutions to the father problem must come is the public one. How are we to change our public institutions, or even the public mind, about a man's capacity for nurturing fathering?

The first step must be made in the education of the children *and* of the grownups. The education of children regarding fathering begins with getting fathers into the learning places, and getting them there early. The easiest way is for school boards and school administrators to make it possible for teachers to open their classrooms and offices to fathers by offering parent-teacher conferences at times when working fathers and working mothers can come together to consult with the teacher, usually the third most important person in the life of the child.

In addition, fathers and fathering have to become part of the curriculum and daily context of the classroom itself. Fathers must be present in the classroom as educators, especially in the critical primary and elementary grades where male teachers are often found only in the gym or the principal's office. This will take affirmative action, money, and active recruiting because of the long-standing resistance, even prejudice, against men teaching children earlier than the fifth grade. The long-standing women-only status of the primary and elementary classroom must be altered by effective male presence. Children (and their parents) could well benefit from the capabilities of men who are *not* their fathers or their coaches to shape and affect young lives. David Giveans of San Francisco, an early childhood educator and editor of a fathering periodical called *Nurturing News*, has prepared a compelling film about men in early childhood education which dramatically demonstrates the real value of such an effort.[4]

Men who are not teachers must also enter the classroom in significant numbers in their more common roles as well. Teachers can invite men, whether or not they are fathers, to help run an activity, talk about their work, and share special interests or skills with children. The fathers' employers can assist such efforts (and enhance their own business's image in the eyes of the community's families) by giving such men the time off to go to the classroom.

Or, the father might bring the mountain to Mohammed and take his children and the classroom children to his workplace. Such events are powerful in purpose and long remembered.

Father presence and effectiveness must also be part of the formal curriculum. Reading texts, audiovisual aids, and filmstrips must be carefully chosen to include fathers in nurturing and caretaking roles, as well as those of the more traditional hunter-gatherer. There are more such texts available now than ever before, but they must be sought out and used to make a difference.

Curricula and family education for older children must change to include infant care instruction early in the middle school years for boys as well as girls, and it should be compulsory.

The Bank Street Family Center and the Collegiate School, both in New York City, offer model courses for school-age boys and girls that accomplish just such a task.

The Germantown Friends School in Philadelphia offers a similar experience as part of its regular curriculum. These courses should be scheduled early enough in the curriculum to prevent the establishment of rigid maternal-nurture, paternal-work stereotypes that are generally well entrenched by mid-adolescence, as seen in Chapter 12. Instructions regarding teenage contraception in the high schools must include some information on parenting for boys as well as girls. A good example is the recent Children's Defense Fund poster that declares, "If you can't be a father then don't make a baby." If sex education classes are taught separately, then the boys' section should certainly be taught by a man.

The message here is not necessarily that boys should become primary caretaking men, although some may choose to or have to. It is rather that child care, even though complicated and worrisome, is also interesting, even fun. It is an opportunity for a special kind of growth, learning, and self-esteem, and it should be accessible to boys as well as girls.

The college curriculum is also sorely in need of repair.

An intriguing effort at the University of Southern California has led to the establishment of a professorship in men's studies in its program for the Study of Women and Men in Society. It is an attempt, catalyzed by the momentum of the women's movement, to use scholarly research to study what it means to be masculine in our society.

After having formal education, men often feel on their own, whether or not they are ready to solve the problems of fatherhood. But there is help available, and much more of it than most of us imagine. The Fatherhood Project of Bank Street College in New York has been in the vanguard of an effort to study, support, and disseminate information on fatherhood at all levels in our society. It has catalogued a remarkable variety of services, programs, and resources for fathers, a brief review of which shows how much can and is being done to begin solving the father problem. It suggests that most major communities will probably have some service that will help fathers work on their fathering skills. Such programs and resources are listed by state in the Fatherhood Project's unique national guide to services for and about fathers, called *Fatherhood, U.S.A.* *

Assistance may also be available from hospitals, child development clinics, health maintenance organizations, and family service agencies. If not, then they should be asked to develop programs that are responsive to the needs of fathers.

Such resources are especially important for the first-time father. Just at a time when he is feeling the need to be strongly protective, adult, and responsible, he usually experiences a loss of intimacy with his wife, who is typically preoccupied with his baby and less available to him as a partner. Most men, for the reasons discussed in Chapter 3, find it very difficult to seek the support, friendship, and "stroking" that they need at this critical point. Consequently, new fathers in particular must be permitted and helped to discuss their difficulties with friends and family, and to use assistance if necessary.

It is hard to conceive of a public setting more important to the solution of the father problem than the workplace. A young Hispanic car salesman whose twin girls were nine months old told with much feeling of the following confrontation with his boss. "I'd been trying to help out at home. Not just 'cause my wife needed me to

---

* Available from Garland Publishing, Inc., New York and London; or from The Fatherhood Project, Bank Street College of Education, 610 West 112th St., New York, NY 10025.

help but because I love those kids, and it's starting to be fun. I asked my boss, who's a family man himself, if I could move my hours around a little bit to work just as much but be home more with the kids when they needed me. I love my job, and I'm good at it, and I'm making money. The boss tells me he's got his eye on me. So I go talk to him and he says 'make a choice, kids or cars.' It's just like he cut me in two, right down the middle!"

It is easy to miss the point here, and many people do. It is certainly not work that is the nemesis of fatherhood any more than it's the nemesis of motherhood. It's the rigidity of the rules of the workplace—of hours, corporate expectations, temporary-leave policies, to name but a few. Here truly is an area ripe for solutions, and some are appearing. Though few and far between, such efforts as Colorado Representative Patricia Schroeder's Paternal and Disability Leave Act of 1986 are a good beginning.

Paternity leave is one solution for some companies, though it's often offered in ways that make it hard to utilize. Catalyst, a New York organization formed to increase the productivity of working men and women by solving career and family dilemmas, surveyed paternity leave policies of 1,500 corporations (about 400 responded) in 1980 and found that women have access to maternity leave in 51 percent of the polled corporations, while 9 percent offered some form of paternity leave.[5] Four years later, 37 percent offered paternity leave, all of it unpaid, though usually with a job guarantee.* But few men are taking advantage of these policies. Husbands usually earn

---

*It is important to remember that these are probably high estimates, as less than one-third of the corporations responded to the survey.

more than wives, so it is more costly to the family for the man to leave his job than for the woman. Most men also believe their careers and promotions will be negatively affected by such a choice, and they are probably right.

Would *paid* paternity leave help? Probably a little, but that seems a remote possibility given the present structure of corporate power and finance. Yet men should be asking, seeking, and challenging paternity-leave policies to increase their options, especially during the early weeks and months of their babies' lives when it matters so much.

Other solutions are making their debut in the workplace, such as on-site day care. The Department of Health and Human Services studied 415 corporations and found 74 of them offered on-site or near-site day-care programs, some subsidized, some licensed, some neither. Interestingly, one-quarter of their users were male. Corporations themselves have become aware that these options are good business because supplying day care reduces, sometimes significantly, their employee turnover rates as compared to those companies who offer no child-care option. If money does talk, this is likely to be a significant addition to the corporate landscape, and soon.

But day care itself is often a less-than-perfect solution. As we've discussed, even when one can find it, the quality is often variable, and adult/child ratios are frequently not what they should be, especially for younger children and infants. Many parents feel, however, that the opportunity to see or be with their child on a lunch break makes up for many of the misgivings they have. Whether it is a better choice for the child is another question.

The last major solution that the business community has offered has been flexible work time. It's rated by many fathers as the *most* desirable work-related aid to their fathering. The flexibility to set one's hours judiciously without jeopardizing one's career can give the family a huge boost in controlling its child care according to its own needs and circumstances. "Flextime" in the job place may be in fact the most valuable of all the business solutions for the children because it permits parents to plan their time for child care in ways *they* choose, not at the convenience of their employers. Such flexibility may, for example, eliminate the need for full-time day care in some two-career families.

A recent issue of *Money* magazine cited ten corporations and businesses as "terrific employers" on the basis of the combination of flexibility of hours, on-site day care, parental leave policies, and job sharing programs: Control Data, Hewlett-Packard, IBM, Merck, State of New York, Procter and Gamble, Stride Rite, Steelcase, Inc., 3M, and the U.S. Navy.[6] Still far from the majority, these businesses are models in how far a company can go for its workers and their families while staying in business.

Changing the way we think of men as fathers is an enormous undertaking. All these solutions are just the beginning. But one hears little hints, sees little clues that the beginning has started. Groups of boys who are popular and masculine bring their Cabbage Patch Dolls to school. Fathers' voices are heard on fast-food radio commercials. Men talk with their children about brushing their teeth on television toothpaste advertisements. Men are photographed with their children in respectful, nurturing, even affectionate poses in the *New York Times'* men's fashion section. Prime-time television sitcoms feature family men who make real decisions for their children, give real help, make real mistakes, and are unabashedly nurturing without being portrayed as powerless martinets. Such evidence, though subtle, is encouragement that profound change may not be impossible.

But the time has come for this change, and the solutions must be real and effective. People laughed at W.C. Fields' jokes about "dog and kid haters" because his humor reflected the diffidence men were supposed to adopt *publicly* toward their children. When it came to being a father in his own family, Fields sent loving letters to his children and longed for their company, writing his daughter after she had borne a son following a difficult labor, "It is impossible, Hat, to tell you how glad I am to know all the worry is over. You are well, ain't it great, Hat? You keep well now and get over this O.K.... I suppose all the worst is over, don't discharge nurse or Dr. too soon.... Tell me how it all happened, how you feel...tell ALL."[7] *That* would not make many people laugh. But it's not funny any more. It's loving and nurturing. Times and fathers have changed.

The paternal child care we see about us reflects a basic change in traditional patterns. This change heralds a shift in values that is real and long overdue. Moreover, it's not just an individual issue for men and women who work out their personal child-rearing dilemmas in the privacy of their own homes. It is a strongly felt, compelling goal toward which our society must strive. Our schools, hospitals, politicians, governing institutions, artists, businesses, writers, grandparents, scientists all know this at some level and must be called upon to help to sponsor the solutions to the father problem.

Nowhere is the father problem in greater need of resolution than in the low-income family. Welfare systems currently in place devalue and denigrate the poor father by giving financial assistance more easily and generously to families when he is gone, thereby trapping him into feeling the single best thing he can do for his family is to leave it.

This is an agonizing trap for the welfare father who is told by this policy that because he can't support his family, his children can't have him, nor he them.

Poor Black, Hispanic, and white fathers first of all need jobs. Then they can be helped to see that they're so important that their absence compromises the well-being of their children, as we've seen so clearly from the father-absence research. Finally, these fathers must be encouraged to be involved and must be supported so that they can see their competence with their own children, in schools, in churches, and the workplace.

Ultimately, specific prescriptions for a little more time here with his children, or a bit more education there, are not the answer. Such advice traps the father into thinking he's doing something when he's just being patronized. Every man who becomes a father can legitimately think of himself as a unique nurturing figure in the life of his child. He is. He must stop thinking of himself as the "babysitter" and must stop being treated as such by society's institutions.

A 32-year-old assistant minister summarized what he felt he required to be a true father to his children. "After Jake was born, I realized that I needed a whole new life—nothing less would do. It really radicalized me. My religion didn't even fit any more. It needed stretching, too. Being a shepherd to my flock took on entirely new dimensions of caring when I became a father." This man, who had never held a child in his arms before he held his own, went on to discuss his "creative gifts as a father," which he'd "discovered daily thanks to Jake and the time to be with him."

Herein lies the heart of this book. Its message is not that all men need to rear their children full time in order to become truly nurturing human beings, but that men must shape, and be allowed to shape, their lives so that they may discover and develop their own full creative talents as nurturing men.

Of course, with such growth comes risk.

More than one man who has experienced the growth of such nurturance within himself and expressed it has found his marriage in trouble when feelings of envy and competition entered the couple's nurturing domain; and sometimes it's big trouble. Some friends will also fall away, made uncomfortable by the man's change in his priorities. Jobs can begin to feel shaky, for reasons we have already discussed. Even asking for paternity leave in most companies will ruffle many feathers. But for most of the men who have begun to express their nurturing selves, there is no turning back. Descriptive phrases like "feeling anchored" come up over and over again when men translate their nurturing sensitivities and impulses into behavior. The pieces of a previously fragmented life fall into place because the father has made whole his unfinished, incomplete self.

Since children both male and female are born with a vigorous predisposition to procreate and nurture, how wise and far-reaching it would be to encourage not just half but the whole human population to embrace this precious endowment. If this could truly come to pass, the flaw in the fabric of a man's life, which rends his cloth into two halves, one doing, the other feeling, could be mended, not just for fathers but all men.

Imagine what such a man could do for his society, his family, his son, his daughter. He would be loving and nurturing without embarrassment or fear, open and vulnerable without being a victim. He could foster in his children the freedom to be strongly feminine or tenderly masculine but, above all, abidingly human.

In so doing, he will help bring forth increasingly humane familial and social environments bent more on nurturing and the fulfillment of meaningful relationships than on the obscene violent posturings of power, envy, and domination. With his own life thus enriched, he bears an enduring gift of a new age for us all.

The journey toward the complete man is now well begun.

Notes

Chapter 1. The Father Problem

1. Graeme Russell, *The Changing Role of Fathers* (Saint Lucia, Queensland, Australia: University of Queensland Press, 1982).
2. Russell Baker, "Fathering," *New York Times Magazine*, June 20, 1982, 14.
3. *Yale Weekly Bulletin and Calendar,* November 19, 1984, 2.

Chapter 2. The Underground Father

1. W. Trethowan and M. Conlon, "The Couvade Syndrome," *British Journal of Psychiatry,* 111 (1965), pp. 57–65.
2. Sanbeth Gottlieb and Morris Wessell, "Gastrointestinal Symptoms Among Expectant Fathers," *Connecticut Medicine,* 46 (1982), pp. 715–718.
3. M. Lipkin and G. Lamb, "The Couvade Syndrome: An Epidemiologic Study," *Annals of Internal Medicine,* 96 (1982), pp. 509–511.

4. W. Trethowan, "The Couvade Syndrome," in *Modern Perspectives in Psyco Obstetrics*, ed. John G. Howells (New York, Brunner Mazel, 1972), 69–93.

5. James Herzog, "Patterns of Expectant Fatherhood: A Study of the Fathers of a Group of Premature Infants," in *Father and Child: Developmental and Clinical Perspectives*, eds. Stanley Cath, Alan Gurwitt, and John Munder Ross, Boston: Little Brown (1982), 301–314.

6. Martin Greenberg and N. Morris, "Engrossment: The Newborn's Impact Upon the Father," *American Journal of Orthopsychiatry*, 44 (1974), 526.

7. Martha Zaslow, et al., "Depressed Mood in New Fathers: Interview and Behavioral Correlates," Paper presented at the Society for Research in Child Development, Boston, April 1981.

8. Ibid.

9. Michael Yogman, "Development of the Father-Infant Relationship," in *Theory and Research in Behavioral Pediatrics*, 1, eds. G. Fitzgerald, F. Lester, and M. Yogman (New York: Plenum, 1982), 221–279.

10. Ross Parke, *Fathers* (Cambridge, Mass.: Harvard University Press, 1981), 35.

11. Erik Erikson, "Human Strength in the Cycle of Generations," in *Insight and Responsibility* (New York: Norton, 1964).

12. Konrad Lorenz, *On Aggression* (London: Methuen, 1966).

13. Michael Lamb, "Qualitative Aspects of Mother-and-Father-Infant Attachments," *Infant Behavior and Development*, 1 (1978), pp. 265–275.

14. Ross Parke and Douglas Sawin, "Infant Characteristics and Behavior as Elicitors of Maternal and Paternal Responsiveness in the Newborn Period," Paper presented at the Society for Research in Child Development, Denver, April, 1975.

15. Henry Biller and Dennis Meredith, *Father Power* (New York: David McKay, 1974).
16. T. Berry Brazelton, "What Makes a Good Dad?" *Redbook,* September, 1984, 32.
17. Frank Pedersen, et al., "Infant Development in Father-Absent Families," *Journal of Genetic Psychology,* 135 (1979), pp. 51–61.
18. Ross Parke, "Perspectives on Father Infant Interaction," in *The Handbook of Infant Development,* J. D. Osofsky, ed. (New York: Wiley, 1979).
19. E. Mavis Hetherington, "A Developmental Study of the Effects of Sex of the Dominant Parent on Sex Role Preference Identification and Imitation in Children," *Journal of Personality and Social Psychology,* 2 (1965), pp. 188–194.
20. Eleanor Maccoby and C. Jacklin, *The Psychology of Sex Differences* (Stanford: Stanford University Press, 1974).
21. Joel Richman, "Men's Experiences of Pregnancy and Childbirth," in *The Father Figure,* eds. L. McKee and M. O'Brien (London: Tavistock Publications, 1982), 89–104.
22. Ibid., 94.
23. Hilda Parker and Seymour Parker, "Cultural Rules, Rituals and Behavior Regulation," *American Anthropologist,* 86, 3 (1984), pp. 584–600.
24. _____, "Father-Daughter Sexual Child Abuse: An Emerging Perspective," *American Journal of Orthopsychiatry* (in press).
25. Mark Gerzon, *A Choice of Heroes* (Boston: Houghton Mifflin, 1982).
26. Arthur and Libby Colman, *Earth Father: Sky Father* (Englewood Cliffs: Prentice-Hall, 1981).
27. James Dittes, *The Male Predicament* (San Francisco, Harper & Row, 1985), ix.

Chapter 3. Teaching the Boys Not To Cry

1. Jeffrey Rubin, Frank Provenzano, and Zella Luria, "The Eye of the Beholder: Parents' Views on Sex of Newborns," *American Journal of Orthopsychiatry,* 44 (1974), pp. 512–519.
2. Laura Sidorowicz and G. Sparks Lunney, "Baby X Revisited," *Sex Roles* 6(1), (1980), pp. 67–73.
3. Eleanor Maccoby (1974).
4. Ross Parke (1981), 56–63.
5. J. Money and A. Ehrhardt, *Man and Woman, Boy and Girl: The Differentiation and Dimorphism of Gender Identity from Conception to Maturity* (Baltimore: Johns Hopkins University Press, 1972).
6. Jean and Jack Block, "The Pinks and Blues: Gender and Sex," *Nova,* WGBH Broadcast, September 30, 1982.
7. Katherine Williams, Marilyn Goodman, and Richard Green, "Parent Child Factors in Gender Role Socialization in Girls," *Journal of American Academy of Child Psychiatry,* 26, 6 (1985), pp. 720–731.
8. Vivian Paley, *Boys and Girls: Superheroes in the Doll Corner* (Chicago: University of Chicago Press, 1984).
9. Phillipe Ariès, *Centuries of Childhood: A Social History of Family Life,* Robert Baldrich trans. (New York: Knopf, 1965).
10. Jonathan Bloom-Feshbach, "Historical Perspectives on the Father's Role," in *The Role of the Father in Child Development,* 2, ed. Michael E. Lamb (New York, Wiley, 1981), 71–112.

Chapter 4. The Nurturing Fathers and Their Kin

1. George E. Vaillant, *Adaptation to Life* (Boston: Little, Brown, 1977), 318.

2. Ibid., 298.
3. Theresa Benedek, "Fatherhood and Providing," in *Parenthood: Its Psychology and Psychopathology*, eds. E. J. Anthony and T. Benedek (Boston: Little Brown, 1970), 167–184.
4. Sally Provence and Audrey Naylor, *Working With Disadvantaged Parents and Their Children* (New Haven: Yale University Press, 1983).
5. Erikson (1964), 113.

Chapter 6. Mr. Mellow, at Twenty-eight, Helen at Six: Life Grows On

1. Anna Freud, "Emotional and Instinctual Development," in *Indications for Child Analysis*, IV (New York: International Universities Press, 1947), 458–488.
2. A. Boehm, "The Femininity Complex in Men," *International Journal of Psychoanalysis*, 11 (1930), pp. 444–469.
3. Edith Jacobson, "Development of the Wish for a Child in Boys," *Psychoanalytic Study of the Child*, 5 (1950), pp. 139–152.

Chapter 11. The Nurturing Father and the Privilege of the Long View

1. Yogman (1982).
2. Frank Pedersen, et al., "Parent-Infant and Husband-Wife Interactions Observed at Five Months," in *The Father Infant Relationship*, ed. Frank A. Pedersen (New York: Praeger, 1980), 65–91.
3. Michael Lamb, "Why Swedish Fathers Aren't Liberated," *Psychology Today*, October 1982, pp. 74–77.

Chapter 12. Gender Versus Role and the Incomplete Self

1. J. Money (1972).
2. Richard Restak, *The Brain* (New York: Bantam, 1985), 244.
3. Doreen Kimura, "Male Brain, Female Brain: The Hidden Difference," *Psychology Today,* November 1985, pp. 50–58.
4. Betty Friedan, *The Second Stage* (New York: Summit, 1981).
5. Ibid.
6. G. Norris and J. Miller, *The Working Mother's Complete Handbook* (New York: Dutton, 1979).
7. Russell Baker, "Not So Up," *New York Times,* February 23, 1985, p. 31.

Chapter 13. Mothers and the Sharing of the Nurturing Domain

1. Simone de Beauvoir, *The Second Sex* (New York: Knopf, 1953).
2. William Alvarez, "The Meaning of Maternal Employment for Mothers and Their Perception of Their Three-Year-Old Children," *Child Development,* 56, 2 (1985), pp. 350–360.
3. Sheila Kamerman and Alfred Kahn and Paul Kingston, *Maternity Policies and Working Women* (New York: Columbia University Press, 1983).
4. United States Census Bureau.
5. Joseph Pleck and M. Rustad, "Husbands' and Wives' Time Use in Paidwork and the Family in the 1975–76 Study of Time Use," Center for Research on Women, Wellesley College, Wellesley, Mass., 1980.
6. Betty Friedan, "How to Get The Women's Movement

Moving Again," *New York Times Magazine*, November 3, 1985, p. 89.

7. J. A. Fulton, "Parental Reports of Children's Post-Divorce Adjustment," *Journal of Social Issues*, 35 (1979), pp. 126–139.

8. Judith Wallerstein and J. B. Kelly, *Surviving the Breakup: How Children Actually Cope With Divorce* (New York: Basic Books, 1980), 853.

9. Lenore Weitzman, *The Divorce Revolution: The Unexpected Social and Economic Consequences for Women and Children in America* (New York: Free Press, 1985).

10. "Infant Care Leaves," *New York Times*, November 27, 1985, p. 16.

Chapter 14. Divorce and the Nurturing Father: The Dangerous Opportunity

1. Wallerstein and Kelly (1980).

2. E. Mavis Hetherington, et al., "The Aftermath of Divorce," in *Mother-Child, Father-Child Relations*, eds. J. H. Stevens and M. Matthews (Washington, D.C.: National Association for the Education of Young Children, 1978).

3. Geoffrey Greif, *Single Fathers* (Lexington, Mass.: Lexington Books, 1985).

4. John Demos, "The Changing Faces of Fatherhood: A New Exploration in American Family History," in *Father and Child*, ed. Cath et al. (1982), 425–450.

5. Cited in J. A. Levine, *Who Will Raise the Children?: New Options For Fathers (and Mothers)* (New York: Lippincott, 1976), 45.

6. Jane Young, "The Father Also Rises," *New York Magazine*, November 18, 1985, p. 72.

7. Kelin Gersick, "Fathers by Choice: Divorced Men Who Receive Custody of Their Children," in *Divorce and Separation*, eds. G. Levinger and O. Moles (New York: Basic Books, 1979).

8. E. Mavis Hetherington (1978).

9. Ann D'Andrea, "Joint Custody as Related to Paternal Involvement and Paternal Self-Esteem," *Conciliations Courts Review* 21, 2 (1983), pp. 41–87.

10. David Chambers, "Rethinking the Substantive Rules for Custody Disputes in Divorce," *Michigan Law Review*, 83 (1984), pp. 477–569.

11. Wallerstein and Kelly (1980).

12. Judith Wallerstein and Joan Kelly, "The Father Child Relationship: Changes After Divorce," in *Father and Child* (1982).

Chapter 15. Solving the Father Problem

1. Alvin Toffler, *Future Shock* (New York: Random House, 1970).

2. Michael Yogman, "Father-Infant Play with Pre-Term and Full-Term Infants," in *Men's Transitions to Parenthood: Longitudinal Studies of Early Family Experience*, eds. Frank A. Pedersen and Phyllis Berman (New York: Erlbaum, in press).

3. Juarlyn Gaiter, "Bonding Behavior of Fathers with Their Critically Ill Pre-Term Infants," Paper presented at the Conference on Men's Transitions to Parenthood, National Institutes of Child Health and Human Development, Bethesda, Maryland, May 1984.

4. David Giveans, ed., *Nurturing News*, 187 Caselli Avenue, San Francisco, CA, 94114.

5. Catalyst, "The Report on a National Study of Parental

Leaves" (New York: Catalyst, 1986), 250 Park Avenue South, New York, NY, 10003.

6. "Going For It All," *Money,* May 1985, p. 144.
7. Cited in Nancy Caldwell Sorel, *Ever Since Eve: Personal Reflections on Childbirth* (New York: Oxford University Press, 1984).

Index